'*The Relational Heart of Gestalt* psychotherapy, making it a co nuances of their existence and fly away into the realm of everyday stimulations. When we say, "the future is now" we say we are living in a universe of interactive agents who, in union, honor a lifetime. The authors of this book flesh out this wonder of earthly relationships of which the psychotherapy relationship is a prime inspiration.'

– **Erving Polster, PhD,** *International Gestalt Therapy Trainer and Founder of the Gestalt Training Center-San Diego*

'All schools of thought need to recognize how they've developed over time. *The Relational Heart of Gestalt Therapy* explores the shift to a more "field-relational" approach – less individualistic, riskier, and more humanly revealing. Peter Cole has assembled a range of talented therapists with different ways of working. Some are "old hands" in articulating this profound shift in values, others discover it with new excitement. Together they reveal the range, integrity, and vitality of Gestalt therapy today.'

– **Malcolm Parlett, PhD,** *Former editor of the British Gestalt Journal, international trainer and coach*

'This engaging and intriguing book combines stories of relational gestalt therapy with its psychoanalytic origins and influences, making both more available to practitioners of both traditions. Many of the best writers in contemporary gestalt therapy appear here, and the reader will be well rewarded with insight and enjoyment.'

– **Donna Orange, PhD,** *Faculty and training and supervising analyst, Institute for the Psychoanalytic Study of Subjectivity, New York*

'Peter Cole's edited book offers a major contribution to the understanding and practice of a relational approach in our present challenged world. This book "unpacks" the process of focusing of "being somebody… rooted somewhere" through an interactive and courageously mutual approach. What also touched me was the humility and inclusiveness of the authors as they describe theory and practice. It is as if they are practicing in the text the very mutuality of this approach; I felt talked with as I read each chapter. The multiple authors offer us perspectives both theoretically and in practice of the living embodied mutuality that is relational Gestalt. It is a description of what is both precious and not precious, uniquely human and yet fully embedded in the contextual situation. I highly recommend this entire volume with its diversity of topics and authors' perspectives on the experience of an engaged process of connection and change.'

– **Michael Clemmens, PhD,** *Author of* Getting Beyond Sobriety: Clinical Approaches to Long-Term Recovery, *Editor of* Embodied Relational Gestalt: Theories and Applications

# The Relational Heart of Gestalt Therapy

This compelling and comprehensive volume is an anthology of current thinking by many of gestalt therapy's leading theoreticians, clinicians, and researchers.

Including many well-known voices in the field and introducing several new ones to the current gestalt therapy literature, the book presents a broad-ranging compendium of essays, scientific articles, clinical applications, and integrative approaches that represent the richness and vibrancy of the field. Each contributor brings intellectual rigor, honest personal reflection, and humanism to their area of inquiry. This ethos—the spirit of relational gestalt therapy—infuses the whole book, bringing a sense of coherence to its seventeen chapters. Following an introduction written by Mark Winitsky, PhD, as an entry point into the field for students and psychotherapists from other schools of thought, the book is organized into three sections: Theory, Clinical Applications, and Integrative Approaches. Readers will encounter new ways of thinking about psychotherapy, new skills they can bring to their work, and new ways of integrating gestalt therapy with other approaches.

*The Relational Heart of Gestalt Therapy* is essential reading for Gestalt therapists as well as other mental health professionals with an interest in Gestalt approaches.

**Peter Cole, LCSW** is the co-director of the Sierra Institute for Contemporary Gestalt Therapy and was an Assistant Clinical Professor of Psychiatry with the UC Davis School of Medicine for 30 years (now retired). He is the co-author of three previous books including *New Directions in Gestalt Group Therapy*, and has published numerous articles.

Gestalt Therapy Book Series

www.gestaltitaly.com                    HCC Italy

Series Editor **Margherita Spagnuolo Lobb**

The Istituto di Gestalt series of Gestalt therapy books emerges from the ground of a growing interest in theory, research, and clinical practice in the Gestalt community. The members of the Scientific and Editorial Boards have been committed for many years to the process of supporting research and publications in our field: through this series we want to offer our colleagues internationally the richness of the current trends in Gestalt therapy theory and practice, underpinned by research. The goal of this series is to develop the original principles in hermeneutic terms: to articulate a relational perspective, namely a phenomenological, aesthetic, field-oriented approach to psychotherapy. It is also intended to help professions and to support a solid development and dialogue of Gestalt therapy with other psychotherapeutic methods.

The series includes original books specifically created for it, as well as translations of volumes originally published in other languages. We hope that our editorial effort will support the growth of the Gestalt therapy community; a dialogue with other modalities and disciplines; and new developments in research, clinics, and other fields where Gestalt therapy theory can be applied (e.g., organizations, education, political and social critique and movements).

We would like to dedicate this Gestalt Therapy Book Series to all our masters and colleagues who have sown fruitful seeds in our minds and hearts.

**Scientific Board**
Vincent Béja, Dan Bloom, Bernd Bocian, Phil Brownell, Pietro A. Cavaleri, Scott Churchill, Michael Clemmens, Peter Cole, Susan L. Fischer, Madeleine Fogarty, Ruella Frank, Pablo Herrera Salinas, Lynne Jacobs, Natasha Kedrova, Timothy Leung, Alan Meara, Joseph Melnick, Myriam Muñoz Polit, Antonio Narzisi, Leanne O'Shea, Malcolm Parlett, Peter Philippson, Erving Polster, Jean-Marie Robine, Jan Roubal, Adriana Schnake, Peter Schulthess, Christine Stevens, Daan van Baalen, Carmen Vázquez Bandín, Gordon Wheeler, Gary Yontef

**Editorial Board**
Rafael Salgado, Billy Desmond, Fabiola Maggio, Max Mishchenko, Georg Pernter, Silvia Tosi, Jay Tropianskaia, Andy Williams, Jelena Zeleskov Djoric

**The Relational Heart of Gestalt Therapy**
Contemporary Perspectives
*Peter Cole*

For more information on the titles in this series, please visit www.routledge.com/Gestalt-Therapy/book-series/GESTHE and www.gestaltitaly.com

# The Relational Heart of Gestalt Therapy

## Contemporary Perspectives

Edited by Peter Cole

Routledge
Taylor & Francis Group

LONDON AND NEW YORK

Cover image: Beyond Heart by Guy-Pierre Tur

First published 2022
by Routledge
4 Park Square, Milton Park, Abingdon, Oxon OX14 4RN

and by Routledge
605 Third Avenue, New York, NY 10158

Routledge is an imprint of the Taylor & Francis Group, an informa business

British Library Cataloguing-in-Publication Data
A catalogue record for this book is available from the British Library

Library of Congress Cataloging-in-Publication Data
Names: Cole, Peter H., 1955- editor.
Title: The relational heart of Gestalt therapy : together in the therapeutic process / edited by Peter Cole.
Description: Abingdon, Oxon ; New York, NY : Routledge, 2022. | Includes bibliographical references and index. | Summary: "This compelling and comprehensive volume is an anthology of current thinking by many of gestalt therapy's leading theoreticians, clinicians and researchers"-- Provided by publisher.
Identifiers: LCCN 2021057657 | ISBN 9781032186931 (hardback) | ISBN 9781032186917 (paperback) | ISBN 9781003255772 (ebook)
Subjects: LCSH: Gestalt therapy.
Classification: LCC RC489.G4 R45 2022 | DDC 616.89/143--dc23/eng/ 20220222
LC record available at https://lccn.loc.gov/2021057657

ISBN: 978-1-032-18693-1 (hbk)
ISBN: 978-1-032-18691-7 (pbk)
ISBN: 978-1-003-25577-2 (ebk)

DOI: 10.4324/9781003255772

Typeset in Times New Roman
by MPS Limited, Dehradun

For Dr. Bud Feder: friend, mentor, colleague, and generous human being.

# Contents

# Foreword

The Relational Heart of Gestalt Therapy has historical implications. It transposes the psychoanalytic search for causation into the immediacy of an effervescent existence. Gestalt therapy's contribution to this movement was its emphasis on the concept of "contact" the spark for interpersonal relationship. Accordingly, the sharply delineated moment of contact amplified the ever-continuous lifetime. The crux of therapy, therefore, became the undoing of stuckness, a freeing of personal fluidity.

This revision of the emphasis on causation was a historic correction of over-intellectualization. As a consequence, no experience was too small or too irrelevant to be excluded from therapeutic attention. This call for sharpness of focus makes all experience count: a tremor of the eye, a grammatically misleading sentence, a despair with contemporary politics, unnecessary repetition, and all the countless avenues available for neutralizing or distorting immediate experience. However, it is a good wind that blows no ill and we discovered that the emphasis on sharpness of contact excluded many important historical and relational experiences. Now, in this book that has been restored and honored, pointing the way toward a larger view of what matters in a person's lifetime.

Now, however, is not just now, it is a spark into the appreciation of relationship, meaningful in the present and inspiring both future and complexity. The reader of this book will see immediate experience joined with an evolving and meaningful relationship. While this relationship is not just folks talking to each other, it is also not abstruse. It incorporates ordinary human experiences such as sadness, humor, dependency, forgiveness, and all those qualities which define an ongoing relationship. This promise is a nudge for the transposition from the elemental into both the mystique and the practicality of ordinary living.

The Relational Heart of Gestalt Therapy is a step in the direction of humanizing psychotherapy, making it a compelling opportunity for people to discover the nuances of their existence and fly away into the realm of everyday stimulations. When we say, "the future is now" we say we are living in a universe of interactive agents who, in union, honor a lifetime. The authors of this book flesh out this wonder of earthly relationships of which the psychotherapy relationship is a prime inspiration.

Hallelujah!

Erving Polster, PhD

# Preface

This book is infused with the theory, spirit, and ethos of relational Gestalt therapy. Relationality is this collection's unifying theme. It is not that each chapter is directly about relationality, rather, each contributor explores their subject through a relational lens. A relational approach values the unique presence and phenomenology of both therapist and client. Accordingly, each of the contributors to *The Relational Heart of Gestalt Therapy* share not only their ideas but something of themselves. By writing from both theoretical and personal perspectives, this book's contributors approach their material with a dialogical attitude that invites the reader into sometimes quite intimate sharing of the author's feelings and vulnerabilities. The result is a book in which the reader gets to know each of the contributors to this volume – both through their ideas and the sharing of their humanity. This integration of the personal and theoretical, emotional and intellectual, the vulnerable and the assertive, is a hallmark of the relational approach in Gestalt therapy. To think with one's heart and gut, to feel with one's mind, to find courage in openness and risk exposure for the sake of connection: these are the integrative qualities that give the relational approach its unique power and beauty. These are the qualities you will find in the essays of this book.

The Gestalt therapy literature broadens and develops as writers, such as the contributors to this book, take the risk of putting their ideas, experiences, and reflections out to the broader community where their writing will be encountered, digested, and responded to over time. This is in no way a linear process. As the editor of this volume, I do not seek final truths or master narratives in the articles contained in this book – instead – I seek enrichment – the sharing of our successes, failures, challenges, insights, and new approaches. In reaching out to the writers of this book, I simply asked if they would write a piece about any aspect of relational Gestalt therapy that feels important to them at this time. The articles that flowed in were remarkable – they reflect the very best of current thinking and practice in Gestalt therapy. All of the contributors to this book are deeply committed to the work of Gestalt therapy, and each have a great many years of clinical and teaching experience. I invite you, the reader, to take your time with this volume. Each chapter provides the opportunity for a unique encounter with an author who shares from a wealth of experience. These short pieces have the potential to open new doors for every psychotherapist who seeks to keep learning, growing, and developing.

In the following section – I briefly describe each chapter in solely my own words and with my own understanding. I have not asked the contributors if they agree with my paraphrasing of their ideas. Please do not take my descriptions as anything more than my limited comprehension of the complex ideas presented by each author. Please enjoy each chapter to derive your own understanding and meaning.

## Introduction: The Emergence of the Relational Perspective in Gestalt Therapy

*The Emergence of the Relational Perspective in Gestalt Therapy* is an introduction by Mark Winitsky who, as a Gestalt therapist and psychoanalyst, brings depth and breadth of knowledge to his subject. I asked Dr. Winitzky to write this introductory chapter primarily for readers such as practitioners from other schools of psychotherapy and graduate students, who may be unfamiliar with the Gestalt approach. Winitsky traces Gestalt therapy back to its roots in psychoanalysis. He introduces the reader to Fritz Perls, Laura Perls, and Paul Goodman. He draws out fascinating parallels and differences between Freud and Perls. He recounts Fritz and Laura's brilliant and impactful careers. In tracing the intellectual developments that gave birth to the relational turn in Gestalt therapy, Winitzky brings humor and many personal observations to this highly informative introduction. Although written for newcomers to the field, those who are well versed in Gestalt therapy theory and history and will enjoy Winitsky's colorful introduction.

## Section I: Relational Gestalt Therapy Theory

Chapter one, *Aesthetic Relational Knowledge and the Dance of Reciprocity in the Therapeutic Field: Post pandemic Gestalt therapy in practice* by Margherita Spagnuolo Lobb, a leading voice in relational work, offers a scholarly and updated look at the sources of suffering in contemporary society and discusses new approaches to treatment. She finds that today's patients often lack a sense of grounding and containment and that they present with more serious disturbances than in previous decades. This necessitates a new emphasis on the field conditions in which the patient functions along with an orientation toward support of the patient's ground. With an appreciation of the beauty of the patient's creative adjustments, the Gestalt therapist brings Aesthetic Relational Knowledge to a reciprocal therapeutic relationship. With her depth and breadth of knowledge in the areas of human development, intersubjectivity, and psychopathology, Spagnuolo Lobb broadens the lens of Gestalt relational work to encompass new understandings of ground support and field considerations.

Chapter two, *Engaged Surrender* by Lynne Jacobs, is a keynote address that she gave to the European Association of Gestalt Therapy in 2019. The theme of the conference was The Fertile Void. In very personal terms, Jacobs explores the meaning of terms such as the *fertile void, creative indifference, zero point* and the *paradoxical theory of change.* Jacobs is well known as one of Gestalt therapy's finest writers and theorists. Her integration of the personal and theoretical is seamless and elegant. She makes it look easy. Always grounded and unassuming, she draws her understandings of what works in therapy as much from her experiences as a client as she does from her experiences as a therapist. In this talk, she covers many areas of interest, but what speaks most to me is her discussion of the paradoxical theory of change, staying with the patient's current commitment, and allowing it to complexify as therapist and client stay with it. There is always much to learn when reading Lynne Jacobs and this chapter will enrich the reader in many ways.

Chapter three, *Being Present to Absence: Field Theory in Psychopathology and Clinical Practice* by Gianni Francesetti, Michela Gecele, Jan Roubal is a rich, challenging, and original article by three researchers who are making important contributions to Gestalt therapy's understanding of field theory and psychopathology. These three European psychiatrists bring a profound re-imagining of Gestalt therapy from a field perspective where the healing process occurs through attunement to that which is missing and not yet assimilated. The unassimilated becomes an "unwelcome stranger at the door" that the "flesh of the therapist" embodies, becoming a support in the patient's processing of previously unassimable material. This approach embraces the Taoist thread present in Gestalt therapy from PHG onward. The therapist attunes to field forces in such a way that the absence can become present, felt, and processed. Francesetti, Gecele, and Roubal bring powerful imagery and lyricism to this piece – infusing their work with a compelling literary quality.

Chapter four, *Gestalt Therapy in an Age of Turmoil* by Gary Yontef applies the principles of relational Gestalt therapy to the sociopolitical, racial, and gender conflicts that have arisen in modern American society. As the original architect of the relational turn in Gestalt therapy, Yontef brings a deep understanding of the potential for taking relational Gestalt principles out of the psychotherapy office and into the broader world to promote dialogue and "working together." He applies Buber's concept of I-it to racism in the U.S. and calls for unity among the races in the struggle against oppressive forces in American society. He utilizes the phenomenological method in unpacking racist projection onto people of color and works with Field Theory as a way of understanding the complexity and context of people's lives. His chapter points the reader toward a renewal of the activism that has always been a part of the Gestalt approach.

Chapter five, *To Hold the Hands that Hold our Hands: Responsivity of Contacting* by Dan Bloom takes a deep dive into Spagnuolo Lobb's *intentionality for contacting* and gives the concept a further nudge with his *responsivity of contacting*. Bloom argues that intentionality for relational contacting encompasses the capacity to respond to the other as well as responsivity. Bloom presents several case examples in which therapist and client make unexpected contact, touching each other's life-world and interconnecting in relational intentionality. Bloom explores the dance of being responsive and responding, touching and being touched at the contact boundary. Bloom's theoretical exactitude and subtlety are on display in this intellectually challenging and clinically astute chapter.

Chapter six, *The Gifts and Risks in Relational Empathy: An historical perspective* by Jack Aylward, is a brilliant look at the history of empathy and relationality in psychotherapy from a Gestalt therapist who, while in many ways sympathetic to the relational perspective, does not specifically identify with the relational approach. Aylward introduces the concept of intimate aggression. He argues that there can be no intimacy without aggression, and that it takes aggression to destructure the old figure so that new figures can emerge. Refreshingly, Aylward discusses Fritz Perls and Paul Goodman at length – reminding relationally oriented Gestalt therapists of the gifts that Fritz's "aggressive" style brought and urging us not to throw out the baby with the bathwater. His chapter is pointed, humorous, scholarly, and a reminder for contemporary Gestalt therapists not to conflate the valuing of empathy with the devaluing of aggression.

Chapter seven, *Living in a World of Meaning* by Friedemann Schulz is a beautiful integration of the personal and the theoretical that exemplifies the very best of the relational Gestalt approach with its highly engaging stories of Schulz's family of origin that bring the concepts he is discussing to life. Schulz presents a discussion of "the between" and the process of transformation that is essential to understanding how therapy works. He locates emotion between what is not yet known and what is conscious – identifying that the exploration of emotion between therapist and client is crucial to making meaning for the client. In my view, Gestalt therapists do not think enough about the process of *transformation* – leaving that potent ground to therapists from the Jungian school. Schulz takes up this important area and finds that the dialogic method is transformational in that new understandings lead to new ways of experiencing the self and being in the world.

## Section II: Applications of the Relational Gestalt Perspective

Chapter eight, *A Classical Beginning and a Relational Turn: A Gestalt therapy case study* by Charles E. Bowman, C. Ann Bowman is a piece that I believe is destined to become a classic of the Gestalt therapy literature.

Bowman and Bowman present the case of Claudia with whom they worked for over ten years during which they gradually shifted emphasis from a "classical" style of doing Gestalt therapy to a relational style. With clarity and scholarship, the authors show the complementarity of the two styles and how the relational style rests on the shoulders of classical style. In the mix, the authors provide a masterful case study of the treatment of trauma. My hope is that Gestalt therapy training programs will look closely at this piece for their syllabi. Trainees will have a great deal to think about, discuss and learn from this compelling piece.

Chapter nine, *When the World Changes in an Instant: Exploring "cracks in the continuity of experience"*, by Michelle Seely is an extraordinarily engaging essay. Seely, working within relational Gestalt therapy's value system in which insight and connection are often forged in the crucible of shared vulnerability, invites the reader into the inner workings of a very personal shame attack. This courageous piece of writing opens the door to the exploration of a universal, but subtle and mostly invisible human phenomenon: when the flow of one's experience comes to a sudden, jolting halt due to some trigger that pulls the rug out from under us and lands us in a traumatized state of mind. Seely's method of utilizing the personal as a passageway to the universal is an example of relational writing at its best.

Chapter ten, *What My Client Taught Me About Dialogic Presence: A case study of client and therapist in relational Gestalt therapy* by Armin Baier is the interweaving of many threads, told with Baier's distinctive intelligence, gentle, self-effacing humor, and generosity. One thread is Baier's experience of barely surviving horrible, homophobic family therapy at a university counseling center in the 70s. Another thread is the story of Baier finding community, support, mentorship, and Gestalt therapy as a volunteer at Identity House, a gay and lesbian crisis counseling center in New York City in the 70s. The form of Gestalt therapy that he learned at that time was liberating, supportive of his nascent gay identity and active in its experimentalism. While Gestalt therapy may have helped save Baier's own life, it did not provide the tools he needed in his intensive work with a sexual abuse survivor, as it did not address issues of shame, trauma, and relational long-term treatment. Ironically, Baier intuitively adopted the methodologies of relational Gestalt therapy in treating this long-term patient – thinking at the time that he was breaking the rules of Gestalt therapy and therefore feeling quietly ashamed. When he eventually encountered the relational approach to Gestalt therapy, it came as a revelation to him that he had discovered in his own way what Yontef, Jacobs, and Bloom had discovered in *their* own ways, that Gestalt therapy must evolve and grow to respond to the changing needs of patients as we meet them in our therapeutic work.

Chapter eleven, *On Regret: A relational Gestalt therapy perspective* by myself, Peter Cole and Daisy Reese is a reflection on working with sorrow, disappointment, guilt, and remorse. Wishes unfulfilled, goals not achieved, injuries caused that cannot be repaired, loves lost, opportunities missed and responsibilities skirted, can weigh heavily on us as we age. Frequently, there is little to be done by way of "fixing" or repairing the damage done. This brings the therapeutic focus to the relationship between therapist and client – to holding the regret together. We often find that this evokes a felt sense of poignancy. We discuss the value of therapists doing our own personal work around disappointment and regret so that we are available to our clients in doing this sometimes emotionally challenging work.

Chapter twelve, *The Encounter Process* by Bruce Aaron is an essay that is close to my heart as it focuses on Gestalt group therapy – a modality that Aaron and I share a passion for. The Encounter Process is a methodology Aaron has developed as a support to better, clearer contact with interactions that have gotten muddied, confused, or hurtful. This exercise supports the awareness of both speaker and listener in clarifying what has been perceived, what is imagined, what is felt and what action the individuals are moved to take. When relational ruptures occur in our treatment and/or training groups, the Encounter Process can be an especially valuable tool. Aaron spells out his methodology clearly and systematically making this chapter highly useful and applicable for Gestalt group therapists at all levels, from trainees to experienced practitioners.

Chapter thirteen, *Shame and Relational Gestalt Group Therapy: Restoring the interpersonal bridge* by Joan Gold, is written with courageous transparency. She walks the walk – believing that facing shame, speaking to it, and sharing it openly is a powerful pathway for healing. In the group therapy that she so eloquently describes, Gold works intensively with group members in unpacking shame in its many relational aspects. She shows that relational Gestalt group therapy is a powerful modality for healing shame with its emphasis on empathy, connection, sensitivity to vulnerability, and support. The relational turn in Gestalt therapy began with Gary Yontef's insights concerning the need for greater attention to issues of shame in Gestalt therapy treatment and training. Gold's group work further develops the synergy between shame theory and relationality in Gestalt therapy.

## Section III: Integrative Relational Approaches

Chapter fourteen, *Embodied Relational Presence in Buddhist Psychology Informed Gestalt Therapy* by Eva Gold and Steve Zahm, is a major contribution from Gestalt therapy's foremost scholars in the field of Buddhist Psychology. This chapter covers a great deal of ground of which I can barely scratch the surface in this one short paragraph. Gold and Zahm explore a variety of ways in which Buddhist Psychology Informed Gestalt

Therapy (BPGT) can support and enhance the therapist's Embodied Relational Presence. BPGT practices deepen the therapist's capacity for wisdom, compassion, equanimity, and love. Mindfulness meditation for example reveals the embodied nature of emotion and aids in attunement to the body/mind such that the therapist may resonate more fully when sitting with a client. Sitting with "what is" – being with our own emotional and physical pain without judgment – naturally gives rise to self-compassion. This in turn may enhance our capacity to sit compassionately with our client's pain. Gold and Zahm draw powerful parallels between Buber's philosophy of dialogue and Buddhist psychology's concept of the buddha nature in all human beings. There are a great many concepts in this chapter that will catalyze your growth as a therapist and as a human being. Gold and Zahm offer a wealth of wisdom in this extraordinarily valuable essay.

Chapter fifteen, *The Here and Now of Sandtray Therapy: Sandtray therapy meets Gestalt therapy* provides an introduction to relational work that moves beyond words into the world of the imaginal with the leading teachers of Gestalt Sandtray in the U.S., Karen Pernet and Wendy Caplin. Pernet and Caplin take the reader through the relational experience of creating Sandtrays, where the therapist supports therapeutic safety through their presence and empathic curiosity. The process is not dependent upon words – the client creates a world in the sand with miniatures while the therapist is present as witness. The authors present an in-depth Sandtray case study in which a client, Sarah, makes many important discoveries about her life and relationships. The authors present an innovative and exciting method that Pernet has named "Cultural Sandtrays." Cultural Sandtrays are designed to support people in exploring their cultural heritage. Cultural Sandtrays can be used individually or can be used in groups with people from diverse backgrounds to help support listening, dialoguing, and connection. This chapter will be of great value for Gestalt trainees as well as advanced practitioners who work with children and adults.

Chapter sixteen, *The Mountain and the River: Stillness and flow and the art of therapy* by Christine Campbell & Jack Fris is a meditation on Gestalt therapy as artistic process. This essay begins with a touching vignette. The authors, Jack and Christine, a married couple, await the availability of a lung transplant for Jack. During these months of uncertainty, they read Finnegan's Wake aloud. Joyce's text frequently does not make narrative sense and the ideas are not always understandable, yet the reading process occasionally yields remarkable moments of beauty that support, inspire and hold them until a donated lung finally arrives and the transplant can take place. For Campbell and Fris, Gestalt therapy is not simply a treatment modality, it is a way of being in the world that is as relevant for the life of the therapist as it is for the client. Campbell and Fris follow in the grand tradition of Paul Goodman, Joseph Zinker, and Erv Polster with their integration of art, literature, and therapy in this elegant essay.

The introduction and sixteen chapters of this book represent a broad spectrum of current thinking in relational Gestalt therapy. The contributors to this volume contributed a great deal of time energy and commitment to this project. I thank them for the excellence of their work, and I wish you, the reader much enjoyment as you encounter their extraordinary essays.

**Peter Cole,** LCSW
Sierra Institute for Contemporary Gestalt Therapy
Oakland, California

# Acknowledgments

First – my deepest appreciation to the contributors who gave so much of themselves to this book. I would like to express my thanks to Jack Aylward and Charlie Bowman who generously gave of their time and expertise with crucial editing assistance. Margherita Spagnuolo Lobb has been an incredible support throughout this project, and I thank her for her friendship, commitment, and help. Many thanks to Stefania Benini with the Gestalt Therapy Book Series for her steady hand in guiding this book through the publication process.

To my mom, Dr. Joan Cole, to our children Ananda, Reese, Alex, Elizabeth, and Hannah and our grandchildren, Sammy, Rowan-Hays, Eleanor, Jack, Abby, and Mateo-Hays I thank you for the joy of our loving family.

My deepest appreciation goes to my wife, co-author, co-parent, co-grandparent, co-therapist, collaborator, and all-around partner in crime - Daisy Reese. Without her unwavering support, this project would never have come to fruition.

# Front Cover art "Beyond Heart"

*Guy-Pierre Tur*

**Guy-Pierre Tur** is a French painter and Gestalt therapist who was born in Algeria and has lived in Mexico City since 1982. His work has been exhibited in several countries. He is currently interested in art as an instrument of peace. His work has illustrated numerous psychotherapy books. He has been a Gestalt therapy trainer for more than 25 years and teaches regularly at a variety of Gestalt institutes throughout Latin America and Europe.

# Introduction

## The Emergence of the Relational Perspective in Gestalt Therapy

*Mark Winitsky*

Gestalt therapy has been a relational approach since its inception. It began as a revision and extension of psychoanalysis that was inspired by psychoanalytic dissidents such as Ferenczi, Rank, Reich, Horney, Sullivan, and Fromm, who distanced themselves from Freud's intrapsychic theories of drives, fantasies, and complexes, and saw psychopathology, and human development, as something that proceeds from interaction with the environment. Two German psychoanalysts, Friedrich "Fritz" Perls, and his wife Lore Posner, later Laura Perls, spent roughly 25 years developing proto-relational psychoanalytic ideas before their new approach, no longer called psychoanalysis, was formally introduced in 1951 with the publishing of *Gestalt Therapy: Excitement and Growth in the Human Personality*. This foundational book established the concepts that differentiated this new system from the psychoanalysis of that time: people were inseparable from the environment, all experience was contact, growth required assimilation of novelty, and pathology was the result of interference in the spontaneous process of contacting and assimilating. Nothing in this new model of psychotherapy was individualistic or intrapsychic; it was profoundly relational. It began as a way of improving psychoanalysis in the treatment of symptoms, it borrowed psychoanalytic ideas to change the way we understand human experience, and it developed into a new movement clearly defined as something separate and apart from psychoanalysis. Over time, with an increased emphasis on the importance of relationality in both Gestalt and psychoanalysis, the two worlds appear to be drawing closer again, both in theory and in clinical practice.

## Gestalt and Psychoanalysis

The word *Gestalt* refers to a form or a shape, and specifically to something that is figural in its relationship with the background from which it emerged. A description of Gestalt therapy therefore invites one to differentiate it as a figure from the background of psychoanalysis, as well as the social, intellectual, and political conditions from which it emerged (see Bocian, 2020).

DOI: 10.4324/9781003255772-1

Psychoanalysis and Gestalt therapy each had a primary founding figure, and they had much in common, but there were also important differences that shaped both the development and content of their theories. Both founders were German-speaking atheists from middle-class assimilated Jewish families, Freud from Vienna, Perls from Berlin. Both were highly educated and read classics in Greek and Latin when young. Both became medical doctors and then psychoanalysts. Freud was, of course, the first psychoanalyst, having invented the term in 1896, when he was forty and Perls was three. Perls became a psychoanalyst in 1926, and developed his ideas as one of the many dissident psychoanalysts until 1950, when he first started calling his approach Gestalt therapy. Each of these founders – Perls preferred to be called the "finder" of Gestalt therapy (Shepard, 1975) – would spend the rest of their lives developing and promoting their creation.

Psychoanalysis was largely invented and, throughout his life, controlled and guided by Freud himself. It began with Freud's interest in a case described to him by Josef Breuer, his onetime mentor, that led to their collaboration on an early book on the treatment of hysteria. Although Breuer's theories eventually turned out to be more in line with contemporary clinical thinking than Freud's (van der Kolk, 2000), he withdrew from treating psychological disorders and Freud was left to continue the work on his own. Freud's psychoanalysis was largely a personal creation that arose out of his own self-analysis, his interpretation of his dreams, and his developing understanding of his clinical experiences with his analysands. Freud considered himself a scientist and admired Darwin, but his heroes were military leaders: Hannibal, Oliver Cromwell, and the fictional Don Quixote de la Mancha. He surrounded himself with loyal followers and expelled those who challenged him or refused to follow. Freud was a brilliant strategist who was dedicated to creating something that would outlive him and make him famous, and he succeeded spectacularly.

Friedrich "Fritz" Perls, on the other hand, was less of a strategist and more of a creative type, an artist or performer. As a student, he was at times brilliant but also rebellious. He was involved in left-wing politics, influenced by the Dada art movement, rode a motorcycle as a teenager, and behaved outrageously throughout his life. Since childhood, Perls had been in love with the theater as a way of finding the real truth under falseness, and in his later life, he often functioned more as a director coaxing authenticity out of his patients, exposing their phoniness, than as a psychoanalyst working through a transference neurosis. Unlike Freud, he constantly integrated anything that he found valuable into his theory, openly crediting those who inspired him, including Freud. Like Freud, Perls wanted to inspire a movement that would liberate people and improve the world, but unlike Freud, he seemed uninterested in establishing and leaving behind an institution that would protect the purity of his theory and method, or in driving away people who contributed new ideas.

In his last decade, Perls seemed most interested in performing in front of audiences whenever possible.

The origins of Gestalt therapy were always present in the ideas of the early psychoanalysts, beginning with Sandor Ferenczi, who was perhaps Freud's closest collaborator. Ferenczi emphasized the active role of the analyst, the importance of the patient's subjective experience, the value of therapist self-disclosure, and the idea that a real relationship was more important than a transference relationship. Otto Rank, another of Freud's closest early collaborators, wrote about the importance of working in the "here and now" – the most basic idea of Gestalt therapy. Karen Horney, Perls' first analyst, influenced his thinking about neurosis as a process of interaction with external forces rather than a conflict caused by intrapsychic drives,[1] and Wilhelm Reich, the last of his four analysts, introduced Perls to the importance of the body and non-verbal communication, as well as the idea that analysts can physically touch their patients. For many years, Fritz and Laura continued to develop their ideas within the boundary of what was considered psychoanalysis, if not orthodox psychoanalysis.

In 1933, as Hitler was rising to power in Europe, Fritz and Laura Perls accepted an offer to establish a psychoanalytic training institute in South Africa and moved to Johannesburg. They spent the next thirteen years there, had two children, and continued to develop their own version of psychoanalysis, which incorporated many of the ideas they had been exposed to in Germany. Their psychoanalysis was strongly influenced by Wilhelm Reich and his theory of *character analysis,*[2] Salomo Friedlander's theory of a *zero point* between polarities and *creative indifference,*[3] and the principles of Gestalt psychology,[4] which Laura had been studying in Frankfurt. In Johannesburg, they discovered and integrated Jan Smut's ideas about holism and field theory.[5] In 1936, Perls traveled to Europe to present a paper at the 13th International Psychoanalytic Congress and to meet Freud. The paper was poorly received and Freud gave Perls a chilly reception, two severe blows to Perls' relationship with the psychoanalytic community. Soon after returning to South Africa, news arrived from Europe that they would no longer be allowed to train psychoanalysts because they had never been trainers in Europe, which further distanced them from Freud's world.

In 1942, in Johannesburg, they published their first book, under Fritz's name only: *Ego, Hunger, and Aggression: A Revision of Freud's Theory and Method.* Although it rejected Freud's libido theory, the heart of orthodox psychoanalysis, it received excellent reviews and sold widely in South Africa. When the book was republished in 1947 in London, it was less successful. A reviewer for the International Review of Psychoanalysis described it as "...a most profound study and of interest from many points of view" but stated that he was "...doubtful as to whether a really fruitful connection can be established between Gestalt-psychology and psycho-analysis" and concluded that "...the book is the clever child of a somewhat inharmonious marriage. A child may succeed in many ways to influence his mother, but will hardly ever change or reform her" (Dreyfuss, 1947, pp. 201–204). He suggested that Perls "…'put his teeth' into the umbilical cord of his newborn spiritual child…" (p. 204) and separate from Freud, which is what happened. Marie Bonaparte, a close associate of Freud's, told Perls, "If you don't believe in the libido theory anymore, you'd better hand in your resignation" (Shepard, 1975).

In 1946, with apartheid on the rise in South Africa, Fritz relocated to New York, and in 1947 Laura followed with the children. There they reunited with Karen Horney and soon found themselves among a circle of "interpersonal" psychoanalysts, including Erich Fromm and Clara Thompson, who rejected many of the tenets of orthodox Freudianism. Fritz became familiar with the ideas of Harry Stack Sullivan regarding existence as aprocess, mental illness as a response to person/environment interactions, and the importance of the therapist/patient relationship, which undoubtedly had a strong influence on him (Clarkson & McKewn, 1993). He and Laura soon had thriving practices as psychoanalysts, supported by referrals from Fromm, Thompson, and others associated with the William Alanson White Institute. Isadore From, one of Perls' early patients in New York, describes a fairly conventional analysis, lying on the couch with Fritz behind him, saying very little. "He told me to describe everything that I experienced but begin each sentence with the words 'here and now.' That's the only thing that surprised me, as the rest of it seemed like my idea of what psychoanalysis was" (Wysong & Rosenfeld, 1988, p. 28). The next year, when Laura arrived in New York, Fritz sent From to work with her, and From said he preferred it. He would still lie on the couch, but Laura sat facing him and often made references to his breathing. "I remember her as being very much more supportive and in direct contact with me. Which at the time was a great help to me" (p. 29).

## The Birth of Gestalt Therapy

Fritz and Laura began hosting gatherings and giving workshops in their apartment where they continued to develop their new ideas about therapy. They became friends with Paul Goodman, an anarchist philosopher and social critic dedicated to changing society through his poems, plays, novels, and essays. Goodman, already an intellectual celebrity, began as Laura's patient, then became a lay therapist in training with them and before long was their closest and most important collaborator. Fritz wanted help in completing a manuscript he had been working on for several years, so he paid Goodman $500 to edit it and asked Ralph Hefferline, a Columbia University psychology professor, to add experiential exercises. In 1951, *Gestalt Therapy: Excitement and Growth in the Human Personality* was published, written almost entirely by Goodman and Hefferline, but based on the ideas of Fritz and also Laura. This book is referred to by Gestalt therapists as "PHG" (Perls, Hefferline, & Goodman) and is generally considered to be the bible of Gestalt therapy. It is a difficult book to read, "impossible to introject," i.e., impossible to read once and take in without processing it, without chewing on the ideas and assimilating them. In the authors' words, the signal contribution of the Gestalt approach was "to shift the concern of psychiatry from the fetish of the unknown, from the adoration of the 'unconscious,' to the problems and phenomenology of awareness" (Perls et al., 1994, pp. viii–ix). *Gestalt Therapy*, like the Bible, served as the glue for a movement that would grow and spread throughout the world, connecting teachers and trainers who would often see things differently with a common set of basic principles and vocabulary.

The gatherings at the Perlses' apartment continued, and in early 1952 they officially launched the Gestalt Therapy Institute of New York. Fritz, Laura, Paul Goodman, Paul Weiss, and Isadore From began traveling regularly to Ohio to train people interested in Gestalt, and in 1954 a second institute was founded: the Gestalt Institute of Cleveland. During these years, Fritz's relationship with Laura and Paul Goodman began to deteriorate and he began to travel, living for several years in Miami, then California, and then Israel. After a visit to Japan to study Zen, Fritz returned to California and settled in at the Esalen Institute, perched high on a cliff over the rocky coastline of Big Sur. There he quickly became a major figure in the "human potential" movement,[6] demonstrating, and often filming, his living philosophy while working with groups of therapists, artists, musicians, and others seeking personal growth. He was known to operate like a Zen master: intimidating, profound, inspiring, unpredictable, and transformative. He behaved outrageously and experimented with meditation and LSD. Mainstream psychoanalysis in the United States at that time was conservative and resisted the counter-culture movement, retaining its place as an important medical specialization that dominated psychiatry. Gestalt therapy, on the other hand, was popularly associated with Eastern religions, cathartic *bataka*[7] fights, drugs, and nudity, and its increasingly famous founding guru was the bearded, rotund, and notoriously libidinous Fritz Perls. In November of 1970, *Time* magazine described the situation:

> One of the newest and most rebellious branches of psychology, Gestalt theory seeks to celebrate man's freedom, uniqueness and potential. This is markedly different from conditioning his behavior, after the manner of B.F. Skinner and other behaviorists, who argue that man is infinitely malleable, or from probing his subconscious and his past, like Freud. The "here and now," according to Perls, is all that matters; the mind and body are inseparably one; converts are commanded to "lose your mind and come to your senses..."

To a large extent, this came to be the public face of Gestalt therapy, for many years overshadowing and obscuring quieter developments elsewhere.

Fritz Perls left behind a complex legacy that required Gestalt therapists throughout the world to go through a process of assimilating and rejecting various aspects of his theory and personality.[8] The ambivalence toward Fritz as a person has sometimes been expressed in charming ways. Virginia Satir once said that "…when Fritz was Gestalting he was magnificent; when he was Fritzing, he could be a bastard" (Gaines, 1979, p. 267). Sylvan Krause called him "an incredible therapist" and "a 24-carat son of a bitch" (Gaines, 1979, p. 42). When Jack Aylward was once asked about his experience of working with Fritz, he responded: "It's like you've been walking in the desert for weeks and you're filthy and you finally come into a town and you really, really need a bath, but all they have is a car wash." Fritz would refer to himself as "a genius and a bum."

At Esalen, Fritz made his films and wrote two more books, *Gestalt Therapy Verbatim* and *In and Out of the Garbage Pail,* both published in 1969. He claimed that working with individual patients was now obsolete, but in New York, Cleveland, and in many other cities Gestalt therapy continued to develop as a mode of individual as well as group psychotherapy aimed not only at maximizing human potential but also at alleviating the suffering of those with psychological disorders. Laura Perls is often quoted as saying: "There are as many Gestalt therapies as there are Gestalt therapists." Eventually, there would be hundreds of Gestalt therapy training institutes throughout the world, organized by local institutional leaders with varied training histories and different relationships to the ideas and styles of Fritz, Laura, and others.

## Contemporary Relational Gestalt Therapy

In psychoanalysis, there has always been a tension between focusing on individual, intrapsychic experience and focusing on relational experience. Philip Lichtenberg (2010), argued that both conservative ("Self-Social Disparity") and radical ("Self-Social Unity") trends existed side by side in the writings of Freud himself.[9] As stated above, the history of psychoanalysis is the history of a movement away from theories based on intrapsychic drives and structures that originate in individuals toward theories based on the idea that all individuality is constituted by relational experience.[10] As we have seen, Gestalt therapy arose out of the most relational of trends in psychoanalytic theory and practice, and can even be viewed as a profoundly relational form of psychoanalysis (Bocian, 2009). So, what does it mean to be "relational" in Gestalt?

One way of looking at relationality in Gestalt therapy is to see it as a counter-response to Perls' aggressive confrontational style of working with his patients; another is to emphasize and expand the relationality already embedded in Gestalt therapy theory. In Gary Yontef's (1993) collection of essays, *Awareness, Dialogue & Process*, he does both, laying the groundwork for what would become known as "relational Gestalt therapy." Yontef rejects the theatrical style of Perls and his imitators – what he refers to as "boom-boom-boom therapy" – and carefully develops the theoretical and clinical implications of the original theory. In an essay from 1976, he describes Gestalt therapy as "clinical phenomenology" grounded in the dialogic principles of Martin Buber[11] and the *paradoxical theory of change*.[12] In a 1981 essay, he writes that "the I-Thou dialogue is to Gestalt therapy what the Transference Neurosis is to psychoanalysis" (1993, p. 201). He vehemently rejects Perls' practice of manipulating and frustrating the patient into taking self-responsibility and instead advocates staying "empathically in the patient's phenomenological world" (p. 220). Yontef emphasizes the importance of working with shame and moves Gestalt therapy away from a "hermeneutic of suspicion" (exemplified by Perls dismissively calling his patients "phonies") toward a "hermeneutic of trust" (Orange, 2011).

The relational trend in Gestalt therapy theory was further advanced with Richard Hycner's (1991) book, *Between Person and Person: Towards a Dialogical Psychotherapy* and his subsequent book, co-authored with Lynne Jacobs, *The Healing Relationship in Gestalt Therapy: A Dialogic/Self Psychology Approach*. These books expanded Martin Buber's ideas about dialogue and psychotherapy, and broadly advanced Yontef's project of assimilating psychoanalytic perspectives, particularly those of Heinz Kohut and Robert Stolorow.[13] Heinz Kohut (1971, 1977, 1984) proposed that our selves are structured by our internalized experience of others ("self-object experience") and that this process continues throughout our lives.[14] This idea had a profound effect on the way one views the therapist/patient relationship. From this principle, Kohut developed the method of "sustained empathic immersion" which, in the simplest terms, emphasized the "inclusion" side of Buber's dialogue, as opposed to Perls' emphasis on presence. Rather than being confrontational, this way of approaching the therapeutic dialogue fostered an exquisite sensitivity to the affective experience of the patient, and especially to the way the therapist was affecting the patient's experience of self. Robert Stolorow, along with George Atwood and others, developed ideas that were, in some ways, parallel to Kohut's and in other ways very different. Their therapeutic system is based entirely on phenomenology and what they call contextualism, something analogous to the field theory of Gestalt therapy.[15] In terms of "relationality," they strongly reject the Cartesian idea that we have separate minds and see all human experience as irreducibly intersubjective, i.e., constituted by our experience of each other and the world we live in. And like Gestalt therapy, their goal is to promote the awareness of disavowed experience, particularly affective experience. In this way of working, the subjective world of the patient is of primary importance. Lynne Jacobs (2001) wrote about the effect of studying with Stolorow:

My work was profoundly altered by this. Instead of listening to patients from the perspective of, "what is this patient trying to do to me (that is, what defenses, manipulations or avoidances is the patient engaged in)?" I began to listen from the perspective of, "what does the patient need from me in order to heal and grow (that is, what developmental striving is being expressed)?" (p. 281)[16]

Staying so close to the experience of the patient, without trying to change it, but rather to "dwell" in it (Stolorow, 2013), has made this approach particularly effective when working with people affected by trauma and the deep shame that is often associated with it. Perls' showmanship had not been very sensitive to shame and this corrective has enhanced the clinical possibilities of Gestalt therapy for those of us who felt that Fritz Perls' "safe emergency" had been too much "emergency" and not enough "safe."[17]

My first exposure to relational Gestalt therapy (or *any* Gestalt therapy) was a lecture and demonstration by Gary Yontef in, I believe, 2005, in Santa Monica, California, when I was in my master's program and training to become a marriage and family therapist. The event was in an auditorium and I have an image of Gary up on a stage dressed in black like Johnny Cash. The friend who invited me there volunteered to be his patient in a live demonstration. She was, to put it mildly, complicated. Sitting across from him, she launched into an affectively intense world of painful memories, metaphors, fantasies, and emotional states that I think would have been a challenge for any therapist. I really liked the way he worked with her: gentle, creative, connected, real. It never felt as if he was showing off, nor did he act as if he was trying to change her or *do* anything to her or make any particular thing happen. But he was very present and seemed to want to know and understand her experience. Now, years later, I know that I had been watching someone deeply committed to staying in a respectful dialogic relationship while exploring the phenomenology of whatever was happening in the moment. As we left, we both agreed that we liked this Gestalt therapy.

Before long, I found my way to a few talks and demonstrations by Erving Polster, which were fun and inspiring, and then a series of small workshops given by presenters from the Pacific Gestalt Institute (PGI), including Gary Yontef, Jan Ruckert, Ann Bartelstein, Lillian Norton, and Friedemann Schulz. I clearly remember my first experience of Lynne Jacobs in one of these small introductory workshops, presenting her ideas in a way that made it seem like we were all already living Gestalt therapy if we could just pay close attention to our experience. Her ideas were very exciting and after the talk I followed her down the hall, trying to keep the conversation going (this happens to her a lot). Soon, I signed up for training at PGI and kept the conversation going another twelve years and have also become a psychoanalyst, trained at an institute emphasizing relational and intersubjective theory.

The term "relational Gestalt therapy" has had many meanings and connotations at different times, in different contexts, for different people. When I began my studies, I thought it was something entirely different than the original "Gestalt therapy" and shouldn't even be called Gestalt. However, Gary Yontef (2002) writes that relational Gestalt therapy is "...not a whole, new system or approach. Rather, it is steeped in what is central to gestalt therapy and has sometimes gotten lost or neglected. It continues the gestalt therapy tradition of assimilating new information into the system..." (p. 31). In this brief introduction, I have focused on the relational perspective as it developed in the U.S., and particularly in Los Angeles, but this "new information" derives from the work of Gestalt therapists writing, training, practicing and researching in many countries throughout the world, supported by large international and regional organizations: IAAGT, EAGT, GANZ, and others.[18] In the following chapters, you will be offered some of this new information and have a chance to come to your own conclusions, to chew on these ideas, and to assimilate them in your own way. I hope and expect that you will find them nourishing.

## Notes

1  Perls' rejection of the libido theory would be the decisive break with Freudian orthodoxy. Eventually, most psychoanalysts would follow.
2  Reich attempted to "...represent character as an armour consisting mainly of muscular contractions" (Perls, 1969a, p. 72). His *character analysis* approach "...consists largely of unblocking and analyzing the structure of the observed behavior" (Perls et al., 1994, p. 13).
3  "In his book *Creative Indifference*, Friedlaender brings forward the theory that every event is related to a zero-point from which a differentiation into opposites takes place... By remaining alert in the centre, we can acquire a creative ability of seeing both sides of an occurrence and completing an incomplete half. By avoiding a one-sided outlook we gain a much deeper insight into the structure and function of the organism" (Perls, 1969a, p. 15).
4  Perls and Goodman list the important insights of Gestalt psychology as: "the relation of figure and background; the importance of interpreting the coherence or split of a figure in terms of the total context of the actual situation; the definite structured whole that is not too inclusive yet is not a mere atom; the active organizing force of meaningful wholes and the natural tendency toward simplicity of form; the tendency of unfinished situations to complete themselves" (Perls et al., 1994, pp. 14–15).
5  "Holism is the term...for an attitude which realizes that the world consists 'per se' not only of atoms, but of structures which have a meaning different than the sum of their parts" (Perls, 1969a/1947, p. 28). About field theory, Smuts (1926) writes: "Every 'thing' has its field, like itself, only more attenuated; every concept has, likewise, its field. It is in these fields and these fields only that things really happen" (p. 18).
6  In 1970, the American Psychiatric Association estimated that in California "...more troubled individuals already seek help from the human potientials movement than from 'traditional sources of psychotherapy'" ("Behavior: Human Potential: The Revolution in Feeling, 1970, p. 2).

7 Batakas are soft "encounter" bats, used to release aggression.
8 Just as all psychoanalysts must form some kind of relationship with the person and legacy of Sigmund Freud.
9 Lichtenberg wrote *Psychoanalysis: Radical and Conservative* in 1969, 10 years before he became a Gestalt therapist. In the preface to 2010 edition, he argues that the "best of Freud's thought is coherent with radical social perspectives" (p. 12) and is the basis for Gestalt therapy.
10 Mitchell (1988), Gergen (2009), and many others.
11 Martin Buber was an Austrian Jewish philosopher best-known for his essay "I and Thou" and for his ideas about dialogue. He wrote "all actual life is encounter" (1970, p. 62).
12 The paradoxical theory of change states that "change occurs when one becomes what he is, not when he tries to become what he is not" (Beisser, 1970, p. 77) and emphasizes trust in the dialogic process over pulling for specific outcomes.
13 This new assimilation should really come as no surprise, as Gestalt therapy has always been closely tied to trends in psychoanalysis and both Kohut's and Stolorow's ideas were derived from the same sources as Perls'.
14 Kohut's ideas about self-object experience echo PHG's idea that the self is a process of contact between a person and the environment, i.e., other people.
15 For many years, their system was known as Intersubjective Systems Theory, but now Stolorow and Atwood prefer to call it Phenomenological Contextualism.
16 It is interesting how ideas need to be rediscovered. In PHG, Perls et al. wrote: "Listening versus fighting. People who listen don't fight, and people who fight don't listen...The 'I'm telling you what you need' would be replaced by 'I'm listening for what you want'" (p. vi).
17 "...the point is for the patient to feel the behavior in its very emergency use and at the same time to feel that he is safe because he can cope with the situation" (Perls et al., 1994, p. 65).
18 IAAGT – the International Association for the Advancement of Gestalt Therapy. EAGT – the European Association of Gestalt Therapy. GANZ – Gestalt Australia and New Zealand.

## References

Behavior: Human potential: The revolution in feeling. (1970). *Time Magazine*. http://content.time.com/time/magazine/article/0,9171,943274,00.html
Beisser, A. (1970). The paradoxical theory of change. In J. Fagan & I. Shepherd (Eds.), *Gestalt Therapy Now*, New York: Harper.
Buber, M. (1970). *I and thou*. NY: Simon and Schuster. (original work published in German in 1923).
Bocian, B. (2009). From free association to concentration: About alienation, Ferenczi's "Forced Fantasies," and "the Third" in Gestalt therapy. *Studies in Gestalt Therapy: Dialogical Bridges*, 3(2), 37–58.
Bocian, B. (2020). From character analysis to interpersonal psychoanalysis to Gestalt therapy: Historical contextualization of various remarks in Perls' book "Skeleton.". In J. Robine & C. Bowman (Eds.), *Psychopathology of awareness*, (pp. 105–136). St. Romain La Virvee, France: L'exprimerie.
Clarckson, P., & Mackewn, J. (1993). *Fritz Perls*. London: Sage.

Dreyfuss, D. K. (1947). Review of the book Ego, hunger and aggression: A revision of Freud's theory and method, by F. S. Perls. *International Journal of Psycho-Analysis*, 28, 201–204.

Gaines, J. (1979). *Fritz Perls here and now*. California: Celestial Arts.

Gergen, K. J. (2009). *Relational being: Beyond self and community*. Oxford, NY: Oxford University Press.

Hycner, R. (1991). *Between person and person: Towards a dialogical psychotherapy*. Highland, NY: The Gestalt Journal Press.

Jacobs, L. & Hycner, R. (Eds.). (2009). *Relational approaches in Gestalt therapy*. New York: Gestalt Press/Routledge, Taylor & Francis Group.

Jacobs, L. (2001). Pathways to a relational worldview. In Goldfried, M. R. (Ed.), *How therapists change: Personal and professional reflection*, (pp. 271–287). Washington DC: American Psychological Association.

Kohut, H. (1971). *The analysis of the self*. New York: Int. Univ. Press.

Kohut, H. (1977). *The restoration of the self*. New York: Int. Univ. Press.

Kohut, H. (1984). *How does analysis cure?*. In A. Goldberg & P. Stepansky (Eds.). Chicago: University of Chicago Press.

Lichtenberg, J. (2010). *Psychoanalysis: Radical and conservative*. Wollongong, Australia: Ravenwood Press.

Mitchell, S. A. (1988). *Relational concepts in psychoanalysis: An integration*. Cambridge, MA: Harvard University Press.

Orange, D. M. (2011). *The suffering stranger: Hermeneutics for everyday clinical practice*. New York: Routledge.

Perls, F. (1969a). *Ego, hunger and aggression*. New York: Random House. (original work published in 1947).

Perls, F. (1969b). *Gestalt therapy verbatim*. Lafayette, CA: Real People Press.

Perls, F., Hefferline, R. & Goodman, P. (1994). *Gestalt therapy: Excitement and growth in the human personality*. Highland, NY: The Gestalt Journal Press. (original work published in 1951).

Shepard, M. (1975). *Fritz*. New York: Dutton.

Stolorow, R. D. (2013). Intersubjective-systems theory: A phenomenological-contextualist psychoanalytic perspective. *Psychoanalytic Dialogues*, *23*, 383–389.

van der Kolk, B. (2000). Trauma, neuroscience, and the etiology of hysteria: An exploration of the relevance of Breuer and Freud's 1893 article in light of modern science. *Journal of the American Academy of Psychoanalysis and Dynamic Psychiatry*, *28*, 237–262.

Wysong, J. & Rosenfeld, E. (1988). *An oral history of Gestalt therapy: Interviews with Laura Perls, Isadore From, Erving Polster, Miriam Polster, Elliott Shapiro*. Gouldsboro, Maine: Gestalt Journal Press.

Yontef, G. (1993). *Awareness, dialogue and process*. Gouldsboro, Maine: Gestalt Journal Press.

Yontef, G. (2002). The relational attitude in Gestalt therapy theory and practice. *International Gestalt Journal*, (25) *1*, 15–34.

# Relational Gestalt Therapy Theory

# Chapter 1

# Aesthetic Relational Knowledge and the Dance of Reciprocity in the Therapeutic Field: Post-pandemic Gestalt Therapy in Practice[1]

*Margherita Spagnuolo Lobb*[2]

## Introduction

This chapter aims to focus on the contemporary relational trend of Gestalt therapy clinical practice. This turn was necessary in our approach around the 80s when clinical needs and social trends changed significantly (Spagnuolo Lobb, 2013). Before that time, all Gestalt therapy methods aimed to support individual power. If a client said: "I feel unable to bring my needs forward: when my boss imposes on me to do something, I'd like to tell him that I see the situation differently, but I stay silent...." The therapist might have replied: "What do you feel in your body while you say that?" "I feel some tension in my legs" "Stay with that tension, breathe, and see where it brings you." The work would have continued with perhaps kicking a pillow and visualising the boss (or the father), until the client experienced a sense of power and a wider sense of self.

Today the scenario has changed. Clients present different problems, which, in turn, call forth different interventions. An example might be: "I feel worried that I will get sick. The doctor says I am fine, but I have a terrible feeling that I will die...." The therapist wants to know more about the "Ground" experience of this client, rather than exploring the figural meanings of his worry and asks: "I see. How do you spend your typical day?" "I wake up early, go to work, it takes one hour and a half to get there. I come back home at 6.30 in the afternoon, I cook something, sometimes I grab a pizza in a place on the way, I go online for a while, chat stupid things with some 'friend'... watch some TV... go to sleep." "How do you feel in telling *me* all this?" "It's strange to speak to someone who listens to you." "Yes, strange! I've noticed that you don't breathe with full lungs, and don't pause or look at me. What you said touches me: 'solitude' is the word that comes to mind. I'd like you to experience being-with me here. Can you breathe fully and look at me while you breath?" The work might continue without much overt intervention but with a feeling of intimacy and a solid feeling ground between therapist and client. This intervention is based on relational aspects ("tell me"... "I feel touched..") rather than on the

DOI: 10.4324/9781003255772-3

development of personal awareness of the client. Generally speaking, traumatic experiences are more widespread today than in years past (Taylor, 2014; Rubino & Spagnuolo Lobb, 2014), and we have integrated new findings from the neurosciences and the relational perspectives of intersubjective approaches to find a hermeneutic way of developing our method.

Next, I will describe in greater detail new clinical tools that have emerged to address both the new needs of society and new manifestations of human suffering that we encounter with today's clients.

## The Emergence of Serious Disturbances and the Relational Turn in Gestalt Therapy

Around the 1980s, Gestalt therapy techniques seemed naïve or even inappropriate to cure the new disturbances. In the face of clients suffering from addictions, personality disturbances or even psychoses, it was ineffective to "talk" with the drug, dialogue with ambivalent parts of the client's self or support creativity in speaking psychotically. Some institutes started to further develop the original theory of Gestalt therapy by studying two theoretical aspects that had been considered out of step with placing a primary value on the "Here and Now." These aspects were the study of child development and psychopathology. Such efforts hermeneutically brought forth a deeper discovery and development of the core relational spirit of the founding book (Perls et al., 1951/1994). Additionally, the concepts of Contact Boundary and Organism/Environment field became more focused. The further development of these two aspects provided theory and methodology for contemporary Gestalt therapists in treating the serious disturbances our clients are coping with in modern society.[3]

The study of *human development* in terms of phenomenological experience (Clemmens, 2012; Spagnuolo Lobb, 2012) and bodily movements (see Frank, 2001, 2016) allowed Gestalt therapists to consider human development as a "Ground" experience of the nowhere and now (Wheeler, 2000), so that to know more about the *ground* provides support in understanding the *figure*. *Psychopathology* is described as the creative adjustment to difficult situations (Perls et al., 1994, p. 6 ff.),[4] and it is connected with social conditions (Perls et al., 1994, p. 7 ff.; Spagnuolo Lobb, 2013, pp. 29–33; 2016a). The vitality implied in this definition guarantees that the therapeutic intervention aims to recognise the "beauty" of the client's adaptation, supporting the vital intentionality that is in each relational disturbance. Psychopathology manifests itself along a continuum of anxious/desensitised experiences (Spagnuolo Lobb, 2016b): from a desensitisation of the contact boundary (lack of awareness) that doesn't allow the person to perceive clearly the situation and herself, to a fixation of the figure that doesn't flow back to the ground experience to be assimilated (as in the case of traumatic experiences, see Taylor, 2014; Kepner, 2003; Bosco, 2014; Militello & Malacrea, 2011).

These developments have been supported by the spread of other studies, especially in the fields of neurosciences (Rizzolatti et al., 1996; Panksepp, 1998; Porges, 2009; Damasio, 2010; van der Kolk, 2014; and others) and intersubjective and relational psychoanalysis (Stern et al., 1998, 2003; Beebe & Lachman, 2001; Tronick, 1989; Orange et al., 1997; Mitchell, 2000) which, in the same decades, have discovered and described important relational aspects of human experience.

These researchers have been good allies in the further development of the relational approach contained within Perls, Hefferline & Goodman (PHG). This phenomenological, aesthetic and field-oriented[5] model provides new understanding in the treatment of current presentations of suffering Gestalt therapists encounter in post-modern society (Spagnuolo Lobb, 2013c).

From all these movements, inside and outside Gestalt therapy, the relational approach emerged as a way to include a better methodology for the treatment of serious disturbances and to address the societal need to increase interpersonal connectedness (Yontef, 1993; Jacobs & Hychner, 2009; Philippson, 2001; Wheeler, 2000). The concepts of contact boundary and organism/environment field became the core principles of the relational approach, and the contribution of the therapist to the experience of the client in the here and now became a tool to work with the field instead of with the individual (Spagnuolo Lobb, 2018a; Macaluso, 2020). As a matter of fact, the feeling of being seen by the other creates in the client (as well as in our lives outside of the consulting room) the feeling of existing for someone. It is here where the unified sense of self is born.

The dilemma which arose inside Gestalt therapy – which was partly created by contradictions inside the founding book itself – was between relational therapeutic praxis and an intrapsychic approach (Wheeler, 2000; Wollants, 2012). In a first moment, they were considered to be different styles of working (cfr. Stemberger, 2018). For instance, when the client says "I feel angry at my mother," one therapist could ask to imagine the mother sitting on the empty chair and tell "her" his anger, another therapist could ask "what do you feel in your body when you tell *me* that you feel angry to your mother?" These two ways of working actually differentiated the styles of Fritz Perls – who used to demonstrate his approach to neurotics in workshops – and his wife Laura Posner – who worked clinically with "real" patients and put much more effort in support, relationship and ground.

Considering the contemporary literature of Gestalt therapy, Macaluso (2020) describes three ways of practicing Gestalt therapy: one is focused on the client, a second is focused on the way the client makes contact with the therapist and a third is focused on the phenomenological field, which expresses the contribution of both therapist and patient to the therapeutic change. Philippson (2017) describes in a similar way three levels of Gestalt therapy training. Even if it is possible to use all of these ways, the above-mentioned differences have become separate currents inside Gestalt therapy:

basically, individualistic models and relational models. With his book *Gestalt Therapy: Therapy of the Situation,* Georges Wollants (2012) has tried to solve the inner contradictions inside the founding text *Gestalt Therapy,* drawing from the phenomenological and Gestalt theoretical concept of situation, which provides a stronger theoretical basis for our relational soul. He states that person and environment are inseparable and parts of the same whole. In our clinical work, we approach not the person of the client but the dynamic between the person and her phenomenological world. Wollants states that we should identify with the relational, situational and contextual perspective described in the first part of the founding book. I fully agree with his definition and I hope that we will be more and more able to develop our very special and unique relational glance, which is procedural, oriented to the concept of the situation (the therapeutic situation), and includes the experience of the therapist as part of it.

Today the "relational" approaches are many, both in the field of clinics and organisations. They are committed to research, both quantitative and qualitative, in particular phenomenological research (see Churchill, 2018; Brownell, 2019; Roubal, 2016; Schulthess et al., 2016; Fogarty et al., 2016; Herrera Salinas et al., 2019). They draw from different psychological and philosophical currents. This development is still in progress. I suggest reading Brownell (2018) for his attempt at describing relational Gestalt approaches applicable to both Gestalt psychotherapy and coaching.

What I have learned from my masters, Isadore From, Erving and Miriam Polster, and from many dialogues with colleagues such as Gary Yontef (1993), Gordon Wheeler (2000), Lynne Jacobs (Jacobs & Hychner, 2009), Ruella Frank (2001, 2016), Jean Marie Robine (2001, 2015), Dan Bloom (2003, 2011), Philip Lichtenberg (1990), Malcolm Parlett (2015), Peter Cole (2018), Peter Philippson (2001, 2017), Michael Clemmens (2019), and others, has inspired me to develop the relational stance into the paradigm of reciprocity, which integrates the focus on aesthetic knowledge (*Aesthetic Relational Knowledge*; Spagnuolo Lobb, 2018a) and intentionality of contact (the *now for next*, Spagnuolo Lobb, 2013) with the attention to the ground experience (*Polyphonic Development of Domains*; Spagnuolo Lobb, 2012) and to the "dance" of reciprocity – the reciprocal intentional movements – between therapist and client (Spagnuolo Lobb, 2019, 2018a, 2017a, 2017b).

## A Contextual Method, the Field and the Aesthetics of Contact

Clinical work is seen by Gestalt therapists in contextual and situational terms[6]: it is not only the client who is unable to reach the therapist with spontaneity but it is also the therapist herself who feels unable to reach the client. Here and now the therapist, with her aesthetic[7] tools, experiences a lack of spontaneity at the contact boundary. The therapist considers herself as involved and part of the same situation (or field) of the client in the therapeutic setting.

The client's suffering is a way of being at the contact boundary, and affects both the client and the therapist. It's a mismatch in the dance, a loss of spontaneity in the reciprocity. It is based on the concept of co-creation of contact boundary between therapist and client in the here and now of the session, with specific limits of two persons in a given time and space. The therapeutic meeting, their contacting, generates an experiential field. The presence of the client is experienced by the therapist who is trained to perceive his/her aesthetic resonance. This is considered in relational Gestalt therapy as the primary diagnostic tool (Spagnuolo Lobb, 2018a; Roubal et al., 2013, p. 87). Diagnosis is a process of "knowing-through" (*dia-gnosis*) the experience of the patient. The Gestalt therapist uses her own senses, alongside her psychological and personal knowledge, to know-through the patient's suffering. An interesting aspect of the contextualised concept of therapeutic intervention is that it explains positively how the diagnosis is influenced by the therapist.[8] What emerges indeed between therapist and client is the co-creation of a relational theme, rather than an isolated behaviour of the patient that is defined as psychopathological. This creates more concrete possibilities for "treating" psychopathological suffering as a phenomenological aspect of the relationship rather than as solely a problem of the patient.

## Contemporary Relational Gestalt therapy: Three Core Clinical Tools for a Contextualised "dance" of Reciprocity[9]

Relational Gestalt therapy approaches new manifestations of clinical suffering by supporting the emergence of a sense of safety that provides sure ground between therapist and client. In order to achieve this, the therapeutic presence-in reciprocal-movement with the patient is valued (Frank, 2016; Spagnuolo Lobb, 2017a, 2017b). The support of the neurophysiological process of contact ("Breathe and feel what happens at the boundary"), which was evident in the work of Laura Perls, is even a more important tool today.

For example, years ago a Gestalt therapist used to ask a client – who was complaining of not being able to decide between moving to another city to work or staying with a partner in his own city – "What do you want? Be responsible of your own wishes and say (even to the partner in the chair) what you want," assuming that the problem of the client was to bring his own wishes forward in front of important "others." Today the problem is not to take responsibility for one's own feelings, to have the courage to break rules, but to feel oneself and have the courage to stay with this feeling in front of another person.

In order to provide the basic physiological support that emerges in contact making, we ask: "Feel your body, breathe, look into my eyes. What do you feel? Continue to breathe while you look at me. Feel your feet on the ground. How do you experience yourself in front of me? What are your feelings and your emotions in this moment in front of me, your therapist and caregiver?" And, since the sense of self is built in contact with another, we need to provide him with our (real) feeling in front of him, like a containing "wall" that allows him to feel himself through the reaction of the other. For instance: "When you look at me, I feel tender," or "I feel disappointed." The resonance of the therapist allows to start the healing "dance" that brings the client to build a sense of solid ground. We re-create a situation where the client is in charge of doing something courageous, in order to be himself in the interaction. Also, the therapist will courageously change the relational schema and allow the client to express himself more spontaneously.

A client can feel a sense of self if we, the therapists, are the wall where he can find a sense of reality, a sense of who he is.

Relying on the foundations of relational Gestalt therapy, I will now consider three core interventions that can meet the needs of today's clients: 1. to work on the ground instead of working on the figure; 2. to use the aesthetic relational knowledge (ARK) in a field perspective (an updated and less naïve way of using our senses); 3. to address the paradigm of reciprocity and consider the "dance" as the locus of therapy, instead of considering what the client or the therapist does.

These are a development of the *phenomenological* root of Gestalt therapy, of its concept of intentionality and its focus on the here and now. They are also an in-depth look at the *aesthetic* tools, which have always been a crucial aspect of Gestalt therapy interventions. In fact, we know the patient and his/her creative adjustment via our senses, a special skill that I have called *Aesthetic Relational Knowledge*. Finally, reciprocity implies a development of the clinical use of the concept of *field*: the therapist becomes part of the situation of the client, and with his humanity and professional competence, co-creates a healing "dance" with him/her, that provides an implicit and aesthetic recognition of the intentionality of contact of the client.

### From Support of the Figure to Support of the Ground

Today the aim of Gestalt therapy has clearly switched from the support of the figure ("be yourself in spite of the others") – which was more needed between the 50s and the 80s – to the support of the ground ("feel your body and stay in contact with me") – a more important and appropriate care for contemporary disturbances, which was already present in the style of Laura Perls. The ground experience is made figural by contacting both somatic feelings (breathing, standing, being tense or relaxed, etc.) and by making contact with definitions of oneself (I am able, I'm not able, I love or I hate, etc.) (see Perls et al., 1994, pp. 156–157).

Today we are faced with manifestations of clinical suffering that express the loss of a sense of oneself. For example, an adolescent who has killed someone without knowing exactly why, or a couple who have not made love in years, or a young successful man who suffers for months with panic attacks at work. These are disturbances of the client's ground experience. Re-establishing the safe ground and a sense of unified self involves the experience of *relying on* the other/therapist and on the ground where they stand. The example in the previous paragraph shows the different styles of Gestalt work that support this basic sense of oneself in contact with the therapist. The therapist provides a presence today which takes care of a neurobiological sense of safety. The experience of the boy who has killed someone without knowing why, may well be an enactment of trauma as opposed to an act of retroflection. He has killed someone as a reaction to the overload of energy (probably related to a personality disorder), not as a consequence of a meaningful anger (a neurotic need to be free from suffocating liaisons). According to the polyvagal theory of Stephen Porges (2007), the sense of safety is an important moderator which influences the efficacy of psychotherapy. Very often our clients don't have access to bodily awareness, and thus lack a basic sense of sureness (see Kepner, 1995, 2002, 2003). This is a problem of regulating arousal and sustaining the bodily conditions of safety in contact and growth. As Gestalt therapists, we need to develop therapeutic skills to provide the perception of safety. Miriam Taylor (2014) reminds us to consider the window of tolerance that pertains to the experience of our client, something that was generally taken for granted years ago. And Ruella Frank (2016) works on the support to the basic relational movements that build up the sense of oneself and the spontaneity in contact making.

The feeling of safety is connected with the experience of being recognised by the other in one's own vitality. Therefore, the question for Gestalt therapists is: how to look at these kinds of difficulties as active expressions of vitality? (Perls et al., 1994, p. 25).

Our clients have acquired specific competencies in their adaptations to their world. These constitute the background of their experience, each competence harmonising with the others. They are domains of competencies, intertwining with each other in a *Polyphonic Development of Domains* (Spagnuolo Lobb, 2012). The way the client sits, moves, looks at the therapist, considers himself in front of the therapist, etc. shows how his previously acquired contacts are available now and supports his intentionality for contact in the session. For instance, a client sits legs crossed, looks and listens to the therapist and nods at each sentence of the therapist. She scratches her head vigorously from time to time, then she goes back to her more static position. The Gestalt therapist is aesthetically taken by that sudden gesture, which expresses some vitality of the ground. The ground experience of this client is made of her crossed legs, her nodding and her sudden scratching, all supporting each other. But the scratching attracts our attention as an "active expression of vitality," and we are curious to see how much that gesture of vitality "is waiting" to be supported, given a surer experience of the ground (that we as psychotherapists will strive to provide).

### The Aesthetic Relational Knowledge to Work with a Field Perspective

The field is activated every time there is a contact boundary (Perls et al., 1994, p. 151). The therapist's and the client's senses are not considered as isolated perceptions, but as individual perceptions that, as far as they are part of a situation, have something in common: they contribute to create a shared reality.

Today our attention is more on how we are co-creators, together with the client, of the contact boundary (instead of how the client creates a contact boundary with us). We are not just partners with our clients, but co-creators.

The field expresses the unitary nature of the therapist/client situation. What the therapist feels is somehow connected with the experiential field of the client, and it can be used as an aesthetic tool. The therapist and client are part of the same situation, and they *both* change. As Perls et al. (1994, p. 35) have stated: "It's meaningless to define a breather without air."

I derive the term ARK from Daniel Stern's[10] term of "Implicit Relational Knowledge" (Stern et al., 1998). He was referring to the capacity of the child and of the mother to know each other via non-verbal aspects, such as movements, tone of voice, interactive schemas, procedural aspects of the interactions. He wanted to support the importance of non-verbal (implicit) ways of knowing each other, giving them the dignity of an autonomous domain of child development, besides the verbal (explicit) domain, which was at that time considered a "superior" capacity (Stern et al., 2003).

I refer to the aesthetic (not implicit) knowledge, that is related to the capacity to know the other via our senses, and our vibrating in the presence of the other. The ARK is the sensory intelligence of the field. It is made of *embodied empathy* and *resonance* (see Spagnuolo Lobb, 2018a).

Here is an example of its use. A client cries finally, and we see how exposed to humiliation he is. The way he looks around and at us informs us that he is on alert, as if he needs to control what we feel. As therapists, we know what the client feels (thanks to our empathic capacity), and we might feel something else in front of that crying and sensitive-to-humiliation client. We might feel annoyed, or tender. We are not led by a rational reason to that feeling, we just feel something that belongs to us rather than to the client. We can understand how much it is a counter-transferential feeling, if it activates our past unfinished business. We are informed about the extent of our sensitivity to the client, and not distracted by our own unfinished business and personal work. Nevertheless, if we experience a particular feeling being activated by the situation in the therapy with a particular client, that feeling also belongs to the field. It belongs to a phenomenological reality. We might say that it expresses the "other side of the moon" of the client's experience, the experience of the "other" which makes humiliation possible for the client.

In other words, we can use our senses, not only to understand the feeling of the client, but also to understand the feeling of other parts of the field, which is made of the organism and of its environment. The way we resonate with a specific client, in a specific moment, is like the waves of the water that "resonate" to the stone thrown into the water. Lynne Jacobs (2018) expresses it well: "To stay in the play as part of the therapeutic situation." Resonance is the contribution of the therapist (a meaningful other) to the situation.[11]

This relational tool is different and can be complementary to the famous Gestalt technique of the empty chair. The latter is focused on the individual and his inner dialogues, rather than on the contact boundary with the therapist (see Macaluso, 2020). The ARK is in line with the situational approach that Perls et al. (1994, pp. 20–21) describe as "contextual method." According to it, we are part of the client's situation. Therefore, when we ask the client: "What do you feel when you look at your father on the chair?", we might add (following Isadore From's lesson): "What do you feel when you look at me now, while you are speaking of your father?" And this is not enough. We can ask ourselves: "And what do *I* feel as the other/therapist?"

### To Focus on the "dance"[12] of Reciprocity: A Switch of Paradigm

In the years, we have switched our therapeutic focus from the client to the phenomenological field that therapist and client co-create and, now, to their reciprocity. In other words, the reciprocal act of moving towards the other is central to the therapeutic process.

The mutual movements of client towards therapist and therapist towards client create a "dance" of reciprocity (Spagnuolo Lobb, 2017a, 2019). What heals is the synchronicity (cfr. Tschacher et al., 2014) and the feeling of being supported that the client gets from the movements of the therapist (cfr. Stern, 2010). There are not predetermined techniques that can give the client the feeling of being supported, it is rather the special gesture that belongs specifically to that therapist, the "signature" as Stern used to say (Stern et al., 2003) that makes the client feel supported by that particular therapist. It is a special implicit and aesthetic knowledge that the two develop in their relationship.

The "dance" between therapist and client takes into account phenomenological and aesthetic aspects of their interaction such as movements, intentionalities, excitement for contact, relaxation when the contact goal is achieved, breathing, time of contact (process), etc.

The concept of reciprocity can be a contemporary realisation of the Gestalt therapy epistemological basis of phenomenology, aesthetics and field perspective. The concept of reciprocity also integrates, current research on relational mind (Seikkula et al., 2015), neurosciences (Porges, 2007; Gallese, 2009), epigenetics (Spector, 2013), therapeutic alliance (Tschacher et al., 2014, 2015, 2016; Flückiger et al., 2012) and intersubjectivity (Stern, 2010; Beebe & Lachmann, 2001).

With the intent of describing this "dance" in terms of the intentionality of their being-with the other over the time-period of their meeting, I consider eight "dance steps," each one of them being identified with proper intentional behaviours. These dance steps describe two main caring interactions: the caregiver/child (Spagnuolo Lobb, 2016c), and the therapist/client interactions (Spagnuolo Lobb, 2017a, 2017b). The dance steps – ideally – are a sequence of intentional movements, but they don't have to happen necessarily in sequence. They are procedural, spontaneous actions of contact between the child and their caregivers or between therapist and client. They are named as follows (see Spagnuolo Lobb, 2016c, 2017a, 2017b): 1. to build together the sense of the ground; 2. to perceive each other; 3. to recognise each other's intentional movement; 4. to adjust to one another; 5. to take bold steps together; 6. to have fun; 7. to reach each other; 8. to let oneself go to the other/to take care of the other.[13]

They allow the therapist to support the regulation of the therapeutic relationship and contact, beyond the single action of one or the other. They help to support each therapeutic "dance" as a unique co-creation, giving dignity to mutual regulative processes and to qualitative aspects of clinical practice.

The use of this concept of "dance of reciprocity," which focuses on the regulative processes of meaningful interactions, is important also in training and supervision: students can be supported to develop their relational mind when they learn psychotherapy. Moreover, to use the "dance steps" to supervise psychotherapists has been proved to be supportive and able to avoid the risk of shame that is so much implied in supervision.[14]

Finally, the "dance steps" are useful to support psychotherapists to trust aesthetic and field oriented feelings in their work, to trust their capacity for being-with, against a narcissistic culture that holds a concept of the therapist who has to do the "right move."

## Conclusion

I've tried to outline the development of relational Gestalt therapy from the support of autonomy of the client, to the capacity to "dance" with her/him, co-creating the sense of safety that is mostly needed today.

The ARK and the paradigm of reciprocity are here presented as recent clinical values of relational Gestalt therapy. We consider ourselves, the healers, as co-creators of the therapeutic situation, and we go into the play as part of the situation, experimenting with specific support for the client's sense of agency, along with a full and spontaneous sense of self. With its relational evolution, Gestalt therapy can continue to provide an innovative contribution to the field of psychotherapy and to society. Relational Gestalt therapy integrates recent studies on the relational nature of the brain, on attachment theories and on the importance of relationship in personal change. It even integrates new research that considers the effects of relationship on genetic change (Spector, 2013). Gestalt therapy, which draws on phenomenology, aesthetics and field theory, is a useful way to help contemporary patients rediscover their vitality, their unified sense of self and their existential safety, in a social context where desensitisation, and dissociations are the most common clinical manifestations.

## Notes

1 This chapter is a revised edition of Spagnuolo Lobb M. (2020). The Relational Turn of Gestalt Therapy Clinical Practice: From the "empty chair" to the "dance of reciprocity" in the field International Journal of Psychotherapy, 24, 3: 17–31. DOI: 10.36075/IJP.2020.24.3.3/Lobb

2 **Margherita Spagnuolo Lobb, Psy.D.**, Director Istituto di Gestalt HCC Italy (Milan, Palermo, Siracusa), Past president and Honorary member EAGT, LAA from AAGT, Honorary president of SIPG, International trainer, Editor of *Gestalt Therapy Book Series* (Routledge) and *Italian Gestalt Therapy Journal*. More about her work: https://www.gestaltitaly.com/margherita-spagnuolo-lobb/ *Address for correspondence:* margherita.spagnuolo@gestalt.it Web sites: www.gestaltitaly.com; www.gestalt.it

3 Other institutes have developed relational models for organisational consulting, applying these two concepts to the relationship between individual and society (see Melnick, 2019; Nevis, 1997).

4 The description of the concept of psychopathology in Gestalt therapy (see Yontef, 2001, 2005; Robine, 2001; Spagnuolo Lobb, 2013a, p. 56 ff.; Francesetti et al., 2013) has allowed us to dialogue with psychiatrists and clinicians, and to create a bridge with the shared language of DSM (see for example Rubino et al., 2014; Spagnuolo Lobb, 2013b, 2015).

5 Literature about the concept of field in Gestalt Therapy is extended, and it would be impossible to quote all contributions. There are various descriptions, which express the debate between individual perception and a shared experience. See for instance Robine (2015), Parlett (2015), Spagnuolo Lobb (2016a), Francesetti (2015), or Rossi (2017) for a in-depth description of general literature.

6 The founders of Gestalt therapy from the very first proposed the "contextual" method, as a hermeneutic circularity between the reader and the book: "Thus the reader is apparently confronted with an impossible task: to understand the book he must have the 'Gestaltist' mentality, and to acquire it he must understand the book" (Perls et al., 1994, p. XXIV).

7  The word "aesthetic" derives from the Greek word αισθετικός, which means "related to the senses." In Gestalt therapy, the term contact not only implies that we are interconnected beings, but also expresses a consideration of the physiology of the experience. Interest in the mentalization of the experience is decidedly replaced by an aesthetic interest in the experience generated by the concrete nature of the senses (Spagnuolo Lobb, 2013, p. 47)

8  Atwood and Stolorow (1993) have described how what is diagnosed, from an intersubjective perspective, is not the patient's psychological organisation seen in isolation but the functioning of the entire therapeutic system. Moreover, Aboraya et al. (2006) have shown how clinician background and training may influence interpretation of symptoms.

9  For an in-depth description of these three clinical tools, see Spagnuolo Lobb (2019, pp. 241–248).

10  Daniel Stern was visiting professor in the post-graduate school that I chair for 9 years. He has been important in my development of Gestalt therapy in relational terms.

11  Ruella Frank (2016) has developed the concept of resonance as a kinaesthetic response. I have developed it as the aesthetic contribution to the knowledge of the field. Michael Clemmens (2019) has developed the concept of "embodied contexts." All three concepts are compatible.

12  I use the word "dance" in a metaphorical way.

13  The "dance steps" model has been validated by studies.

14  This method is used in the international programs for Gestalt Therapy Supervisors organised by the Istituto di Gestalt HCC Italy (www.gestaltitaly.com), accredited by the European Association for Gestalt Therapy.

## References

Aboraya, A., Rankin, E., France, C., El-Missiry, A. & John, C. (2006). The Reliability of Psychiatric Diagnosis Revisited: The Clinician's Guide to Improve the Reliability of Psychiatric Diagnosis. *Psychiatry*, *3*(1), 41–50.

Atwood, G. & Stolorow, R. (1993) *Faces in a Cloud: Intersubjectivity in Personality Theory*, 2nd ed. Northvale, NJ: Jason Aronson.

Beebe, B. & Lachmann, F. M. (2001). *Infant Research and Adult Treatment: A Dyadic Systems Approach*. Hillsdale, NY: The Analytic Press.

Bloom, D. (2003). "Tiger! Tiger! Burning Bright" – Aesthetic Values as Clinical Values in Gestalt Therapy. In Spagnuolo Lobb, M., & Amendt-Lyon, N. (Eds.), *Creative License. The Art of Gestalt Therapy* (pp. 63–78). Wien, NY: Springer.

Bloom, D. (2011). One Good Turn Deserves Another… and another… and another: Personal Reflections on Relational Approaches to Gestalt Therapy. *Gestalt Review*, *15*(3), 296–311. 10.5325/Gestaltreview.15.3.0296

Bloom, D. (2016). The Relational Function of Self: Self Function in the Most Human Plane. In J.-M. Robine (Ed.), *Self, A Polyphony of Contemporary Gestalt Therapists*. St. Romain la Virvée, France: L'Exprimerie.

Bosco, F. (2014). Translating Somatic Experiencing® and Gestalt Therapy for Trauma Resolution into Music Therapy Practice with Adults. In Bloom, D. & O'Neill, B. (Eds.), *The New York Institute for Gestalt Therapy in the 21st Century: An Anthology of Published Writings Since 2000*. Queensland, Australia: Ravenwood Press.

Brownell, P. (2018). *Gestalt Psychotherapy and Coaching for Relationships*. New York, NY: Routledge/Taylor & Francis Group.

Brownell, P. (Ed.) (2019). *Handbook for Theory, Research and Practice in Gestalt Therapy*. 2nd ed. Cambridge: Cambridge Scholars Publishing.

Churchill, S. D. (2018). Explorations in Teaching the Phenomenological Method: Challenging Psychology Students to "grasp at meaning" in Human Science Research. *Qualitative Psychology*, *5*(2), 207–227. 10.1037/qup0000116

Clemmens, M. (2012). The Interactive Field: Gestalt Therapy as an Embodied Relational Dialogue. In T. Bar-Yoseph Levine (Ed.), *Gestalt Therapy: Advances in Theory and Practice*. (pp. 39–48). NY: Routledge.

Clemmens, M. (2019). *Embodied Relational Gestalt: Theories and Applications*. New York: Gestalt Press.

Cole, P. H. & Reese, D. (2018). *New Directions in Gestalt Group Therapy. Relational Ground, Authentic Self*. New York: Routledge.

Damasio, A. (2010). *Self Comes to Mind: Constructing the Conscious Brain*. New York: Pantheon/Vintage.

Flückiger, C., Del Re, A. C., Wampold, B. E., Znoj, H., Caspar, F. & Jörg, U. (2012). Valuing Clients' Perspective and the Effects on the Therapeutic Alliance: A Randomized Controlled Study of an Adjunctive Instruction. *Journal of Counseling Psychology*, *59*(1), 18–26.

Francesetti, G., Gecele, M. & Roubal, J. (2013). Gestalt Therapy Approach to Psychopathology. In Francesetti, G., Gecele, M. & Roubal, J. (Eds.), *Gestalt Therapy in Clinical Practice. From Psychopathology to the Aesthetics of Contact* (pp. 59–75). Siracusa, Italy: Istituto di Gestalt HCC Italy Publ. Co, www.gestaltitaly.com.

Francesetti, G. (2015). From Individual Symptoms to Psychopathological Fields. Toward a Field Perspective on Clinical Human Suffering. *British Gestalt Journal*, *24*(1), 5–19

Frank, R. (2001). *Body of Awareness. A Somatic and Developmental Approach to Psychotherapy*. Cambridge, MA: Gestalt Press.

Frank, R. (2016). Moving Experience: Kinaesthetic Resonance as Relational Feel. In Spagnuolo Lobb, M., Levi, N. & Williams, A. (Eds.), *Gestalt Therapy with Children. From Epistemology to Clinical Practice* (pp. 87–99). Siracusa, Italy: Istituto di Gestalt HCC Italy Publ. Co., www.Gestaltitaly.com.

Fogarty, M., Bhar, S., Theiler, S. & O'Shea, L. (2016). What do Gestalt Therapists do in the Clinic? The Expert Consensus. *British Gestalt Journal*, *25*(1), 32–41.

Gallese, V. (2009). Mirror Neurons, Embodied Simulation, and the Neural Basis of Social Identification. *Psychoanalytic Dialogues*, *19*, 519–536.

Herrera Salinas, P., Mstibovskyi, I., Roubal, J. & Brownell, P. (2019). Researching Gestalt Therapy for Anxiety in Practice-Based Settings: A Single-Case Experimental Design. *Psychotherapie-Wissenschaft*, *9*(2), 53–67. 10.30820/1664-9583-2019-2-53b

Jacobs, L. (2018). Comment to My Other's Keeper: Resources for the Ethical Turn in Psychotherapy, by Donna M. Orange. In Spagnuolo Lobb, M., Bloom, D., Roubal, J., Zeleskov Djoric, J., Cannavò, M., La Rosa, R., Tosi, S. & Pinna, V. (Eds.), *The Aesthetic of Otherness: Meeting at the Boundary in a Desensitized World, Proceedings* (pp. 37–40). Siracusa, Italy: Istituto di Gestalt HCC Italy Publ. Co. (www.Gestaltitaly.com).

Jacobs, L. & Hycner, R. (Eds.) (2009). *Relational Approaches in Gestalt Therapy*. New York: Gestalt Press Book.

Kepner, J. (1995). *Healing Tasks: Psychotherapy with Adult Survivors of Childhood Abuse*. San Francisco, CA: Jossey-Bass.

Kepner, J. (2002). *Energy and the Nervous System in Embodied Experience*. www. pathwaysforhealing.com/pdfs/Phenom%20of%20NS.pdf

Kepner, J. (2003). The Embodied Field. *British Gestalt Journal*, *12*(1), 6–14.

Levinas, E. (1946). *Time and the Other*. Pittsburgh, PA: Duquesne University Press.

Lichtenberg, P. (1990). *Undoing the Clinch of Oppression*. New York, NY: Peter Lang Publishing Inc.

Lyotard, J.-F. (1979). *La condition postmoderne: rapport sur le savoir*. Paris: Minuit.

Macaluso, M. A. (2020). Deliberateness and Spontaneity in Gestalt Therapy Practice. *British Gestalt Journal*, *29*(1), 30–36.

Melnick, J. (2019). Gestalt Approach to Working with Organisations. In Spagnuolo Lobb, M. & Meulmeester, F. (Eds.), *Gestalt Approaches with Organisations* (pp. 51–66). Siracusa, Italy: Istituto di Gestalt HCC Italy Publ. Co., www. Gestaltitaly.com.

Militello, R. & Malacrea, M. (2011). Il trauma dell'abuso e il delicato processo della riparazione: come ridare voce e corpo al bambino violato. *Quaderni di Gestalt*, *XXIV*(1), 11–21. DOI: 10.3280/GEST2011-001002

Mitchell, S. (2000). *Relationality: From Attachment to Intersubjectivity*. New York: Analytic Press.

Nevis, E. C. (1997). *Organizational Consulting: A Gestalt Approach*. London, UK: Routledge.

Orange, D. M. (2018). My Other's Keeper: Resources for the Ethical Turn in Psychotherapy. In Spagnuolo Lobb, M., Bloom, D., Roubal, J., Zeleskov Djoric, J., Cannavò, M., La Rosa, R., Tosi, S. & Pinna, V. (Eds.), *The Aesthetic of Otherness: Meeting at the Boundary in a Desensitized World, Proceedings* (pp. 19–32). Siracusa, Italy: Istituto di Gestalt HCC Italy Publ. Co., www.Gestaltitaly.com

Orange, D., Atwood, G. & Stolorow, R. (1997). *Working Intersubjectively: Contextualism in Psychoanalytic Practice*. Hillsdale, NJ: The Analytic Press.

Panksepp, J. (1998). *Affective Neuroscience: The Foundations of Human and Animal Emotions*. New York, NY: Oxford University Press.

Parlett, M. (2015). *Future Sense: Five Explorations of Whole Intelligence for a World That's Waking Up*. Leicester: Troubador Publishing.

Perls, L. (1992). *Living at the Boundary*. New York: Gestalt Therapy Press.

Perls, F., Hefferline, R. & Goodman, P. (1994, or. ed. 1951). *Gestalt Therapy: Excitement and Growth in the Human Personality*. New York: Julian Press.

Philippson, P. (2001). *Self in Relation*. Highland, NY: Gestalt Journal Press.

Philippson, P. (2017). Three levels of training. *British Gestalt Journal*, *26*(1), 3–6.

Philippson, P. (2013). Comment to Gestalt Therapy Approach to Psychopathology, by Gianni Francesetti, Michela Gecele and Jan Roubal. In Francesetti, G., Gecele, M. & Roubal, J. (Eds.) *Gestalt Therapy in Clinical Practice. From Psychopathology to the Aesthetics of Contact* (pp. 76–78). Siracusa, Italy: Istituto di Gestalt HCC Italy Publ. Co., www.Gestaltitaly.com

Polster, E. (1987). *Every Person's Life is Worth a Novel*. New York: W.W. Norton & co.

Porges, S. W. (2007). The Polyvagal Perspective. *Biological Psychology*, *74*(2), 116–143.

Porges, S. W. (2009). The Polyvagal Theory: New Insights into Adaptive Reactions of the Autonomic Nervous System. *Cleveland Clinic Journal of Medicine, 76*(Suppl 2), S86–S90. DOI: 10.3949/ccjm.76.s2.17

Rizzolatti, G., Fadiga, L., Gallese, V. & Fogassi, L. (1996). Premotor Cortex and the Recognition of Motor Actions. *Cognitive Brain Research 3*, 131–141.

Robine, J.-M. (2001). From Field to Situation. In Robine, J.-M. (Ed.), *Contact and Relationship in a Field Perspective* (pp. 95–107). Bordeaux: L'Exprimerie.

Robine, J.-M. (2015). *Social Change Begins with Two*. Siracusa (Italy): Istituto di Gestalt HCC Italy Publ. Co., www.Gestaltitaly.com

Rossi, S. (2017). *La pulsazione del campo. Dalla Gestalt therapy alla Field Therapy*. Pisa: ETS

Roubal, J. (Ed.). (2016). *Towards a Research Tradition in Gestalt Therapy*. Newcastle upon Tyne, UK: Cambridge Scholars Publishing.

Roubal, J., Gecele, M. & Francesetti, G. (2013). Gestalt Therapy Approach to Diagnosis. In Francesetti, G., Gecele, M. & Roubal, J. (Eds.) *Gestalt Therapy in Clinical Practice. From Psychopathology to the Aesthetics of Contact* (pp. 79–108). Siracusa, Italy: Istituto di Gestalt HCC Italy Publ. Co, www.Gestaltitaly.com

Rubino, V. & Spagnuolo Lobb, M. (2014). Autoregolazione, intenzionalità e co-creazione del confine di contatto come antidoto alle esperienze dissociative. La proposta della psicoterapia della Gestalt. *Idee in Psicoterapia, VII*(1), 77–86.

Schulthess, P., Tschuschke, V., Koemeda-Lutz, M., von Wyl, A. & Crameri, A. (2016). Comparative Naturalistic Study on Outpatient Psychotherapeutic Treatments Including Gestalt Therapy. In Roubal, J. (Ed.), *Towards a Research Tradition in Gestalt Therapy* (pp. 335–355). Cambridge: Scholars Publishing.

Seikkula, J., Karvonen, A., Kykyri, V.-L., Kaartinen, J. & Penttonen, M. (2015). The Embodied Attunement of Therapists and a Couple within Dialogical Psychotherapy: An Introduction to the Relational Mind Research Project. *Family Process, 54*, 703–715.

Spagnuolo Lobb, M. (2001). From the Epistemology of Self to Clinical Specificity of Gestalt Therapy. In Robine, J.-M. (Ed.), *Contact and Relationship in a Field Perspective* (pp. 49–65). Bordeaux: L'Exprimerie.

Spagnuolo Lobb, M. (2012). Toward a Developmental Perspective in Gestalt Therapy Theory and Practice: The Polyphonic Development of Domains. *Gestalt Review, 16*(3), 222–244.

Spagnuolo Lobb, M. (2013a). *The Now-for-Next in Psychotherapy. Gestalt Therapy Recounted in Post-Modern Society*. Siracusa, Italy: Istituto di Gestalt HCC Italy Publ. Co., www.Gestaltitaly.com

Spagnuolo Lobb, M. (2013b). Borderline. The Wound of the Boundary. In Francesetti, G., Gecele, M. & Roubal, J. (Eds.), *Gestalt Therapy in Clinical Practice. From Psychopathology to the Aesthetics of Contact* (pp. 617–650). Siracusa, Italy: Istituto di Gestalt HCC Italy Publ. Co.

Spagnuolo Lobb, M. (2013c). From the Need for Aggression to the Need for Rootedness: A Gestalt Postmodern Clinical and Social Perspective on Conflict. *British Gestalt Journal, 22*(2), 32–39.

Spagnuolo Lobb, M. (2013d). Human Rights and Social Responsibility in Gestalt Therapy Training. In Klaren, G., Levi, N. & Vidakovic, I. (Eds.), *Yes we care!. Social,*

*Political and Cultural Relationships as Therapy's Ground, a Gestalt Perspective* (pp. 71–83). The Netherlands: European Association for Gestalt Therapy.

Spagnuolo Lobb, M. (2015). Gestalt Therapy Perspective on Depressive Experiences: An Introduction. In Francesetti, G. (Ed.), *Absence is the Bridge Between Us. Gestalt Therapy Perspective on Depressive Experiences* (pp. 35–63). Siracusa, Italy: Istituto di Gestalt HCC Italy Publ. Co., www.Gestaltitaly.com.

Spagnuolo Lobb, M. (2016a). Psychotherapy in Post Modern Society. *Gestalt Today Malta, 1*(1), 97–113. ISSN 2519-0547.

Spagnuolo Lobb, M. (2016b). Self as Contact, Contact as Self. A Contribution to Ground Experience in Gestalt Therapy Theory of Self. In Robine, J. M. (Ed.), *Self. A Poliphony of Contemporary Gestalt Therapists* (pp. 261–289). St. Romain la Virvée, France: L'Exprimerie.

Spagnuolo Lobb, M. (2016c). Gestalt Therapy with Children. Supporting the Polyphonic Development of Domains in a Field of Contacts. In Spagnuolo Lobb, M., Levi, N. & Williams, A. (Eds.), *Gestalt Therapy with Children. From Epistemology to Clinical Practice* (pp. 25–62). Siracusa, Italy: Istituto di Gestalt HCC Italy Publ. Co., www.Gestaltitaly.com.

Spagnuolo Lobb, M. (2017a). From Losses of Ego Functions to the Dance Steps between Psychotherapist and Client. Phenomenology and Aesthetics of Contact in the Psychotherapeutic Field. *British Gestalt Journal, 26*(1), 28–37.

Spagnuolo Lobb, M. (2017b). Phenomenology and Aesthetic Recognition of the Dance between Psychotherapist and Client: A Clinical Example. *British Gestalt Journal, 26*(2), 50–56.

Spagnuolo Lobb, M. (2018a). Aesthetic Relational Knowledge of the Field: A Revised Concept of Awareness in Gestalt Therapy and Contemporary Psychiatry. *Gestalt Review, 22*(1), 50–68.

Spagnuolo Lobb, M. (2018b). Comment to My Other's Keeper: Resources for the Ethical Turn in Psychotherapy, by Donna M. Orange. In: Spagnuolo Lobb, M., Bloom, D., Roubal, J., Zeleskov Djoric, J., Cannavò, M., La Rosa, R., Tosi, S. & Pinna, V. (Eds.), *The Aesthetic of Otherness: Meeting at the Boundary in a Desensitized World, Proceedings* (pp. 41–44). Siracusa, Italy: Istituto di Gestalt HCC Italy Publ. Co., www.Gestaltitaly.com

Spagnuolo Lobb, M. (2019). The Paradigm of Reciprocity: How to Radically Respect Spontaneity in Clinical Practice. *Gestalt Review, 23*(3), 234–254. DOI: 10.5325/Gestaltreview.23.3.0232

Spagnuolo Lobb, M. & Lichtenberg, P. (2005). Classica Gestalt Therapy Theory. In Woldt, A. L. & Toman, S. M., *Gestalt Therapy: History, Theory, and Practice* (pp. 21–40). Thousand Oaks, CA: SAGE Publications.

Spector, T. (2013). *Identically Different: Why You Can Change Your Genes.* New York: Overlook Press.

Stemberger, G. (2018). "Wie hätte sich die Gestalttherapie wohl auf Gestalttheoretischer Grundlage entwickelt?" – Zu Leben und Werk von Georges Wollants (1941-2018). *Phänomenal – Zeitschrift für Gestalttheoretische Psychotherapie, 10*(2), 33–39. ("What kind of Gestalt therapy would have been developed on the basis of the Gestalt theory of the Berlin School?" – On Life and Work of Georges Wollants.)

Stern, D. N. (1985). *The Interpersonal World of the Infant: A View from Psychoanalysis and Developmental Psychology.* NY: Basic books.

Stern, D. N. (2004). *The Present Moment in Psychotherapy and Everyday Life*. New York: Norton.

Stern, D. N. (2010). *Forms of Vitality. Exploring Dynamic Experience in Psychology and the Arts*. USA: Oxford University Press.

Stern, D. N., Bruschweiler-Stern, N., Harrison, A., Lyons-Ruth, K., Morgan, A., Nahum, J., Sander, L. & Tronick, E. (1998). Non-interpretive Mechanisms in Psychoanalytic Therapy. The "something more" than interpretation. *International Journal of Psychoanalysis, 79*, 903–921.

Stern, D. N., Bruschweiler-Stern, N., Harrison, A., Lyons-Ruth, K., Morgan, A., Nahum, J., Sander, L. & Tronick, E. (2003). On the Other Side of the Moon. The Import of Implicit Knowledge for Gestalt Therapy. In Spagnuolo Lobb, M. & Amendt-Lyon, N. (Eds.), *Creative License: The Art of Gestalt Therapy* (pp. 21–35). Vienna and New York: Springer.

Taylor, M. (2014). *Trauma Therapy and Clinical Practice. Neuroscience, Gestalt and the Body*. London: Open University Press, McGraw Hill.

Tronick, E. Z. (1989). Emotions and Emotional Communication in Infants. *American Psychologist, 44*, 112–119.

Tschacher, W., Rees, G. M. & Ramseyer, F. (2014). Nonverbal Synchrony and Affect in Dyadic Interactions. *Frontiers in Psychology, 5*, 1323.

Tschacher, W., Haken, H. & Kyselo, M. (2015). Alliance: A Common Factor of Psychotherapy Modeled by Structural Theory. *Frontiers in Psychology for Clinical Settings, 6*, 421.

Tschacher, W. & Pfammatter, M. (2016). Embodiment in Psychotherapy – A Necessary Complement to the Canon of Common Factors? *European Psychotherapy, 13*, 9–25.

van der Kolk, B. (2014). *The Body Keeps the Score: Mind, Brain and Body in the Transformation of Trauma*. New York: Viking Penguin.

Wheeler, G. (2000). *Beyond Individualism: Toward a New Understanding of Self, Relationship, and Experience*. Hillsdale, NJ: The Analytic Press.

Wollants, G. (2012). *Gestalt Therapy. Therapy of the Situation*. London: SAGE Publications.

Yontef, G. M. (1993). *Awareness, Dialogue and Process. Essays on Gestalt Therapy*. Highland, NY: The Gestalt Journal Press.

Yontef, G. M. (2001). Relational Gestalt Therapy. In Robine, J. M. (Ed), *Contact and Relationship in a Field Perspective* (pp. 79–94). Bordeaux: L'Exprimerie.

Yontef, G. M. (2005). Gestalt Therapy Theory of Change. In Woldt, A. L. & Toman, S. M. (Eds.), *Gestalt Therapy: History, Theory and Practice* (pp. 81–100). Thousand Oaks, CA: Sage Publications.

## Chapter 2

# Engaged Surrender[1]

*Lynne Jacobs*

What follows is the keynote talk that I gave at the EAGT conference in Budapest in September of 2019. I was the caboose in a train of six keynote talks. I did not write a formal paper for EAGT. I mostly allowed my associative process to take me where it would. I wanted to cover a few thoughts that were stimulated for me by our assigned topic, the fertile void. The thoughts are in no particular order, and none so rich as to provide a jumping-off point for an in-depth paper, so I have chosen to offer here simply a mildly edited version of my spoken remarks (I owe thanks to the planning committee for recording the talk, and to Heather Keyes for translating the recording).

### Introduction

I am humbled and appreciative about being asked to participate as a keynote speaker. I am also aware, as I stand here, that I am the fourth native English speaker you will listen to. Most of us were born in the US, and three of us still live there. I feel a bit embarrassed by that, it seems like a bit of an imposition on you.

I know there are many factors to take into account when you decide about keynote speakers, and I don't know what went into making these decisions, but I want to offer you what I started to think about as I watched the panoply of speakers. I think it's one of these moments where I've realized my age. All of the speakers are from the seniors' community. I think maybe you chose us in order to honor us? I feel humbled because I do feel honored. And maybe part of my role here is to receive that honor and to try to offer some wisdom and then to pass the torch along.

There are people in your European Association of Gestalt Therapy (EAGT) community who are full of creative ideas. But to offer your creativity to this community and the wider Gestalt therapy community, written English is required. Thus, native English speakers are more widely read. Increasingly, Europeans and others for whom English is a second (or even third!) language, are writing in English. People like Margherita Spagnuolo-

DOI: 10.4324/9781003255772-4

Lobb have encouraged others to write in English and have arranged for occasional translations from native languages into English. I cannot tell you how grateful I am to those of you who are brave enough to write in English! I am learning so much. I think there is very rich intellectual ferment in Gestalt therapy all across Europe. Frankly, I am in awe of some of you for what you are bringing to us all.

On another matter, I realize we are also all suffering together a time of great tumult, disruption, even a sense of impending collapse—of democracies and of the habitability of our planet. And yet the energy I have seen this week, from so many of you, to use your living, breathing, rich Gestalt therapy to contribute to healing, is impressive, and has enriched me, so thank you for that.

The theory of the zero point in consciousness and its relevance to Gestalt therapy has already been thoroughly covered by Nancy and by Kathleen and it is one of many strands of exploration of our human situation that Perls, Hefferline and Goodman draw on. Fritz Perls, Laura Perls and Paul Goodman were amazing. They gathered all the different sources that had influenced them and they didn't just do what I'm going to do today, which is to take bits and pieces and do riffs on the topic. They wove their sources and inspiration together into a coherent whole that continues today to lead to new thinking! For instance, I look closely at one strand. I am particularly interested in exploring and explicating the implications of the relationality—especially the implications for the therapy relationship—of the organism-environment field as the source of phenomena. But that's just one strand among many interrelated strands of our theory, and I am spending my entire clinical life trying to work that out. Each of can take one strand and spend your entire clinical life working with it.

So why, I ask, is the notion of the fertile void so compelling to us this week? Why has it garnered our attention? For one thing, the idea of polarities, which is intrinsic to the fertile void conversation, emerges from the epistemology of Gestalt psychology, which is a cornerstone of Gestalt therapy. Polarities are figure and ground. They live in a figure-ground relationship. That is fundamental to perception. Our entire experiential world is organized in terms of figure and ground.

However, I think there is something more important, which is the language (at least the English words), the words "fertile void." The phrase, those two particular words put together, has its own romance to it. It bursts the bounds of Cartesian clear and distinct ideas. Nancy and Kathleen really made clear and distinct presentations about Friedlander's ideas, and so, I am not talking about the *concept* of the fertile void, I am talking about the juxtaposition of those two words. There is something romantic, dare I say mysterious, about putting those two words together.

I think our attraction to that is because it's an attempt to find a place for what cannot be fully grasped, what cannot be fully named or known. It is that "something" that lives "just prior to" and works its shaping influence on the forming Gestalt. Every Gestalt is an individual act of perception, but it is something that emerges from a larger shared world in which that fertile void has a place. The fertile void both constitutes and emerges from what Jean-Marie Robine (2011) calls, the "Id of the situation." Technically we can call this "forecontact," obviously "fertile void" has a little more romance to it. We might also call it "intuition." When we pay attention, we can sense the coming presence that we call forecontact. We can feel the sense of the room. We are affected by it. This may be an example of a word that's controversial at this moment, "atmosphere." I know that it's a politically laden term, but experientially, it is a word that points to another way to attempt to find our way into, and be sensitive to, the shaping power of forecontacting. And yet, we can never fully know how forecontacting shapes the figure. I shall speak a bit more about our struggles with the limits of our knowledge a little bit later.

## The Feeling of Words

While I've spoken abstractly so far, I actually want to stay close to both experience and clinical practice pretty much from now on. I will start with how I experience the notion of the fertile void. What happens to me is that the word "void" frightens me. I don't know all about what's frightening to me about "void." Certainly, it implies unknowing and uncertainty, but those two words don't frighten me. Those words disrupt me and excite me. "Void," frightens me. Part of my association to the word, "void," is that I only know the void of trauma. A couple of speakers this week played with differentiating between the void of trauma and the fertile void. In trauma, for me, it's a void in which there is no imagination, no breath, no future. And that's my association to the word "void."

I also have to say that I have a despairing, bodily-sinking when I am confronted with the phrase, "creative indifference." In this case again, it's personal—and I guess this is important—language is personal. There was too much indifference in my household when I was young, so the word, "indifference," is not a neutral one for me, and it's not one that's full of possibility. It is full of estrangement and isolation. I say this not to argue with those words as concepts, but I'm playing with walking through experientially why those words are not words that show up in my theorizing, at least not often. "Fertile void" may have never shown up. For me, the opposite of the traumatic void is not—at least initially—the fertile void. When I pay attention, it's more a sense of expansive openness, free and easy breathing, a sense of aliveness, and vibration. Thus, I wouldn't use the word, "void," and my awareness is not empty. There is a humming sense of unformed shapes and of vague motion—I was going to use the word "movement" but "movement" is even too defined. Motion. There is a sense of fallowness, like a field lying fallow, and that's the fertile part of it. It is not empty, there is a sense of fertility, and the word, "void" doesn't capture that moment for me.

Why does this matter? It leads me to try to think about what might replace, "fertile void," in my own theorizing. I see how polarities and figure/ground are fundamentals of consciousness. And I recognize that the zero point (I still wish it wasn't called "zero") is a place of balance, not stasis, but a sense of bobbing about, of wiggling back and forth instead of massive swings back and forth between poles. We want our patients to have that capacity for balance and for flexibility.

However, when I was in workshops as a beginning Gestalt therapist—eons ago, of course—I remember a sinking feeling, a sense that my suffering was being too easily dismissed when it was being cast as one side of a polarity. So, although I see the value in thinking of polarities, I am quite cautious in "playing" with them with my patients.

## Paradoxical Theory of Change

I realize that my grounding is not polarities, but instead, I notice something else. I notice the investments, the commitments, that my patient and I have. And oftentimes those investments are held quite intensely, in a way that shrinks one's field of vision, thus foreclosing the complexity that is intrinsic to any experience.

For instance, let us take the example of someone who is deeply invested in and committed to presenting and living as a "good girl." I notice that. Obviously, there's a polar opposite to that; The Janice Joplin "bad girl" that a lot of good girls listen to at night in their bedrooms. But I am interested in how the patient holds to these investments quite intensely, reducing complexity and narrowing their field of vision.

My pathway in my own life and with my patients then is to try to support staying engaged with that current commitment; not aiming at loosening it, not aiming at hinting that there's another side (except when I'm frustrated, which means I have become too invested in a particular outcome). When the patient and therapist stay engaged with the current commitment, go more deeply into it, it will complexify and ultimately, the other pole will enter awareness. I am actually staying at one pole, the pole the patient identifies with, but the way it begins to complexify, of course, is that as you stay with it and are exploring it, you get a greater awareness of the felt significance of the commitment. You might get a sense of how it originated, and how it continues to be maintained, how it functions in the patient's life. You start to get some sense of the cost of adhering to the commitment, and of course an exploration of how the commitment gets invited into our work. We begin to identify how the way we are together inviting the patient to make a commitment to being a good girl in the room with me. And all these things together, by broadening awareness, by complexifying, helps the patient gain more choice-fulness about when and where to use that commitment, and greater capacity to entertain other commitments—like the polar opposite, for instance.

I think perhaps this approach represents one of my investments, my commitment to the paradoxical theory of change. I know in my life as a patient, I wanted to dive more deeply into the investments, the commitments I had, in the hopes of riding through a dark tunnel to get to the other side. The thought of "trying on" the other polarity was an experiment that did nothing for me other than to reinforce my belief that my concerns, my investments, my commitments were silly and wrong.

By the way, I do not mean to say that experimenting with polarities goes against the paradoxical theory of change. Done with an experimental attitude, there is no problem. What I am saying, is that I realize how much it has meant to me in my own life as a patient, when the therapist stayed with what I was presenting, rather than looking for the other pole. That approach suited me better, and it was a pathway that led me to the paradoxical theory of change as a mainstay in my approach to Gestalt therapy.

## Bounded Self and Enlightenment

I want to circle back to the idea that the notion of the fertile void is an effort to catch phenomena that do not have words. I think that the combination of words is itself paradoxical, perhaps even an oxymoron. To me, a void is empty. Fertile suggests potential. Potential exists, thus, the void is no longer empty. But here, maybe I am just being too picky. I think the idea of the fertile void is attractive to us because it makes a space for that which exists in forecontacting; that which has not yet spoken itself, which is still shapeless, wordless and almost present. It is an influence on us that we cannot fully grasp.

One of the curses that the Enlightenment Project brought upon us, is a view of human beings as encapsulated selves. We developed human beings into disembodied, isolated monads. Notice I said we "developed" human beings this way. I've heard, around this conference space, people saying, "human nature." I prefer to speak of the human situation, rather than human nature. I don't know what we can say about universally, unequivocally and immutably about human nature, but we can say something about our shared situation, things we have in common. I think human beingness itself is incredibly malleable.

Generations of philosophers, historians, therapists, etc., have tried to help us find our way out of our encapsulation. Certainly, our founding theory was centrally concerned with this issue, hence, we have the organism/environment field, and importantly, a radical redefinition of self-as-process, emergent of organism/environment field. By now, most of us do not believe we are bounded, encapsulated selves. But through those centuries of the development of Enlightenment thought, until pretty recently, we've developed this sense of having a bounded self—of being a bounded self—and it is difficult for us and our patients to grasp, at a profound experiential level, the "co-emergent selfhood" Perls and Goodman championed.

## Gestalt Therapy and the Place of Agency

There is a social-activist psychoanalytic psychologist named Phil Cushman, who calls this bounded, encapsulated self, the "sovereign self" (a metaphor that I love). The sovereign self exists within a worldview that holds that, as individuals, we are fully in charge of the direction of our lives, our actions, etc.

There are some conflicts within our original Gestalt theorizing, some ideas that don't sit easily with the notion of emergence. One example is Sartrean existentialism that averred that you create your life—the ultimate sovereign self. He would say that you are not responsible for the rain, but you are responsible for how you live with being rained on. He made that into the *sine qua non,* of being human. You are fully responsible for your life. In a milder form, we value the notion of response-ability. Still, field theory and phenomenology point us less to how we make our lives, but more on how we are also made-in-relation (or made-in-context). We make our lives, and we are made. The "making" that is favored in existentialism gives less power to context than do field theory and phenomenology.

Co-emergent selfhood, thus, complicates the question of agency. While I do not want to hew to Sartre's extreme position, nor do I want to totally surrender the idea of agency. I think that having a *sense* of agency is crucial to our capacity to look for and adapt "best fit" solutions as we navigate our lives. Sartre represented one end of a polarity, the other end being that context determines us entirely. Peter Philippson (see for example, 2001) reminds us repeatedly that we are a part of the context, that our actions are part of what is making/being made.

As I said earlier, philosophers, psychoanalysts and historians have been trying to help us break out of our encapsulation now for over a century, maybe longer. And we're only partly successful. The sovereign self is such a tempting orientation. Clinically, when we live in the world of the sovereign self, we can define what therapy is and how it works because you can develop an instrumental set of definitions; we have found out experimentally that, "when I as a therapist do 'x', the majority of patients respond in 'y' way." Clear and distinct ideas can be used to form a foundation for instrumental therapy, instrumental relationships.

When we are no longer trying to live as the sovereign self, and we are treating the person who appears to have impairments in their agency, we have to grapple newly with the questions that have always plagued psychotherapy, which is, "how does psychotherapy work?" and "what is its purpose and meaning?" I'm eager for those questions to be alive in our more contextually embedded, contextually emergent way of thinking and carrying ourselves now. I have to say at this point, I don't even want to try to answer these questions, I just want to keep them floating around. All I can say that I know, is that the art of intimate and meaningful dialogue is the reason I get up in the mornings. And people are willing to take the time, to pay me money and keep me company to have these conversations all day. What could be better? The insurance companies and national health programs are still locked into the instrumentality mindset, which puts quite a strain on us since that's not the mindset we live in, that's not the way we walk the therapy talk.

But another question that becomes very important is: what is a place of the *sense* of agency? What is the place of agency when we also recognize that we are emergent of field and context? What are the conditions at play in this particular field, in my particular field in this moment? How can I ever fully know them? How do I work, knowing that I cannot know them? We pick out certain strands of awareness that we can grab hold of, but we swim in uncertainty.

We are more and more interested in forecontact these days, in part because that is where the antidote to the sovereign self resides. So we want to try to learn more about it and we're fumbling around for ways to do that. Let's keep fumbling. We're struggling to find words and concepts that capture the invisible, the ineffable. These questions—or uncertainties—affect not only how we hope to help empower our patients, but also affects how we understand our therapeutic practice. We are struggling to find words and concepts that capture the ineffable aspects of the process of emergence, of the phenomena that underlie every moment.

### The Situation

We talk often about presence, about being with the patient in dialogue. Perhaps moments of sitting together in a fertile or a traumatized void. But "presence," is too simplistic. I am often present with others when I am not a therapist. Aren't you? But we emphasize presence and dialogue because we are still reminding ourselves that the old instrumentalist approach to therapy is not a Gestalt approach. We are present with an intention. We are there in the service of the other's awareness (or, the other's being).

I have found some direction in Jean-Marie Robine's notion of the" id of the situation," (2011, p. 141) and Georges Wollants' (2012) exposition of "the therapy of the situation." Their ideas have been incredibly helpful and that'll be the next part of my talk. In this idea of the situation, there are things I can hold on to in my work as a therapist that are more concrete. When Jean-Marie refers to the "id of the situation," that is the forecontacting. He's offering us some ways to think about forecontacting (and I hope I am understanding him correctly). In the id of the situation, phenomena are barely beginning to take shape, and the question of who belongs to what is not yet defined.

Therapy is a *particular* situation. Whatever else may be in the background of any situation, the background of the therapy includes particular freedoms (for instance, the freedom to speak forbidden truths) as well as constraints in our contact. Social psychologist Kenneth Gergen (2009, p. 73) writes about how even the most spontaneous—even impulsive—speech follows rules of engagement. The rules are structures and norms that make communication possible and meaningful. If you come to sit with someone who is grieving, and you suddenly start doing cartwheels or reciting your alphabet, your response would be so discrepant from the demands of the situation as to seem psychotic. All situations have formal and informal rules of engagement as part of what structures contacting moment-to-moment.

The situation of therapy is comprised by its structure. I realize that some of you work in the community, that you may be meeting teenagers on the park bench somewhere, something like that. I'm going to use the more quotidian, ordinary therapy situation for the moment. The structure is usually a certain time, a certain place, the same furniture, the regularity of the meeting, a fee structure and perhaps some external ethical and legal constraints. That structure is a containing environment and not just for the patient, but for us as well. For instance, I have capacities to be present in certain very difficult situations in part because I know the session will end. I don't have to go home with my rageful patient. I don't have to deal with their rage over the dinner table.

The situation in therapy is also structured in large part by norms. I have tended to underrate the value of norms in terms of their importance for sustainability, until President Trump became elected, and we've begun to see, in the US and elsewhere, that norms, even more than our system of laws, are what keeps our fragile democracies going. I think certain norms, for instance, ethical norms, drew us to this work in the first place. Here I don't mean the legislative ethical system which is sometimes problematic for our genuine ethics. I am referring to the primal ethic that Levinas named, which is: "the face of the other constitutes an ethical command," and we therapists respond, "I am here." I don't think you get into this work unless you are compelled by that ethic. I didn't know it was an ethic, I just thought my passion for this work was driven by my love of intimate meaningful conversation and my care. It turns out that Levinas locates it as the central ethic of being a human being.

Norms require our art, our creative engagement, our integrity and the Levinasian ethic, all of which to say—and here it's kind of paradoxical—the situation is bigger than we are. We can't predict and control it. It has a compelling force upon us yet it's also contingent on us, on the qualities and intentions that we bring. Once again, we are shown there is no inside and no outside of the situation. The situation lives through us and we co-create the situation, so it's making and being made at the same time. I hope this makes sense or opens up some associations to play with. We do comprise an aspect of the situation. We affect and are affected by it. It is bigger than us, and yet our intention is an intrinsic factor—without which, it would not be a *therapy* situation.

Margherita Spagnuolo-Lobb and others who have studied with her, have taught us that there is always directionality in our contacting (see, for example, Spagnuolo Lobb, 2013; Francesetti et al., 2013). On some level we have known this, but they have lifted it into the foreground. The direction is always both a response and an initiation. We are never *not* responding, we are never *not* being affected by your situation, even though we are also initiating. Importantly, also, we are always living in a non-indifferent world. Our senses are only drawn towards things that are making a difference. Thus, there are always aspects that will remain out of awareness. The significance is that we are always working uncertainly. And yet, all we have to draw on is that by which we are affected. I can never fully know the context my patient and I share, including the id of the situation.

Why does that matter? Because when a patient says something to me that reflects an aspect of one of their enduring relational themes, a repetitive theme, *that theme is also a response to this context, including this moment.* An important implication of this is that since all experience is contextually-emergent, then even the patient's repetitive character themes (and mine, as well,) reflect something in *this* context, in *this* situation, at *this* moment. The patient and I together can discover what in or being-together makes this reaction make perfect sense now, in our situation together. Nothing that emerges is beyond our context, even if it is a common and repetitive phenomenon. It is emerging now, between us, here.

So instead of creative indifference, as I possibly have misunderstood the term, I am more interested in asking this question: "what it is about how we are being together," and sometimes much more specifically, "what is it about how I am being with you, that brings this particular theme into the foreground now?"

Even if the experience at question is a familiar, repetitive experience, it's not an experience they have every moment of their lives. So, what is it in this moment? That is a valuable question to ask is because we are making and being made by each other together. As we explore and make sense of it, our exploration includes how the therapist is participating in the evocation of this particular repeating experience. When the therapist can understand their part in whatever difficult repeated moment is occurring, the patient often accrues a greater sense of agency (and sometimes the therapist learns something about themselves, or may accrue a sense of humility).

Gaining a sense of agency is empowering and dignifying. A sense of agency also tends to support the patient to see more options for interpreting situations and for acting. The norms of the therapy situation provide a relatively safe ground where we can both explore the experience making/being made together. We can look at how much agency we have and we don't, we can also build a greater sense of agency. Sally Denham-Vaughan captured this process beautifully with her notion of both will and grace, in an article of the same name (2005). We do not have total Sartrean agency, nor are we totally passive surrender to our situations and contexts. To me, fluid polarities have the qualities of both will and grace.

### Engaged Surrender (and the Double Nature of the Power of the Situation)

Clinically thinking, instead of "fertile void," or "creative indifference," I prefer the notion of "engagement and surrender." As I've said before, I love the art of therapeutic dialogue. And part of that art includes moments when I speak with intensity to a patient, where I offer an argument or a tear. And then I let go. I'm able to open myself to whatever comes next, even if what comes next does not match what I had hoped or what I was striving for in the intention of my movement toward the patient. It had direction. There is directionality, a movement towards where I think is a good idea to go. But once I take the step in that journey, I can emotionally withdraw that investment, because now I become interested in just what happens next, even if it's not what I had hoped for. Because now is a new moment. I just surrender to this moment. I hope that makes some sense. It's a process of investment, of invested engagement and surrender. When I let the intention of my moving-toward recede, a new interest in the next moment, the coming moment, is what attracts my attention.

Something will always attract my attention. Remember, we live in a non-indifferent world. And we are always coming from a perspective. Our moving-toward or moving-away is a reflection of an investment shaped by a perspective. Some things emerge as figures and some things don't because they are not of interest to us. What does this mean clinically? For example, let's say that you see tears in the eyes of your patient. How you respond to that has different qualities, depending on your investment (co-emergent from the shared situation). You might say something. You might say, simply, "I see tears." Do you say it as if you believe you are a neutral observer? Or is it a resonant moment, softly acknowledging, "I see tears?" Or is it a slight, delicate question, "I see tears?" All of these different ways of noting the exact same observation position you differently. You're never neutral. This idea that we live in a non-indifferent world is one of the ideas I love from American pragmatism. We are never without prejudice, we are never without bias.

### A Short Case Example

There is a two-sidedness to the rules, norms and ethics that party structure the therapeutic situation. I mentioned freedom earlier, I also mentioned constraints. When I'm at a cocktail party and I am not satisfied with a conversation, I can move on. Not so in a difficult or unpleasant therapeutic situation. In that therapeutic situation, there is no escape from the conversation. I cannot escape my part in whatever difficulties we are having. I am, to a certain degree helpless in the face of how I am activated by the pressures of the situation, and yet it's also the situation that supports me to simply sigh and admit ruefully my problem.

With one patient I was reactive to his stubborn hunger for me to find the right way to meet him, and his angry refusal to respond in a welcoming way to any effort I made to reach towards him. After some time, I became stubbornly withholding, myself. And finally, at the end of one of our grueling and tense sessions, I said, "I don't like the way I am being with you. I'm angry and withholding and I don't like this." I couldn't leave the situation and I was out of other ideas. So, what's left? Be myself. So, I told him. And in that case, a therapeutic turn happened. At the next session he told me that he had thought, up until my remarks, that I knew exactly what I was doing at every moment, and he had felt oppressed by my "knowing," or what he had thought was my knowing. Since I felt lost with him a lot of the time, that was interesting an interesting surprise. It makes me wonder if I might have been coping with feeling lost by adopting a more "know-it-all" stance. I don't know. We didn't actually pursue that part, he wasn't interested. He was just so excited about our conversation and his discovery, we just went on from there. Hid response wasn't a response I would have expected or predicted.

What I have come to know, is that in difficult situations that I have learned to trust the honest dialogue done with underlying goodwill. That somehow takes us to a new possibility. That is about staying within the situation in the paradoxical theory of change. I gave up trying to change myself or him, I just spoke my truth.

To end, rather than using the idea of zero-point or fertile void, my trust is with the paradoxical theory of change, which I believe requires a kind of engaged surrender. I live my investment pretty full for a moment, and then I let go. And now, I'm free to let go. Thank you very much.

## Note

1 This paper was previously published by Gestalt Review – Vol. 24, No. 2 (2020). Thanks to Gestalt Review for permitting its republication here.

## References

Denham-Vaughan, S. (2005). Will and Grace. *British Gestalt Journal, 14*(1), 5–14.
Francesetti, G., M. Gecele & J. Roubal (2013). *Gestalt Therapy in Clinical Practice: From Psychopathology to the Aesthetics of Contact*. Vol. 2. FrancoAngeli Milan.

Gergen, K. J. (2009). *Relational Being: Beyond Self and Community*. Oxford, United Kingdom: Oxford University Press.

Philippson, P. (2001). *Self in Relation*. Highland, New York: The Gestalt Journal Press.

Robine, J. M. (2011). *On the Occasion of an Other*. Gouldsboro, ME: The Gestalt Journal Press.

Spagnuolo Lobb, M. (2013). The Now-for-next in Psychotherapy. *Gestalt Therapy Recounted in Post-Modern Society*. Milano, Italy: FrancoAngeli.

Wollants, G. (2012). *Gestalt Therapy: Therapy of the Situation*. Newbury Park, CA: Sage.

# Chapter 3

# Being Present to Absence

## Field Theory in Psychopathology and Clinical Practice

*Gianni Francesetti, Michela Gecele, and Jan Roubal*

## Introduction

Field theory has been a core concept of Gestalt therapy since the beginning of its development (Robine, 2001; Wollants, 2008; Parlett & Lee, 2005; Staemmler, 2006; Francesetti, 2019b; Francesetti & Roubal, 2020), and it has been used with different meanings by various authors to the point that this theoretical domain can lead to a Babylonian confusion (Staemmler, 2006). This is not just a sign of lack of definition and clarity, but indicates the richness of this concept that can have multiple understandings and applications (Philippson, 2016). We claim in this paper that field theory is not only a bedrock of our approach, but one of the possible paradigms that informs clinical practice in Gestalt therapy, in psychotherapy, and in psychiatry. We can identify other paradigms: i.e., the mono-personal and the bipersonal paradigm, that we have discussed elsewhere (Francesetti & Roubal, 2020; Roubal & Francesetti, forthcoming). In this chapter, we want to focus on the implications of the field paradigm for psychopathology, psychotherapy, and psychosocial perspectives. According to field theory the self is not a structure, but an emergent process (Philippson, 2009; Robine, 2016; Höll, 2020). The consequence of this conceptualization is that there is a dimension of the ongoing process of the emergence of self when self and world are not yet differentiated and from where the poles of self/world (or me/other or subject/object or organism/environment) emerge. We think that this paradigm is revolutionary for understanding human suffering and for clinical practice.

This chapter is based on some papers already published (Francesetti, 2015, 2019a, 2019b; Francesetti & Griffero, 2019; Francesetti & Roubal, 2020; Roubal & Francesetti, forthcoming; Francesetti et al., forthcoming; Gecele, 2013, 2021), to which we refer the reader who is interested in more in-depth study.

DOI: 10.4324/9781003255772-5

## Some Preliminary Definitions

Let's start with some definitions at the outset in order to clarify the terms that we use and the perimeter of our exploration.

### The Phenomenal Field

The phenomenal field is the horizon of phenomenal events for a given situation, the boundary of possibilities within which certain phenomena tend to emerge, while others do not. For example, at a party with friends, it is easier for jokes and jests, moments of good cheer, and feelings of lightness to emerge, during which time will tend to flow quickly. At a funeral wake, it is more likely that feelings of heaviness will emerge, along with the slowing or rarefaction of time, gloominess, and immobility. The phenomenal field is perceptible by the senses as the atmosphere of the situation, in which the forces that condition the emergence of phenomena move. With black holes, the force that bends the events' horizon is gravity; with the phenomenal field, it is the intentionalities at play that bend it. In the therapeutic encounter, those forces – embodied intentionalities – move both the patient and the therapist who are functions of them. In this paradigm – in which the self is not a structure but a process that emerges in the situation – the forces in the phenomenal field are in motion before the subjects are differentiated and defined. Therefore, we can say that the therapist and the patient emerge, "are made", within the situation and are moved by the forces of the field. The phenomenal field is *pathos*: it is suffered and not chosen (Waldenfels, 2011).

### The Phenomenological Field

The phenomenal field (*where I am subject-to*) can be transformed into the phenomenological field (*where I am the subject-of*) that is, into a field where it is possible to reflect on what is happening and make choices, where the sphere of possibilities can expand. Such a transformation is enabled by the capacity to be aware of the phenomenal field, to notice the forces at play that move us, to be curious about what is happening. We could say that the phenomen-o*logic*al field is the phenomenal field + "*logos*", i.e., from the Greek, the possibility to bring order, meaning, sense, to think, reflect, and to give words. That passage from the phenomenal to the phenomenological field is close to what Fonagy (Fonagy & Target, 1997) describes as the capacity for reflection and mentalization. Nevertheless, from the perspective that we propose, the ability to reflect and verbalize is not only a passage to a cognitive competence, since it is combined with an embodied awareness of the sensorial phenomena in motion.

### The Psychopathological Field

The psychopathological field is a phenomenal field where it is not possible to be present one to the other, either because perception or emotion is dulled or restricted, or because people cannot be fully constituted as differentiated and connected subjects belonging to a common world (in which case the experience has a psychotic quality). It is a phenomenal field where an absence is struggling to become present. Psychopathology can be seen as an expression of the ways in which we can be absent at the contact boundary. Psychotherapy then is a situation in which the therapist can be present to those absences.

Psychopathological suffering is not existential pain, it is not discomfort ensuing from the limitations or losses that we all experience in our lives (Salonia, 2013; Francesetti, 2019e). Psychopathology starts when the experiences that emerge in difficult situations cannot be processed and assimilated: when the other, needed in order to afford and to process the sensorial and affective elements, is not there.

Psychopathology starts when the other is missed. The sensorial and affective elements are proto-feelings[1] that cannot be assimilated and remain as more or less chaotic and disorganized sensorial footprints. We have some systems to protect ourselves from such chaos: we are able to put them aside, in order to render them minimally disturbing. They are dissociated and "packed up" in patterns of symptoms, syndromes, and personality. The tables of content of the nosographic psychiatric systems present a list of the forms of those packages.

Psychopathological forms are the result of our ability to creatively adjust to what could not be fully experienced and processed. With such transformations, the absent-other becomes the absence in the present contact. A person becomes blind, absent, less existent, and less alive in those not-processed experiential points. Such absence is the emergent psychopathology that we experience when meeting our clients. There, the absences become present, and so therapy can be seen as a way of allowing the absences to become present.

We can see two main origins of absences emerging in therapy.

## The Stranger[2] Knocking on the Door

The first origin of absences in therapy is connected to the impossibility of processing an experience.

Taking inspiration from both Gestalt Psychology and American Pragmatism, Gestalt therapy has rooted its anthropology in the description and analysis of the process of experiencing, i.e., the process of *Gestaltung* and the sequence of contact. To *experience* is a process starting from the emergence of a new figure. In order to process the novelty that we meet we need support (Perls, 1992): the novelty, indeed, must be sensed, perceived, approached, chewed, assimilated, and in the process of assimilation the organism also changes and grows. But what happens if such support is not available? The result of facing the novelty without enough support is that the experience cannot be processed and assimilated. The bodily excitement remains unprocessed and an unfinished business remains open, waiting for the chance to be closed. In order not to be disturbed by it, we can put it aside, we dissociate those unprocessed feelings (proto-feelings), that cannot become integrated in our personality's archives, thus they cannot become "past". All traumatic experiences, (but not only them) present this lack of environmental support and sensorial activation such that these experiences find no place in the memories that are integrated into the personality function.[3]

These proto-feelings are packed in rigid forms in order not to occupy too much space, time, and energy in one's life. They become absences at the contact boundary: inaccessible corners of our life's landscapes, mute strings that cannot resonate, blind spots in our sight. These dissociated sensorial impressions are unformulated since the experiences take their form during the process that ends with the assimilation: the personality function weaves the sensorial impressions of the id function and makes it possible to create a narrative form of the experience. From a field perspective, the novelty is not met as something external, objective, separated from the organism, it is an emerging phenomenon already influenced by the personality function, that is both supporting the process of meeting the novelty and hindering it with its structures and previous forms.

When there is not enough support, the body of the client is *not enough* to allow the process of Gestaltung to proceed toward assimilation. So, in the therapeutic meeting, the unformulated proto-feelings call the flesh of the therapist to emerge and to come into existence. They are like a stranger knocking on our door. Therapists lend their flesh[4] to the field forces in order to allow the stranger to appear. The stranger knocking on the door is often disturbing: perceived as out of place,[5] inappropriate, embarrassing, shameful, etc. But "A poet does not reject an image that stubbornly but 'accidentally' appears and mars his plan; he respects the intruder and suddenly discovers what 'his' plan is, he discovers and creates himself" (Perls, Hefferline & Goodman, herein after PHG, 1951, p. 137).

The disturbing stranger knocking on the door is the welcome guest at the therapeutic meeting. It is a process belonging to the undifferentiated level of experience – it is not of the client, neither of the therapist – until *somebody* is available to receive it in order to allow it to become present. In this moment, the absence becomes present and it is not absent anymore. The stranger knocking on the door is finally admitted to life, in a unique and unpredictable way, since it takes its form when coming into existence in this unique therapeutic meeting.

Therapy, in this perspective, is the special time and space where these field forces are free to move. The task of the therapist is to lend flesh to them and not to step in the way of the process. "We reiterate that the suggestion is a spectacularly conservative one, for it is nothing but the old advice of the Tao: 'stand out of the way'" (PHG, 1951, p. 24). This "art of doing nothing" (Roubal & Francesetti, 2021 forthcoming) is however a very active psychotherapeutic attitude since the therapist needs to transform their way of being in the session. They need to build enough self-support to be able to allow themselves to be used by the field forces, to embody the absences, and make them present.

## The One Who Is Always There

"*Madness is rare in individuals – but in groups, parties, nations, and ages it is the rule*": this quote by Friedrich Nietzsche[6] is a good introduction to this paragraph. The second possible origin of absences in therapy is indeed connected with the social context at many different levels. The most simple, "normal", one is what each society and culture take for granted. What is taken for granted can be more or less available to awareness and awareness can be more or less supported in different societies, for different issues, for different groups, and for different people. What is normally taken for granted becomes invisible, and is not experienced as existing. Like water for fish. It is the ground that enables societies and cultures to grow and perpetuate themselves. However, what enables societies to grow is also the possibility, sometimes for some of its members, to find new ways, to change something, or just to be aware of the possibility for humanity to have different ways of living. The less this possibility is present and shared, the more the society and the culture create blind and fixed spots. The more societies, nations, and cultures are powerful, successful, and self-referential, the less this possibility is accessible for people. Such blind spots in a culture, a society, a group, a political party, or a family, can be easily detected by a third party, i.e., by everybody outside either the confluence or the influence (Gecele, 2002, 2021).

For example, when we watch a video from the 60s we immediately notice what was impossible to notice if we were in that time and culture. The fashion, the words, the attitudes, were peculiar maybe strange, and clearly different from other times. But the atmosphere, or the *Zeitgeist*, is invisible when you are inside it.[7] Also the forces that maintain the atmosphere are invisible, since they are acting on – and acted by – everybody. What exceeds this normality is easily put aside as weird, out of place, odd, irrelevant, useless, dangerous, unreal, crazy, etc. It becomes a minority with less voice. It has, indeed, more truth to speak (Francesetti, 2013).

The consequence is that there are pieces of experiences or perspectives that are dissociated on a social level. What is beyond the horizon of the common world is neglected or rejected.

This horizon of the common social world supports some ways of being in relationships and prevents some others so that societies have specific and normal ways for people to relate to each other.[8] There are omnipresent forces in a society that influence personalities to prefer a specific shape, to accept some feelings, beliefs, views, and to reject others. For example, aggression can be neglected or rejected, as stated by PHG (1951), and this dissociated feeling comes up as a social tendency – powerful even though invisible – toward destructive and suicidal wars.

These kinds of absences are difficult to detect and, at the same time, crucial to consider. They are field forces omnipresent both in the client's and the therapist's lives. Water for fishes. *The one who has always been there.* And they are important for psychopathology: "The disturbances are in the field (...). The lapse of community in political societies is not reducible to the neuroses of individuals, who indeed have become 'individuals' because of the lapse of community; nor is it reducible to bad institutions, for these are maintained by citizens; it is a disease of the field, and only a kind of group-therapy would help" (PHG, pp 134–135). Different societies have different forces, exerting different pressures on the process of the emergence of individual personalities.

In a liquid society (Bauman, 2002), fragmented and complex (Morin, 2008), accelerated (Rosa, 2010), with porous boundaries and disembodied (Gecele & Francesetti, 2007), bipolar (Francesetti, 2019d), the personality cannot but be unstable, threatened by dissolution: the sense of identity becoming vague, uncertain, ephemeral. Two opposite risks arise: discontinuity, emptiness, and vagueness of the sense of self; or, at the other pole, the risk of adhesion to strong and salvific narratives. The first is more often met in therapy (people suffering from personality disorders) and the second in politics (people needing a man of strength in a powerful position). In therapy, all the actual clients come from such a social field and the therapists too. This is why personality disorders can be considered the ethnic disorder of our time (Gecele, 2013, 2016), they have eroded the classical neurotic and psychotic functioning and ways of suffering. It is more and more important not to consider just the symptomatology or the disorder (as listed in the Axe 1 of the DSM IV), but to understand them in the frame of the personality functioning and traits of our clients.

The basic issue in therapy is no longer to gain a personal freedom from a rigid and limiting social context, as it was when Perls was working in Esalen. Today it is rather to achieve a sense of *being somebody rooted somewhere*, with some more or less clear and persistent boundaries and sense of belonging. Our personality function cannot integrate all the accelerated, contradictory, ever-changing, disembodied stimuli that we receive without the pauses needed to assimilate them. The consequence is that we continuously change our focus of attention and we split vertically different unfinished pieces of experience. More than the problem of the removed (the experiences that are pushed down, as happened in Freud's times), we have today the problem of the splitting between infinite not-integrated fragments of experience, that are continuously put aside (Gecele, 2019). This is the background to be considered behind every figural experience of suffering with our clients.

Being aware of this issue is a support for the therapist from the very first meeting: it offers the possibility of seeing the background that the client brings, the background from where the anxieties, depressive experiences, obsessive-compulsive behaviors, eating disorders, relational problems, etc. arise. Being aware of this common ground makes it possible for the therapist to rely upon a frame, to calm down, to stay rooted in the personality of the situation, and to offer very simple and surprisingly very effective feedback to the client. And, most importantly, being aware of dwelling in the same landscape as the client, he has the chance not only to experience it but also to bring some *logos* to it.

## The Transformation of Absences in Presence

We have described two kinds of absences.

We called the first "*the stranger knocking on the door*", which we refer to as a proto-experience that couldn't be processed and that is pushing in order to be embodied and to emerge in the session.

We called the second kind of absence "*the one who is always there*", which we refer to as the common and shared social ground where parts of possible experiences are neglected or rejected. In both cases, these absences are un-formulated proto-feelings that cannot be fully present without some sup-port. They are pushing as intentional forces of the field in order to emerge, increase the presence and develop the potentialities of the actual field (PHG, 1994, p. 151).

The task of the therapist is neither to change the client nor the absences (Francesetti, 2015, 2019a; Francesetti & Griffero, 2019; Francesetti & Roubal 2020; Roubal and& Francesetti, forthcoming), it is rather to become aware of those absences in order to allow them to become present and to follow their journey toward being processed and transformed. Without the therapist's awareness the absences remain absent and are reenacted in the therapeutic process, with a reiteration that can increase or reinforce the absences in the field.

We won't describe here the theory and the passages in the modulation of the therapist's presence, the reader can refer to Francesetti and Roubal (2020) and to the mentioned bibliography.

A couple of clinical examples may help to understand this process in therapeutic practice.

### *"You must be angry!"*

In a group, Roman, a 60-year-old monk, has taken many roles of responsibility, both as a teacher and as an Abbot. Now he lives in another community where the Abbot is much younger and less experienced than him and who was his student years ago. The actual Abbot is leading the community by often humiliating the members. Roman strongly contributes to community life, including financial support. Some months ago his laptop broke down and, after many frustrating requests for permission to buy another one, he was finally successful. The Abbot, in front of many other people, humiliated him by saying in a contemptuous and mocking way, "how ingenuous you are brother Roman to buy such a stupid laptop. You waste the money of this community!". Roman couldn't reply, felt very hurt, and was unable to recover from that episode. From that point on, he has had declining energy, his voice has faded, he feels sad and exhausted, has experienced sleeping disorders, and has progressively withdrawn from the community's life. He is very critical toward himself: "Why am I not able to recover from that episode? Has all the work that I have done on myself been useless? Why have I learned so little? Do I have so big an *ego* that I am not able to go beyond my narcissism?"

While listening to him, I feel pain and anger: first, pain for him and anger toward the Abbot. Then, suddenly, something changes: he was humiliated, and instead of protecting himself he feels inadequate, not good enough, guilty, he invalidates and devalues his feelings and his own value. How many times have I seen these dynamics in closed communities, not only religious ones? I share that I feel some anger and I ask what effect this has on him. He says that he understands. I ask him whether he feels anger too. He doesn't know. I feel a wave of anger: he should be angry, but he is not. Why is he so mild, gentle, and submissive? I feel this wave as too strong, out of place, so I wait... and after a while, I realize that what I am doing is what he is already doing to himself: I want him to feel something else other than blaming himself. Since he is not able to feel something different, I invalidate his way of being. Roman is like that: he is not angry, it is just me who feels anger. He is profoundly gentle. Why should he feel the same as I feel? Or what I think it is right to feel? I am putting into the field the same invalidating force that the Abbot uses, and that Roman uses against himself too... And now I feel pain for what I was doing, I stay with this, I breathe, my anger calms down. Then, while looking at him, a vague fantasy comes to my mind, something like a little flame in the darkness. I share it with him and then I say: "Maybe your persistent pain and your humiliation that cannot be overcome are the ways of not letting the violence be normalized... Somebody in the community must do it". Roman changes his eyes, he looks at me as if a new horizon has opened up. "Oh... I see... indeed the other brothers are accustomed to it... they are humiliated and this seems normal to them..."

He cries now. The pain has meaning now, it can flow. Now his feelings are "right". Everything becomes meaningful, included his movements – that now he shares with me – to leave this community and to found a new one. He was ashamed for that wish and vision, now he understands that maybe it is not a narcissistic illusion of too big an ego.

The therapist is taken by the force of invalidation, and he is about to act on it, of course with good therapeutic intentions (*"you should be angry!"*). He could even push the client to become angry, and in doing so he would just repeat – with good intentions – the invalidating and humiliating pattern. The perception of something out of place, too strong, supports the therapist to wait for what comes next, and the awareness of being invalidating again of Roman's experience becomes clear. This opens the door for feeling pain for the invalidation that Roman has received, that he himself was doing, and even the therapist was about to do. In this case, the stranger knocking on the door is the pain of the invalidation: while this pain cannot become present the invalidation will continue to circulate. In this process the therapist modulates his own presence: he is available to be taken by the field forces, he doesn't re-enact them, he waits and allows something more[9] to emerge that opens the door for the transformation.

### *"It's not me!"*

Another example is more connected to the second kind of absence, the one that is always there.

In the first session, Katy, a young woman who has just very successfully finished her studies in economics says: "I feel disoriented, I don't know who I am, I can't sleep anymore, I live in continuous anxiety, I don't know why! With my boyfriend things are going worse and worse, even though nothing bad has happened... I feel desperate, I cannot recognize myself.... it's not me!".

She is very upset, and for the first half of the session her intense and unmanageable feelings occupy all the available space, and the therapist is not able to intervene in any way. Then, he offers her just a simple and obvious reminder: "Katy, you said that you have just finished the University and that it was very stressful. So, in this moment you may be very tired and also uncertain about the direction you will take in your life".

Katy, after 30 minutes of strong tension in her body and an accelerated unstoppable talking, finally breathes out and leans on the chair.

She pauses and then says "Do you think so?".

"Yes, I think so..."
"Oh, I am so relieved...".

As we discussed elsewhere (Roubal & Francesetti, 2021, forthcoming), what matters in the therapeutic intervention is the quality of the therapist's presence:

from where the words come, more than the spoken words. But what makes such a simple, even obvious, intervention effective? Let's consider the therapist's experience: for the first half hour the therapist is very tense, almost not breathing, taken along with Katy by the tornado in the room. Slowly he notices his own bodily tension, almost a kind of disembodiment, he tries to relax but he can't. So, after some struggle he let his experience be. At this point, some memories of scary and disorienting turning points in his life come up. He becomes aware that he is meeting Katy in her landscape, he comes back to his perception: he is taken by the same tornado, he doesn't know what to do, but he can feel, now, his and Katy's need to root somewhere. This awareness opens up some new possibilities, he breathes, he roots himself in his body and in the same unsupportive ground of contemporary time and society. In this case, the therapist is aware of the unsupportive social ground that the client and he share. He is now able to feel Katy's fearful disorientation, even her terror of no longer being the person that she once was. The therapist can calm down now. He senses his body and, very simply recognizes a possible meaning for Katy's situation. A possible meaning that is not necessarily catastrophic. The therapist has taken a little journey from disembodiment and disorientation to a feeling of being part of the same world as Katy. At this point, he can ground himself in his somatic and emotional experience. Only as a result of the process of awareness of all that has emerged in the session is he able to support the personality function of the situation: now the feelings can be contained and a first provisional and possible shape of the experience begins to emerge.

## Conclusions

In this chapter, we have tried to describe how we understand psychopathology as quality of absence in the phenomenal field, and therapy as modulation of presence. We have also identified two possible roots of these absences. Therapists, in this perspective, are not the agents of change, nor the co-creators of the change.[10] They are rather at the service of the field forces: they lend their flesh to these intentionalities in order to let them produce the transformation. Therapy, in this view, can be understood as the "art of doing nothing". Nevertheless, this is not a passive attitude. On the contrary it is a very active one, even though often invisible from the outside. In psychotherapy, we are like artists who are in the service of the therapy process itself. Here, we come back to our foundations: "(...) we reiterate that the suggestion is a spectacularly conservative one, for it is nothing but the old advice of the Tao: 'stand out of the way'" (PHG, 1951, p. 24). Change can grow from our humble, grateful, and joyful acceptance of what is. From a field theory perspective, the crucial point is that the therapist's acceptance does not only refer to the client, but to whatever emerges in the session, because everything that emerges is a function of the field dynamics. Accepting the client in fact means accepting everything that happens with us in the presence of the client. And the art of therapy is to be aware of what is happening without reiterating the rejection of the *stranger knocking on the door* or the invisibility of the one who is always there. Being present to absence: this is the very simple, even though often not easy, core of the therapeutic process in a field theory perspective.

## Notes

1 According to Damasio's definition of the stage of proto-self (when self and world are not separated and defined yet in the process of perception), we call proto-feelings the feelings that are not processed, nor arrive at a clear definition, and remain as a vague sensorial impression not clearly belonging to the person (Damasio, 2010; Francesetti & Griffero, 2019; Francesetti & Roubal, 2020).
2 We have chosen the word 'stranger' even though, in some of the literature quoted, the same concept is expressed by the word 'alien' (Waldenfels, 2011).
3 Trauma, by definition, is an overwhelming event that cannot be processed. But also an experience that is not traumatic (and doesn't activate the psychophysiological responses typical of trauma) can be unprocessed. I.e., a child who lives in a family where an emotional dimension is forbidden doesn't have the support to feel, recognize, name, communicate it, and it remains unformulated and unprocessed. This is, for example, what usually happens in Panic Disorders that are not always connected to traumatic experiences, but to the impossibility to relationally process the feelings of solitude and so to recognize it (Francesetti, 2007; Francesetti et al., 2020).
4 'To lend the flesh' is a specific philosophical concept developed by Jean Luc Marion (2003). In a personal communication with one of the authors, he recognizes the important role that the phenomenon of lending the flesh (that he calls the 'Erotic Phenomenon') can have in therapy as conceptualized in Francesetti (2019a, 2019b, 2019c) and in Francesetti and Roubal (2020).
5 We developed the concept of *atopon* (*out of place* in Greek) elsewhere (Francesetti, 2019a; Francesetti & Griffero, 2019; Francesetti & Roubal, 2020).
6 Friedrich Nietzsche Quotes. (n.d.). BrainyQuote.com. Retrieved August 11, 2020, from BrainyQuote.com Website: https://www.brainyquote.com/quotes/friedrich_nietzsche_134058
7 This is connected to the fact that history cannot be written until it is past.
8 See the concept of Basic Relational Mode (Salonia, 2007, 2013).
9 We called this second feeling 'the second wave' (Francesetti & Roubal, 2020).
10 We don't see the three paradigms of change (mono-personal, bi-personal, field theory based paradigm) as alternative or competitive at all. The three are equally important and in figure in different moments of the therapeutic process. See Francesetti and Roubal (2020) and Roubal and Francesetti (2021), forthcoming.

## References

Bauman, Z. (2002). *Liquid Modernity*. Cambridge: Polity Press.

Damasio, A. (2010). *Self Comes to Mind. Constructing the Conscious Brain*. New York: Pantheon Books.

Francesetti, G. ed. (2007). *Panick Attacks and Post-modernity. Gestalt Therapy Between Clinical and Social Perspectives*. Milano: FrancoAngeli.

Francesetti, G. (2013). *The Emergent Suffering. Field Perspective on Psychopathology in Gestalt Therapy*. In Klaren, G., Levi, N. & Vidakovic, I. eds., *Yes We Care! Social, Political and Cultural Relationship as Therapy's Ground. A Gestalt Perspective*. The Netherlands: EAGT.

Francesetti, G. (2015). From Individual Symptoms to Psychopathological Fields. Towards a Field Perspective on Clinical Human Suffering. *British Gestalt Journal, 24*(1), 5–19.

Francesetti, G. (2019a). The Field Strategy in Clinical Practice: Towards a Theory of Therapeutic Phronesis. In Brownell, P. ed., *Handbook for Theory, Research and Practice in Gestalt Therapy* (2nd edition). Newcastle Upon Tyne, UK: Cambridge Scholars Publishing.

Francesetti, G. (2019b). *Fundamentos de psicopatología fenomenológico-gestáltica: una introducción ligera*. Madrid: Los Libros del CTP.

Francesetti, G. (2019c). A Clinical Exploration of Atmospheres. Towards a Field-based Clinical Practice. In Francesetti, G. & Griffero, T. eds., *Psychopathology and Atmospheres. Neither Inside nor Outside*. Newcastle Upon Tyne, UK: Cambridge Scholars Publishing.

Francesetti, G. (2019d). Interview with Miguel Benasayag. In Francesetti, G. & Griffero, T. eds., *Psychopathology and Atmospheres. Neither Inside nor Outside* (pp. 164–177). Newcastle Upon Tyne, UK: Cambridge Scholars Publishing.

Francesetti, G. (2019e), La metamorfosi del dolore. In Conte, V. & Sichera, A. ed., *Avere a cuore. Scritti in onore di Giovanni Salonia* (pp. 109–118). Cinisello Balsamo, MI: Edizioni San Paolo.

Francesetti, G., Alcaro, A. & Settanni, M. (2020). Panic Disorder: Attack of Fear or Acute Attack of Solitude? Convergences Between Affective Neuroscience and Phenomenological-Gestalt Perspective. *Research in Psychotherapy: Psychopathology, Process and Outcome, 23*, 77–87.

Francesetti, G. & Griffero, T., eds. (2019). *Psychopathology and Atmospheres. Neither Inside nor Outside*. Newcastle Upon Tyne, UK: Cambridge Scholars Publishing.

Francesetti, G. & Roubal, J. (2020). Field Theory in Contemporary Gestalt Therapy. Part One: Modulating the Therapist's Presence in Clinical Practice. *Gestalt Review, 24*(2), 113–136.

Francesetti, G., Gecele, M. & Roubal, J., eds., *Gestalt Therapy Perspective on Psychotic Experiences*. Newcastle Upon Tyne, UK: Cambridge Scholars Publishing, forthcoming.

Fonagy, P. & Target, M. (1997). Attachment and Reflective Function: Their Role in Self-organization. *Development and Psychopathology, 9*(4), 679–700.

Gecele, M., ed. (2002). *Fra saperi ed esperienza. Interrogare identità, appartenenze e confini*. Torino: Il Leone Verde Edizioni.

Gecele, M. (2013). *Introduction to Personality Disturbances. Diagnostic and Social Remarks*. In Francesetti, G., Gecele, M. & Roubal, J., eds., *Gestalt Therapy in Clinical Practice. From Psychopathology to the Aesthetics of Contact* (pp. 601–608). Milano: FrancoAngeli.

Gecele, M. (2016). Intersections. Gestalt Therapy Meets Ethnopsychiatry. *GTK Journal of Psychotherapy, 5*, 97–104.

Gecele, M. (2019). Chasing Joy in the Liquid Time of Emptiness: Obsessive-Compulsive Experiences in Postmodern Era. In Francesetti, G., Kerry-Reed, E. & Vazquez Bandin, C., eds., *Obsessive-compulsive Experiences: A Gestalt Therapy Perspective*. Madrid: Los Libros del CTP.

Gecele, M. (2021). *Gli sfondi dell'alterità. La terapia della Gestalt nell'orizzonte sociale e culturale: tra frammentazione e globalizzazione*. Roma: Giovanni Fioriti Editore.

Gecele, M. & Francesetti, G. (2007). The Polis as the Ground and Horizon of Therapy. In Francesetti G., ed., *Panick Attacks and Post-modernity. Gestalt Therapy Between Clinical and Social Perspectives*. Milano: FrancoAngeli.

Höll, K. (2020). The Gestalt of the "Self" in Gestalt Therapy: A Suggestion for a New Configuration of Theory. *Gestalt Review, 24*(1), 33–59.

Marion, J.-L. (2003). *The Erotic Phenomenon*, Chicago, IL: University of Chicago Press.

Morin, E. (2008). *On Complexity*. Cresskill, NJ: Hampton Press.

Parlett, M. & Lee, R. G. (2005). Contemporary Gestalt Therapy: Field Theory. In Woldt, A. L. & Toman, S. M., eds., *Gestalt Therapy. History, Theory, and Practice* (pp. 41–63). Thousand Oaks, CA: Sage.

Perls, F., Hefferline, R. & Goodman, P. (1951). *Gestalt Therapy. Excitement and Growth in the Human Personality*. Gouldsboro, ME: Gestalt Journal Press, 1994.

Philippson, P. (2009). *The Emergent Self. An Existential-Gestalt Approach*. London: Karnac Books.

Philippson, P. (2016). *Revisiting the Field*. Topics in Gestalt Therapy Book 1. Manchester Gestalt Centre, e-book.

Perls, F., Hefferline, R., & Goodman, P. (1951/1994). *Gestalt Therapy: Excitement & Growth in the Human Personality*. New York: The Gestalt Journal Press.

Perls, L. (1992). *Living at the Boundary*. Highland, NY: Gestalt Journal Press.

Robine, J.-M. (2001). From the Field to the Situation. In Robine, J.-M., ed., *Contact and Relationship in a Field Perspective* (pp. 95–107). Bordeaux: L'Exprimerie.

Robine, J.-M. (2016). Self: Artist of Contact. In Robine, J.-M., ed., *Self. A Polyphony of Contemporary Gestalt Therapists* (pp. 213–232). St. Romain-La-Virvée: L'Exprimerie.

Rosa, H. (2010). *Alienation and Acceleration: Towards a Critical Theory of Late-Modern Temporality*. Aarhus: Aarhus Universitetsforlag.

Roubal, J. & Francesetti, G. (2021). *Field Theory in Contemporary Gestalt Therapy. Part Two: Paradoxical Theory of Change Reconsidered*. Gestalt Review, forthcoming.

Salonia, G. (2007). Social Changes and Psychological Disorders. Panic Attacks in Postmodernity. In Francesetti, G., ed., *Panic Attacks and Post-modernity. Gestalt Therapy Between Clinical and Social Perspectives*. Milano: FrancoAngeli.

Salonia, G. (2013). Social Context and Psychotherapy. In Francesetti, G., Gecele, M. & Roubal, J., eds., *Gestalt Therapy in Clinical Practice. From Psychopathology to the Aesthetics of Contact* (pp. 189–200). Milano: FrancoAngeli.

Staemmler, F. M. (2006). A Babylonian Confusion? On the Uses and Meanings of the term Field. *British Gestalt Journal, 15*(2), 64–83.

Waldenfels, B. (2011). *Phenomenology of the Alien: Basic Concepts*. Evanston, IL: Northwestern University Press.

Wollants, G. (2008). *Gestalt Therapy. Therapy of the Situation*. London: Sage.

# Chapter 4

# Gestalt Therapy Theory in an Age of Turmoil

*Gary Yontef*

We live in an era of crises, tumult, and strife. Our era is characterized by the presence of oppressive forces and hateful rhetoric in which politicians do not talk with each other respectfully, but with acrimony and strife. We are coping with a worldwide pandemic. We experience divisive political reactions to large waves of immigration. We witness institutional discrimination and violence against minorities, including the murder of black people by police in the U.S. We experience crises of violence against people of color, against Muslims and Jews. In such an age, no group is free from either having some of its members become victims of violence or of some of its members committing violence.

Since the onset of Gestalt therapy and throughout its history, Gestalt therapists have been allied in spirit with forces of liberation and equality, and in opposition to oppressive forces. Although the Gestalt therapy literature does not specify how to govern at an institutional level or how to organize in the larger political world, the principles of Gestalt therapy provide guidance as to how people can productively relate to each other and how to distinguish less productive patterns of behavior. Above all, Gestalt therapy principles can provide some clarity as to ways in which people may come together around their differences and similarities, work together, talk to each other, and creatively make things better.

In clinical practice as well as in person-to-person contacts outside of the therapeutic situation, Gestalt therapy principles can provide guidance. In its clinical practice, the foundational principles of Gestalt therapy provide support for addressing relational patterns that emerge in the clinical situation by paying attention to situational variables in our patients' lives such as diversity, multiculturalism, social class, and economic differences. Gestalt therapy theory's organizing principles help support the exploration of situational factors of difference and diversity at play between therapist and patient. Additionally, Gestalt therapy theory helps to facilitate exploration of these situational factors as they operate in our patients' lives. Gestalt therapy principles also provide guidance in relating to diverse political views of both patient and therapist as they arise in session. How can we

DOI: 10.4324/9781003255772-6

understand and prepare for the diversity of cultures that our patients are embedded in? My purpose here is to make explicit and to clarify how the basic principles of Gestalt therapy can be helpful in working with difference and diversity in these difficult times.

In this chapter, I discuss the three principles of Dialogue, Phenomenology, and Field Theory and how they apply in modern practice and sociopolitical conversation.

> Dialogue: Working together dialogically.
> Phenomenology: Moving from habitual understanding to explicating a clearer sense of actual experience.

Field theory: Taking a field theory perspective on the complexities of actual situations: Developmental, historical, and current. This includes sociopolitical, cultural, racial, gender, sexual orientation, religious, racial, socioeconomic, and linguistic factors.

## Dialogue

### Working Together

A relational perspective is at the heart of Gestalt therapy theory and practice. At the center of this perspective is the idea and practice of people working together. In this outlook, attention to task, technique, advocacy, and desired outcome are subsumed under the process of how the participants relate to each other. The therapist manifests a respectful and caring interest in understanding the experience of the patient while presenting their own authentic presence and perspective. Dedication to what emerges in the therapeutic dialogue rather than a goal-prescribed outcome is the sine qua non of Gestalt therapy. This mode of relating between therapist and patient is the most powerful therapeutic variable. It makes the other aspects of the clinical work possible and successful. We must *work together*.

In clinical practice this *working together* provides a worthy alternative to the stance of the therapist as the unidirectional expert agent of change, intent on curing the other. *Working together* also presents an alternative to the therapist who takes the stance of only being an empathic listener who trusts change to happen "naturally." Clinical *working together* is a meeting of the perspective of the patient, the perspective of the therapist in the service of the task, and the change that emerges from that meeting. All Gestalt therapy methods including dialogue, focusing on the awareness continuum and the use of experiments, are carried out in the spirit of *working together*. Any other agenda of the therapist, political or otherwise, no matter how worthy, is put in brackets (see discussion in section Phenomenology).

In the clinical situation, issues of diversity with regard to cultural background, race, class, caste, religion, and ethnicity call for a therapist who is curious, open, and inquisitive. The therapist brings these qualities to appreciate the patient's situation and the reality of their experiences in an often intolerant world. Concurrently, the therapist needs to be aware of their own socio-cultural position, and how that position may be a factor in the dialogue. The Gestalt therapist seeks to dialogue with the patient about aspects of their own culturally-based assumptions of which they may have been previously unaware. What is it like if the therapist encourages directness with a patient from a culture in which directness is thought to be rude? How is that suggestion affected by the status, gender, age, or culture of the therapist? What is it like if the patient is a person of color and every day, because of color, is treated differently than the white therapist?

Working together does not mean we are all the same, in agreement, or have the same wishes and values. Working together means knowing and accepting both similarities and differences. When there is conflict, we take special care about being congruent and respectful with each other.

Does this *working together* in the spirit of dialogue apply outside of the clinical situation, e.g., when there are political differences? The dialogic attitude certainly excludes demonizing and name-calling. When people not only present their own viewpoint but also have interest and respect for the viewpoint of those with opposing views, then compromise and creative alternatives can emerge. There can be the dynamic of thesis, antithesis, and then an emerging new synthesis.

Currently, this attitude is too often missing. When it is missing, people talk at the other not with the other, those with opposing viewpoints are ignored or treated as the enemy, and the atmosphere is marked with divisiveness and acrimony. I often see this pattern occurring at the beginning of conjoint therapy and it is a significant barrier to therapeutic progress. The conversation in these cases often devolves into attacking the character of the other rather than attacking the issue and searching for understanding and creative solutions. Frequently the result is a pattern of repetitive circular interactions, animosity, often escalating hostility, and lack of resolution — a lack of creative adjustment.

### Treating People as an It

Gestalt therapy is influenced by Martin Buber's thesis that there is no "I" except the I of I-Thou and the I of I-It. The Gestalt therapy philosophy is an attitude of dialogue that pragmatically includes necessary I-it transactions, but does so within a dialogic matrix. Not treating people solely as an "it" is central to the Gestalt therapy relational attitude.

Therapeutically this implies that we do not reduce patients to a group identity, i.e., identity by categorical grouping. In the Gestalt approach, diagnosis (our understanding of patterns of behavior and thought) is used to sensitize and alert the therapist to possible enduring relational patterns. Diagnosis is not used to presume a truth about the individual patient based on the therapist's assumptions concerning group characteristics. Making such assumptions has the effect of reducing and reifying the patient in the eyes of the therapist. The reduction of the individual patient to a categorical understanding is not truth but approximation, bias, and guesswork disguised as fact. This especially applies to unaware assumptions, biases, and prejudices accorded to gender, culture, race, religion, and socio-economic status. These are all forms of reducing people to "thing" or "it."

There have been a series of movements over the last approximately 60 years in which there has been a recognition of the toxic form of I-It that has oppressed people solely based on group identity. This includes recognition of the discrimination against women, against LGBTQ people, and currently a long-overdue recognition of the widespread and systematic oppression of people of color. Assuming an individual's characteristics based solely on his or her race, religion or ethnic background reduces the person to an "it." Treating or considering an individual based solely on the category one assigns to them is an I-it attitude that goes against the whole philosophy of Gestalt therapy.

Currently in the U.S., there is a long-overdue protest against the institutional racism that people of color are subjected to. This institutionalized racism constitutes a serious and toxic form of I-it. A Gestalt therapy viewpoint about intergroup tensions, e.g., black and white, calls for real talk and genuine contact between different groups of people. Contact, real relating, is the key to change and a form of *working together*. Without the contact of diverse individuals and groups, we are usually left with stereotypic biases, fears, defensive anger, and hatred.

Conceptualizing black and white as being inherently against each other is not only divisive but makes a true alliance of anti-oppressive forces more difficult to coalesce. Group identification without individuals who relate and make contact with one another makes differentiating among the people of various groups difficult. Understanding and advancement happen when people work together. "Together" means actually meeting the other, acknowledging and appreciating differences, agreements, and likenesses – with the other treated as an individual who is equal in worth, value, and virtue.

Gestalt theory would indicate that this kind of person-to-person contact between the police and members of the black community on an ongoing basis would be extremely useful. Knowing individuals from the other group supports movement away from the systematic institutional violation of basic human rights. These rights include both each person's legal rights and their rights by natural law to be shielded from institutional racism, violence, and discrimination. Changing everyday manifestations of individual biases, including those based on ignorance and fearful assumptions, will be difficult and perhaps impossible without actual contact between individuals of different ethnic and racial groups.

### Essential Aspects of Dialogic Relating

According to Martin Buber, relating dialogically has the following essential aspects:

#### Inclusion

One person opens as fully as possible to experience what the other person experiences without losing the autonomous sense of his or her own experiencing. In other words, inclusion involves experiencing the other as if the other's experience was a part of the therapist's own body. The Gestalt therapist simultaneously experiences this approximation of the patient's experiences while maintaining his or her own sense of self.

#### Confirmation

Practicing inclusion renders the other person's existence real by imagining it, thus making it an understandable and shared human experience. In Gestalt therapy, inclusion confirms the patient in several ways. First, the therapist accepts the actuality and recognizability of the patient's experience. Second, the therapist confirms the patient's potential for change. In sum, confirmation affirms that the patient firmly belongs in the human community, and can be understood by other humans.

#### Presence

In dialogue, one person relates to the other with open, authentic, and disclosing presence – of course with discrimination about the context, demands, and limitations of the situation. In the clinical situation, the Gestalt therapist makes choices concerning self-disclosure based on the therapeutic task, the patient's strength and state, the clinical needs, and ethical limitations. I believe inclusion, confirmation, and presence in therapy are most effective when the therapist feels and shows genuine warmth, tenderness, respect, and caring.

In situations in which there is conflict, a dialogic attitude includes taking the risk of congruent and authentic presence. When there is incongruence between what is explicitly expressed and a dissonant sentiment that is kept hidden, the dialogic atmosphere is negatively affected by such discrepancy.

#### Commitment to Dialogue

The difference between a dialogic and a rhetorical process is that a rhetorical process aims for a predetermined outcome, while a dialogic process allows an outcome that emerges spontaneously as opposed to one that is predicted or planned. In political debate each participant is trying to win; in the dialogic process, people come together and outcomes are created by that which emerges in the process of contacting.

When people give up trying to control the outcome and instead surrender to what emerges from the dialogue, the dialectic formation of new wholes is likely. In therapy, the dialogical approach does not seek to move the patient to some predetermined vision of health in which only the patient is expected to change while the therapist, being above it, stays the same. In a true dialogic therapy, both patient and therapist are influenced and changed by the therapeutic interaction. This is especially important when there is dis- agreement, e.g., in therapy when the patient is critical of or disappointed with the therapist. Similarly, in the political sphere, such dialogue can lead to compromise and breakthroughs in getting things accomplished.

### How Can This Work in Political Discourse?

In attempts to win elections and pass legislation, the discourse usually fol- lows the dictates of rhetoric, not the dictates of dialogue. The goal comes down to winning. However, even in this context, there is something to be said for being more dialogic — more civil. When those who take part in the process of governing treat those with differing viewpoints as enemies who are worthy of ridicule, censure, and personal attack, governing itself be- comes more contentious and dysfunctional. We certainly suffer from such in 2020, both in the U.S. and elsewhere in the world.

In person-to-person conversation, even those relating to political issues, the attitude of dialogue can be a guide. I am disappointed when I observe discourse in which people "talk at" one another rather than entering into a more respectful dialogic interaction. Often "talking at" the other in the political sphere results in divisive and repetitive arguing rather than fos- tering the emergence of understanding, compromise, and community.

Subtle or overt political exhortation by the Gestalt therapist, whether they are serving in the role of group leader, individual therapist, or trainer, is antithetical to the Gestalt therapist's commitment to the therapeutic task. In therapy and training relationships, commitment to the therapeutic task, guided by the principles and methodology of Gestalt therapy, lead to an atmosphere of mutually respectful dialogue which does not include the Gestalt therapist's insistence on any form of political persuasion.

## Phenomenology

One of the tripod legs that supports Gestalt therapy is thinking that builds on a phenomenological attitude and adopts a phenomenological method. This thinking is, in part, a reaction against Cartesian thought. Descartes organized his thinking around finding a truth that cannot be denied, a truth that is both beyond experience and that causes experience. He considered experience to be the problem, and logic, the solution. The phenomenological response is that actual experience is the solution, not the problem.

Truth is perspectival. There is no awareness from nowhere, it is always from a perspective. Truth is probabilistic, corrigible, and partial. It is imbued with ambiguity and contradictions. Truth is socially constructed, framed, and interpreted. Truth is not absolute. While these qualities of truth are difficult to keep in mind during intensely emotional situations, they are vital to keep in mind if we are to have dialogue rather than monologue and soliloquy disguised as real discussion.

The Gestalt therapy phenomenological method identifies the assumptions organizing or coloring people's orientation in a "natural outlook." Its awareness method aims to clarify actual experience. The so-called *natural outlook* very often does not differentiate observation from inference while it confuses an initial affect or thought with what the person holds more deeply. The person's more meaningful underlying, central affects, thoughts, and senses of self are hidden in the background and not immediately available to awareness. The phenomenological method supports bringing into awareness that which is genuinely important to the person, and is subtly activated by the current interaction.

## Bracketing (Epoché)

Bracketing is a practice in which one notices assumptions and biases as such and "put them in brackets," to "hold them lightly." It is a procedure in which one notices these biases and holds them aside in order to be open to another perspective. It enables being more precisely aware of just what is actually observed, what is inferred, and what is triggered. Bracketing supports holding lightly the assumptions that might be determining first reactions. Such assumptions might have personal meaning that prevents one from making new connections and adopting new perspectives. Bracketing enables the investigation of as yet unexplored beliefs and reactions that might be influencing and limiting one's accurate perceptions. Bracketing allows one to step away from the belief that a particular perspective is an objective truth.

The phenomenological method is employed to increase the clarity of actual experience ("phenomenological reduction") allowing for the relating of self to another person, of self to otherness in general, and of being open to differing perspectives.

A true dialogic conversation requires one to become aware of previously unaware assumptions, including those derived from one's social position, class, cultural, racial, religious, and ethnic factors operating in the background and frequently out of awareness. Real dialogue requires the ability and willingness to get under reflex and be open to new discoveries of both self and other. The immediate expression of partial thoughts or affect without this clarity, as if it is truth, limits the depth of understanding and dialogue. For example, criticizing the other when one's actual core experience is of hurt or shame makes dialogue less possible.

This issue is important in our current crises with respect to racism. Assuming characteristics of someone of another race can become a self-fulfilling prophesy. If a white person assumes that black people face the same conditions as they have, then they might assume that the problem is just within the black culture. With that misconception, one might hear that if the black community would cure its violence, work harder, get more education, there would be no racial problem. Such assumptions can function as blinders that block awareness of institutional racism in which the conditions that a black person faces are not the same as those of a white person in our culture. Despair, hopelessness, and anger are frequently caused by oppressive social and economic conditions that are so pervasive that they might be difficult to bring into awareness for those who do not have to cope with systematic racism on a daily basis.

The phenomenological method includes a procedure that allows us to become aware of the awareness process itself. For instance, expressing anger may serve as a cover for, and a defense against the experiencing of shame. The processing of awareness is necessary for engaging in dialogue. So too, awareness of assumptions, especially assumptions about the other person, can enable interpersonal contact that is based on actual recognition of the situation, behavior, motivation, and affect of both parties to the conversation. This awareness enables the clarification of one's actual inner experience, intent, and motivation, rather than merely inferring the motivation of the other by way of unexamined assumptions. This awareness is a vital tool in navigating situations we face in our current social crises – situations in which feelings can become highly explosive and communication can readily get stymied.

One person's behavior (verbal or non-verbal) may have the impact of causing hurt, shame, anger, or sadness in the other. Working together to explicate awareness can differentiate intent from impact, inform the person who was unaware of the impact of his or her behavior, and lead the impacted person to differentiate the immediate trigger from more intense, more central feelings, thoughts, and senses of self that have been activated or brought into focal awareness in the current situation.

Gestalt therapists are familiar with phenomenological awareness work in therapy. After all, such awareness work lies at the very core of Gestalt psychotherapy. But how is phenomenological awareness relevant to the much more difficult hurly-burly of ordinary life, politics, and situations that we live without the principles and structure of therapy to help guide the process? Getting clarity about one's assumptions, biases, observations, and associations, enables us to become being open to new discoveries of self, other, and the "relational between." Awareness requires contact with people of other cultures and/or scholarly exploration of diverse cultures. It is this contact and awareness that enables the dialectical emergence of new understanding and creative solutions. Such contact and awareness are vital possibilities that are often dangerously missing in the current contentious social and political environment.

For example, people of color are often met by white people with an attitude of suspicion, fear, and hate. Some will assume the person of color is dangerous, dishonest, or uneducated. Even when just walking down the street, shopping, or hailing a taxi, people of color are frequently met with feelings that are not based on fact or actual person-to-person contact but on largely unexamined assumptions. These assumptions often result in toxic interactions. In the extreme, but all too frequently, suspicion, fear, and hate result in the police shooting of innocent black men and women who are not in actuality behaving provocatively.

Assumptions about the other that are not vetted by dialogic exchange and phenomenological inquiry make likely alienation and the reifying reduction of the other rather than relating more fruitfully toward understanding. Here are other examples of dangerous assumptions (in addition to those about people of color): Jews are smart, calculating, and cheap. Muslims are terrorists or terrorist supporters. Native Americans are alcoholic. Poor people are stupid and/or lazy. WASPS are unfeeling. And, of course, there are multiple gender assumptions. In all these examples there is usually a lack of contact with actual people of the other group and a lack of dialogue along with divisive, unexamined but sometimes vehemently voiced assumptions.

### The Here-and-now and the There-and-then

One of the most misrepresented Gestalt therapy concepts has been what is meant by the "here-and-now." The action of contact and awareness work happens at moments in time within a given situation. However, the focus is not just what is happening in the moment, but bringing into awareness the situations of a person's life: The past situations that still influence mind and body, concurrent situations, and prospects for future situations. The "here-and-now" is a lens that offers a view into the whole dynamic field of a person's life.

The directing of awareness work, and the mode of interaction involved, is informed by the patient's life experience. For example:

In U.S. society there is an obvious dichotomy between the way people who are white and people who are black are treated. There is structural inequality. At the extreme there is the shooting of black men and women without cause, e.g., for "driving while black." And in a more quotidian perspective, people who are white have a relative freedom to go out and not worry about being singled out as suspicious or dangerous. Black people do not enjoy such freedoms in that they are constantly perceived as dangerous or "less than." This distorted view is common even among white people who do not hate black people nor consider themselves to be racist.

Factors of a person's life are best explored by working together in dialogic phenomenological explication. Coming together around differences requires all parties to work together.

### Field Theory

Field theory in Gestalt therapy represents a way of thinking and a point of view. It conceptualizes the situation, and person-in-situation, as being complex, multifactorial, always changing, with the individual having impact on the whole situation and while simultaneously being impacted by the whole. This complex relational perspective is a natural fit for the current awakening about multiculturalism, diversity, and related considerations. Field theory provides a way of understanding the actual situations of people's lives, their childhoods, embedded cultural mores, and the different actualities that are organized by these forces. It is the antidote to individualistic, ethnocentric, simplistic perspectives.

Field theory is a way of thinking about situations in which a person is understood in relation to the whole context. To understand an individual, one must know the context in which he or she is living and has lived. In addition, social and political situations can be better understood in relation to how they are organized and powered by both groups and individuals. To really understand a social situation, one must understand how individuals are impacted and how they impact the social situation. Clear understanding of the social situation and its various parts is achieved through assessing relationships within the whole.

To clarify semantics: The "situation" is the context that is "out there" as collectively understood. The situation as experienced is the "phenomenal field." The term "the field" sometimes refers to the former and sometimes to the latter. Modern usage in Gestalt therapy distinguishes semantically between the "situation" and the "phenomenal field."

All of the forces of the situation affect each other. The causality is complex and non-linear rather than simple. Causal processes are not regarded as being simple: A precedes B and A causes B. The more frequent situation is non-linear and circular: A causes B causes A causes B and so forth.

Dialogic contact and phenomenologically clarified experience require taking into account the current impact of past and current situations that people live through. Conversely, true field understanding requires contact and clarified awareness.

Dialogue and awareness require some degree of understanding concerning the situation and how people experience it. Conversely, field theory understanding requires the discipline of dialogue and phenomenological clarification. One cannot adequately understand a culture by observation without contact with the people of that culture in order to understand their perspective.

Political rhetoric is rife with simplistic statements of causality. These can stir up political support and inhibit sophisticated and constructive thinking that could be creative in finding solutions. The paradigmatic statement has the form: If you/we only do X, then the problem will be solved. But in actual fact, this is usually not the case. Statements such as "if you just be nice" "if you just say no" "just throw them in jail" are almost always far too simplistic. In my experience the prescription that starts with "if only ..." is never accurate or effective enough.

### Self of the Field

In Gestalt therapy theory, people are not seen apart from their situation. Never is there a person without environment and never is there a psychological environment without being considered from some person's perspective. In slightly modified classical Gestalt therapy language: "the person is of the field." The self is the contact of a person in situation, the sense of self forms always in a situation that includes both the individual and their environment. The situation is always experienced from some perspective; the person always exists as part of a situation.

From this perspective, understanding the behavior and rhetoric of societal factions always involves the interaction of environmental force and individual behavior. That complexity opens questions about power and responsibility in managing and directing the situation.

## The Situation: Support and Power

Support is that which makes something possible. Everyone and everything needs support from the situation. This includes the physical environment, other people, and structure.

Everyone needs support from others, not just the weak. It is sometimes thought that the weak are needy and the strong have the power to provide. That narrative favors a view in which need equals inadequacy (shame) while simultaneously reinforcing a top-down view of power. That view camouflages the neediness of the so-called powerful and diminishes the power exerted or potential power that might be exerted by the so-called "weak."

Sometimes power and/or powerlessness are assumed. Looking through a field-oriented lens at the situation, one might ask: How is power being used in this situation? How is the power or potential power of resistance being manifested?

Those whose social status gives them power and capacity to influence what happens in a given situation can use their power to dominate, for self-aggrandizement, to defend against any discomfort, or that power can be used to facilitate working together to improve the situation. People who are impacted by the lack of situational support, especially those who are aware of how power is exercised by the advantaged, have the potential to become agents of resistance. That resistance can promote working together to reorganize the forces of the situation or can take more divisive forms that have less probability of promoting desirable structural change.

## Valuing Other and Otherness

In complex situations, such as psychological and political situations, a core variable centers around how differences are regarded. In situations in which differences are not welcomed or not respectfully discussed, the situation often gets organized in patterns marked by acrimony and negatively escalating circular causality. Openly receiving and being affected by differences increases wisdom and creativity.

What is the life experience of the other? How are current beliefs, values, and behavior shaped by social learning or by behaviors modeled in one's early environment, through verbalized expectations and moralities, behavioral reinforcements, or current life situations? The variables are multiple and often out of awareness until explored. In therapy, we need to be interested, curious, and able to inquire rather than to ignore and assume. Understanding complex political social situations require a similar openness, knowledge, interest, and caring about the circumstances of how the other lives currently and has lived in the past.

Understanding and working constructively with the complexity of multicultural, multiracial, and multiclass makeup of society, requires an openness to exploring differences, a toleration for complexity, and guarding against ingrained and fixed invalidation of alternative ways of thinking, feeling, and behaving. This includes a non-judgmental understanding of diverse cultural mores and practices. What are the expectations and limitations of another's culture with regard to honesty and directness versus politeness? What are the limitations of age, gender, and class? How are differences dealt with? What are the styles of emotional expression? How does the other's life experience lead them to assume how they will be treated?

Within one's own culture, intuitive understanding may well make working together easier. But what about understanding the whole life experience of someone from a different culture, different race, different ethnicity, different religion, different socio-economic class, different gender, different sexual preference?

Whether in the role of therapist or in everyday interactions, one cannot and should not count on his or her expertise in understanding the particular culture of another. Even if familiar with that culture, there are subcultural, familial, and individual variations. And with various backgrounds, one cannot reasonably presume to know the experience of the other. But what a person can offer, whether in or out of therapy is curiosity, inquiry, and working together for the purpose of gaining understanding.

In clinical situations, the therapist can offer guidance to bring out the patient's implicit knowledge of cultural variables. The patient contains the same potential for increased awareness of the therapist if the patient senses the therapist's openness to examining his or her own biases. That is, there is the possibility of phenomenological exploration in a two-way dialogue, especially if it includes an awareness of such influences and their importance, a workable knowledge of how to explore, and a method for working with awareness around such variables.

Doing this not only fosters curiosity and interest in such differences, but also supports humility and recognition of resistances and deflections concerning uncomfortable truths about one's own perspective. Assuming that we know, often leads to a more superficial understanding while the appreciation of differences requires two principles I have discussed earlier in this paper: Working together dialogically and practicing the phenomenological method.

Outside of the therapy context, Gestalt therapy principles work toward understanding, respecting, and appreciating the different cultures, races, religions, and more that come together in cross-cultural situations. In the U.S. there are forces that pull for uniformity and for eliminating individual, cultural, religious, and racial differences. It is as if being a "real American" means being at least middle class, white, Protestant Christian, straight, and in some contexts male. Gestalt therapy principles stand for the opposite of this divisive and ethnocentric attitude. Thankfully Gestalt therapy does not stand alone in this regard.

## Healthy Aggression and Creativity

A central element in Gestalt therapy theory and practice is the need for healthy aggression and creativity. In Gestalt therapy usage, "aggression" refers to the use of biological, psychological, and spiritual energy. It does not denote or connote hostility as in the common usage of the word. Adjusting to the actuality of social, political, and personal conditions and/or changing the situation, takes the initiative and energetic application of personal intelligence, motivation, and values.

Obviously not all ways of doing such are equal. The relational principles of dialogue, phenomenology, and field theory help distinguish between different uses of aggression. Some applications of aggression attack problems, others are divisive attacks on people. In political rhetoric, sometimes people can harness a positive application of aggression that is consistent with an appreciation for differences, respect for the opposition, and while vigorously expressing reasoned analyses, remaining open to working together toward compromise and emergent solutions. A key factor is to understand and respect others with courtesy in receiving and expressing wishes, values, thoughts, and preferences. Understanding the value and validity of differences makes coming together more likely.

For current issues of racism, religious conflict, or antisemitism, we might benefit from imagining: What is it like to be of another gender, race, religion, political persuasion, or class? Does one have a true interest in the other? Can one hold one's ground while also respecting and imagining the actuality of another reality or perspective, i.e., knowing that one's perspective is not the only reality?

## Conclusions

Over the 70 years of Gestalt therapy, there have been attitudes that have been modified and transformed. The liveliness of the late 60s groups and cliches were modified by theoretical clarification of ideas, such as dialogue and the general clarification of the relational basis of Gestalt therapy. Catharsis-oriented "experiments" gave way to more phenomenological experiments. There have been new attitudes and more sophisticated practice constructs, e.g., in conjoint, individual, and group modalities, as well as in the training of Gestalt therapists.

At the present time, we are integrating new understandings with regard to racial, gender, ethnic, religious, and class diversity in the teaching and practice of Gestalt therapy. Dialogue, phenomenological exploration, and field theory are still central and vital as they are being applied to current conditions and concerns.

# Chapter 5

# To Hold the Hands that Hold Our Hands: Responsivity of Contacting

## Dan Bloom

Touch touching touch being touched. Gestalt therapy has much to say about this. Copernicus moved the earth from its privileged place at the center of the solar system and showed how it revolved around the sun as one planet in relation to the others. (Bloom, 2009) The so-called "relational turn" (see, for example, Yontef, 1993; Jacobs & Hycner, 2009; Jacobs, 2019) in Gestalt therapy, while surely not the earthquake of a "Copernican Revolution," nevertheless marked the emergence of a new paradigm. Gestalt therapy pivoted from a focus on the dynamics of a single person to the experiences of persons-in-relation, from an intrapsychic to an intersubjective model. The individual is not the center of the universe but is a person-in-relation. There have since been turns within turns within turns – the dialogical turn (Hycner, 1985; Yontef, 1993), the esthetic turn (Spagnuolo Lobb & Amendt-Lyon, 2003; Spagnuolo Lobb, 2014), the esthetic/estheological turn (Francesetti & Griffero, 2019), the ethical turn (Bloom, 2013), and the pathic turn (Francesetti, 2015b). It seems that once spun on its axis, there are no limits to Gestalt therapy's spins. And this ought to be so long as each turn broadens Gestalt therapy's perspective. Each time it pivots, Gestalt therapy re-orients to the needs of specific clinical, social, political, or cultural conditions. In this chapter, I offer a nudge to Gestalt therapy's spin by looking at the responsivity of contacting.

I will reconsider some of the essential concepts of the clinical phenomenology[1] of Gestalt therapy. Consequently, I will look closely at the *intentionality for contacting* (Spagnuolo Lobb, 2014) in terms of its emergence of the contact-boundary of the organism/environment-*lifeworld* field. I will present *relational intentionality* and suggest further that relational intentionality includes not only the potential for *responsivity*, but the ability to *respond*, which are the basis for a responsivity of contacting. This perspective on Gestalt therapy is possible within a *responsive phenomenology* (Waldenfels, 1996, 2011, 2016). When we see relational intentionality in terms of responsive phenomenology, relationality appears as being responsive to as well as responding to the other.

DOI: 10.4324/9781003255772-7

The potentials to be responsive and to respond are entwined with intentionality to constitute the interpersonal essence of *relational contacting*. This animates the esthetic ebb and flow, back and forth, of the sequence of relational contacting of the field-emergent self (Philippson, 2009). This is the rhythm of relational contacting. It is the rhythm of being responsive and responding, of being receptive, welcoming, acting, and answering – of holding the hand that holds our hand. These intertwining gestures of interpersonal contacting are the heart of this chapter.

## Contact-boundary and Field

Intentionality for contacting accounts for how contacting is directed, with what qualities meanings, forms, with what, with whom (Bloom, 2020). As an organizing structure of contacting, intentionality is emergent of the contact-boundary. Necessarily, intentionality for contacting is shaped by the complexities of the contact-boundary and the field, as I will describe. The contact-boundary's importance to responsive intentionality is pivotal. It is impossible for contacting to emerge as if pristine from the contact-boundary.

The contact-boundary's centrality to Gestalt therapy's theory and practice is indisputable. Its novelty as a concept, remarkable. The contact-boundary is the basis for Gestalt therapy's claim to be experiential psychotherapy. Gestalt *Therapy, Excitement and Growth in the Human Personality* (Perls et al., 1951 hereinafter PHG), Gestalt therapy's founding text, affirms that experience occurs at the boundary of the organism and its environment..." (PHG, p. 227) Later, PHG offers various other perspectives on the contact-boundary. For example, "...the contact-boundary ... *is the organ of a particular relation of the organism and the environment* ... this particular relation is growth." (emphasis in original) p. 229, "Growth is the function of the contact-boundary..." p. 230. "The self is the contact-boundary at work; its activity is the forming figures and ground." p. 235; "... the contact-boundary is ... the specific organ of awareness." p. 259.

It ought to go without saying that the contact-boundary is not a "boundary" per se in the sense of dividing a "this" from a "that," a "Dan" from a "Tom," a "horse" from a "cow," or even the "ocean" from the "land." I can tell my neighbor to "respect the boundaries" of our properties, that is, the limit that separates what is his from what is mine. We can remark that a patient becomes anxious when she is faced with "making" boundaries. These are boundaries that are made, lines that can be drawn, categories that can be constructed to sort things. These are boundaries that differentiate and separate. These are boundaries that account for differences of things we can count. They are boundaries that can be crossed in both directions – back and forth. They are the boundaries of the Cartesian world.

This is not what is intended by contact-boundary. The contact-boundary is a "boundary" of a wholly different order. It is the "location" of the emergence of experience – of the intentionality of contacting itself. It is a *topos*,[2] a phenomenal space or region. Instead of "space," it has "spatiality" (Heidegger, 1962, p. 53; Moran & Cohen, 2012, p. 303). The contact-boundary is unitary. That is, it is without an inside or outside, an up or a down. It is without a place that can be marked, measured, or mapped. It is *neither* material *nor* immaterial (Bloom, 2019c). It is the ground of the field-emergent relational self. Further, since the self is a sequence, a temporal sequence (PHG, p. 403), the contact-boundary is a process with its own time or "temporality" (Husserl, 1970; Drummond, 2010, p. 200; Schalow & Denker, 2010, p. 17). That is, just as it lacks physical dimensions that can be measured in inches or millimeters, it lacks time that can be measured in minutes or hours (clock time). The dash, "-," in the word differentiates the contact-boundary as a phenomenal or experiential boundary from Cartesian boundaries.[3] "Contact-" is not an adjective modifying "boundary"; it is intrinsic in "boundary." This is the creative invention of Gestalt therapy's basic clinical epistemology that disappears with the disappearing dash.

So, you and I do not "have" a contact-boundary. We cannot "make" one together. The contact-boundary isn't an achievement. You and I, rather, are emergent processes *of* the contact-boundary. The contacting process that includes you and me, then, is *of* the contact-boundary. That we are of a common contact-boundary ensures our relationality. Further, the contact-boundary is the condition for the very possibility of contacting and consequently self emergence. At the same time and reciprocally, the contact-boundary is enriched by ongoing contacting. The "aftermath" of contacting is assimilated to the ground and becomes part of the ongoing basis of the contact-boundary from which contacting is emergent. How else could we have continuity of personal, interpersonal identities? Or history? Or a past to recollect? Contacting emerges of a contact-boundary that is always already a rich field nourished by previous contactings. Responsivity and the capacity to respond are emergent functions of this richly structured phenomenal "boundary" of emergent contacting. Intentionality of contacting is emergent of this contact-boundary, and of course, it cannot be other than relational intentionality since of this contact-boundary nothing non-relational can exist.

When we say that "we meet at the contact-boundary," we mean that our experience of "meeting" emerges of a place that is described by PHG on p. 229 as a particular *relation of* "the organism/environment field," that is, the contact-boundary.

Contact-boundary emergent of...

The contact-boundary is usually understood in Gestalt therapy as the "organism/environment field." This paradigm is incomplete for the approach I am proposing. "Environment" is too broad a word to capture the potentialities and possibilities of self emergence (Bloom, 2016, 2019a, 2019b). At least in English, the material connotations of "environment" are too limiting. The environment supports me as a biological organism, and of course, it is a mistake to consider an organism as separate from the environment. But as much as I live in an environment with this climate, with this oxygen and am sustained by these nutrients, I dwell, thrive, love, make meaning and suffer in my home, with my family, my loved ones, my culture, my language, my history – my world. When I travel far away, I may get lonely and homesick. I rarely say I miss my environment. I can dig a hole in the ground and that is rarely a hole in the "environment." When I bury a dead person in it that hole, it becomes something else: it becomes a grave. When I hold the hand that holds my hand, we touch and form a world that belongs to us. Is there a name for it?

We ought to have another term that is more suitable for our work as psychotherapists. The Baltic German biologist Jakob von Uexküll (1864–1944) introduced *Umwelt* to describe the surrounding world of a biological organism that is *not only* its environment but includes its world of significance (Harrington, 1996, p. 44). Edmund Husserl (1859–1938) imported *Umwelt* into his phenomenology and further developed this as *Lebenswelt*, lifeworld. (Husserl, 1970; Moran & Cohen, 2012, p. 189) Lifeworld is the world of our actual practical living as human beings in a community who intersubjectively make meaning together, who form relationships, share histories, and dream of the future. Husserl's horizon is the spatial, temporal, historical, and cultural context of particular experience (Moran & Cohen, 2012, p. 9). It is the world of life, lived-history, social bonds, culture, and so on. It is our personal horizon that surrounds each of us, each person, each relationship, each family, each group, each community. It is the world as given as well as "the pre-given basis for all experience" (Gadamer, 1976, p. 245) where "pre-given" is past "lived-experiences" that make present experiences possible" (Luft, 2011, p. 109). It is also "pre-given" in the sense of the naïve subjective world before we add meaning to it; that is, the world that is there prior to our own sense-making. The lifeworld is the gathering or meeting of personal horizons as the horizon of all horizons, which connects us in a whole fabric of humanity. It is both the visible everyday world right in front of our faces and the invisible hidden world we see when we clear our eyes and find enchantment in unexpected places. Consider, then, the contact-boundary as emergent of and including this extended field, the organism/environment-lifeworld field.

Lifeworld deserves to be appended to "environment" so that the "organism/environment-*lifeworld* field" more accurately reflects how contacting, self, and relationality are world-embedded processes. The meeting of the organism and its environment becomes the personal and relational organism/environment-lifeworld field. And the contact-boundary can be understood as an already richly populated human *horizon* (Moran & Cohen, 2012, p. 147) out of which the figure of relational contacting emerges. The lifeworld is the extended worlded fringe around the focus of figural attention, which stretches to the margin or edges of awareness. Further, responsive intentionality of contacting is emergent of the contact-boundary of the organism/environment-lifeworld field since responsivity itself is intrinsic in the contact-boundary as "the organ of a particular relation of the organism and the environment" (PHG, p. 229). Consequently, relational intentionality for contacting has to be understood to include both the openness of responsivity as well as the activity of responding. I will return to this important point, below.

## Relational Intentionality for Contacting

It is a familiar experience. We know someone is in the room before we recognize her by shape and then, by face. We had *already* breathed the air of the same lifeworld, our feet were on the same ground, our seeing was already lit by the same light before I recognized her by name. I and she were, *a la* Merleau-Ponty, as if two hearts beating in one body. She and I were organs of one single "intercorporeity" (Landes, 2013, p. 176).

### Relational Intentionality to Responsive Intentionality

Since intentionality emerges of the contact-boundary of the organism/ environment-lifeworld field, it must also be considered relational intentionality since every intentional object of contacting is a *social* object of the lifeworld. This keyboard under my fingers, for example, is part of the social world of keyboards users. This coffee cup is part of the world of coffee drinkers and cup users. They are given to me as objects of the lifeworld already surrounded by a network or horizon of shared, relational meanings (Husserl, 1989, pp. 205–207). The keyboard is useless until I know terms of its use by others in this world. The keys and this cup stand out as figures against a background world of others without which they are meaningless. Every figure/ground of contacting inevitably has this horizon of the lifeworld as background. This is what Husserl referred to as *horizon-intentionality* of the lifeworld – the context for all relational intentionalities[4] (Gadamer, 1976, p. 189).

Even further, I did not merely want to contact the keys, but I *intended* to make meaning for others by writing. Every word I am forming contains other's voice as an echo even as I repeat it and reform it into my own (Waldenfels, 2020) every sub-vocal sound in each phrase I type is a "saying" to another of the lifeworld. Each word on this page stands out from within a community of meaning-makers, language users, speakers, writers, and so on. It is unlikely – impossible – that I would be writing were I not in a world of others. My relational intentionality of contacting this keyboard is a function of the lifeworld that is not merely threaded by a network of social references, but alive with others who are always already there, including you, the invisible readers of this chapter who are affecting me as I write this paper – to *whom I am being responsive.*

I worked with Alice face to face for years. During the covid-crisis, she and I meet at the contact-boundary of tele-phenomenological field. One day she said that unlike after the sessions in which we met face-to-face, she felt alone. after our online sessions. She felt ashamed that she spent so much time talking about herself.

"After sessions in your office, I used to have the chance to go around the corner and sit in the coffee shop and take some time for myself. There were people all around. But now the session ends and I am all alone."

I asked Alice to take a moment and look around my office particularly look at the objects, their shapes, colors. Could she identify what they are? Consider that they were mine or not. Could she tell me something about them and me? Then I asked her to do the same with what was in her own room.

The objects she noticed soon took on social meanings as the horizon of her personal lifeworld became clearer. Some objects were hers, some her husband's, and some from various times in her life and as if extracted from her pre-given lived-history, which is her vital past that mains part of her life, yet just beyond the edges of her memory. Those social objects of the lifeworld were in the dark background and came forward into the foreground light of the contacting process.

Her room itself was no longer "her" room, but the room in her family's house and the room in a home in which her parents had condemned her for being selfish whenever she didn't do all the household chores. Her room became crowded and noisy with previously unheard sounds of people, some of which were now disturbing.[5]

The others were always already there (Heidegger, 1962) as they are always part of the intrinsic social dimension of the contact-boundary and part of the invisible ground to which she was responsive. Our experiences pass into the memory of the last moments, hours, days, months, years, and back into the lived past, which is available to recollection or awareness. "The past is never dead. It isn't even past" (Faulkner, 1951). Since social contacting becomes the ground for the emergence of all future contacting. The world of the others-in-relation is always already there, seen and unseen. This is the horizon-intentionality, mentioned above, that is the context or fringe contextualizing relational intentionality. Responsivity is the fundamental basis for our ability to respond to our milieu (Friesen, 2014). Without responsivity, relational intentionality would be lost, empty, and aimless. And would be condemned to isolation.

Consequently, I am not deaf to the voices of the lifeworld nor blind to the hands that reach toward my hands reaching toward them. Responsivity and the ability to respond are entwined in relational intentionality. To hold the hand that holds our hand exceeds the limit of our grasp. This becomes clear from the perspective of responsive phenomenology

… in which intentionality (intending, grasping something as something) is transformed into responsivity (responses to claims). *What* we respond to is always more than the *answer* we give under certain circumstances and within certain [situations]. Rationality can thus be understood as responsive rationality stemming from the creative answers themselves … (Waldenfels, as quoted in Parent (1996) p. xvii).

## Responsive Intentionality: Clinical Willingness

To hold the hand…

It is easy to experience the phenomena of responsive intentionality's responsivity and capacity to respond. We know that "contact" is derived from the Latin, *contactus*, "a touching." https://www.etymonline.com/word/contact. We demonstrate contacting in various ways. I touch one hand to the other.[6] A world of sensations and experiences of being touched and touching opens up. Warmth *and* pressures. Push *and* weight. I reverse the touching and the touched and mirror the experience. Sensing hand and sensible hand. My felt hand is a *sensible* object just like any other object I can touch; my *sensing* opens different worlds of experience, unseen.

Now I clasp my hands together and there is even a time when I don't know which hand is which. I experience myself as a body "inserted into the world," feeling *and* felt, seeing *and* seen, *invisible and in*visible as the chiasm or enfolding of Merleau-Ponty's phenomenology by which he resolves the mind/body dualism (Merleau-Ponty, 1968). This is the *interleafing* of being responsive and responding, touched-being-touched-touching at the contact-boundary of the organism/environment-lifeworld field.

This experience is taken to another register when I touch the hand of another person or look into another person's eyes. It is at this level that the capacity to respond and potential for responsivity reveal a different perspective on the relational field. It is an example of the emergence of responsive intentionality of the organism/environment lifeworld field.

Responsive intentionality characterizes a clinician's willingness (Orange, 2018) to go along with the developing figure, not merely as a partner, not as someone who retreats to the background as a listener nor as someone who reflects back to the patient what he or she has "heard." The therapist is along with and fully engaged in the figure/ground process, as touched and touching, responsive and responding. The Gestalt therapist Ruella Frank demonstrates a version of responsive intentionality in her training when she asks two people to balance a large ball between them by supporting the ball with both of their hands. She asks them to vary the pressure of their grip and notice their sense of the other. Invariably each person experiences the other as part of one whole experience – poised in intersubjective equilibrium by the dance of responsivity and responding in responsive intentionality. Each person is committed to a willingness to go along with the sense of the other emerging of the contact-boundary.

Acknowledged or not, this cannot be otherwise in clinical situations since patient and therapist *undergo* a common situation and resonate to the kinesthetics of the horizon extending in all directions at the contact-boundary of the organism/environment-lifeworld field. Responsive intentionality is a function of this undergoing of the situation. "To undergo" stresses the simple phenomenality that responsivity is an experience of something that happens rather than done. That is, it is

> something which provokes sense [meaning] without being meaningful itself yet still as something *by which* we are touched, affected, stimulated, surprised and to some extent violated. I call this happening *pathos*, *Widerfahrnis* or af-fect, marked by a hyphen in order to suggest that something is done *to us.* (emphases in original)
> (Waldenfels, 1996, p. 74 in Friesen, 2014, p. 72)

Responsivity, then, is a functioning of the dative self, that is the self to which something is given. Responding, on other hand, is a function of the agentic or active self. In terms of the awareness-consciousness continuum of contacting, responsivity is linked to wariness, watchfulness, responsiveness to the situation. Awareness. Responding is deliberate, choiceful, and more or less conscious (Bloom, 2019a).

The pre-given and *then* felt a sense of the situation, the affective atmosphere of the organism/environment-lifeworld field is the temporal predecessor or *prius* of the therapy relationship. It comes *upon* the therapist and patient. How often do we therapists experience ourselves seized by sadness or overtaken by anxiety even prior to those moods becoming clear to us and our patients? (Ratcliffe, 2015; Spagnuolo Lobb, 2018). This is a function of the pathic field, the field of undergoing the weight, pathos, or suffering of the other (Orange, 2011; Waldenfels, 2011; Francesetti, 2015a, 2015b, Bloom, 2018, pp. 119–128).

> Something touches me; I feel it in the pit of my stomach. The way he walks and sits down? Maybe. Then I hear his voice; its hollow tone touches me. Now his words are heavy and the sound like rocks falling on the ground. I imagine they were falling on me.

> "Henry, I suddenly had trouble following what you were saying to me. I knew the meaning of your words, but I couldn't connect them anymore. What is your sense of what is happening now?

> "Hmm. Let me see... (pause... he swallows hard...) It's hard for me to swallow....(He tries again and clears his throat.) .... A few moments.... Look, there's something I don't want to talk about."

"Uh, huh." I utter sounds rather than words. This is not deliberate. I extend my arms, palm sides up.

"Hmm." He looks right at me and meet my eyes. "You seem as if you are interested." His voice inflected upward in a quasi-question

I smile "yes."

The air has cleared. His voice is now full and resonant.

"There is no pathos, be it joy, love, pain or jealousy without provoking a certain response and there is no response without a certain pathos to which it points back." (Waldenfels, 2016, p. 22). The rhythm of my and Henry's interaction in the ebb and flow of the responsive field reflects the emergence of responsive intentionality. Responsive intentionality is the movement of the relational field – of responsivity to the scents and senses of the atmospheres of the lifeworld. Responsivity and response are the esthetic movements of responsive intentionality, where esthetic is the sensed and felt experience of the emerging relational figure (Spagnuolo Lobb, 2014, 2018; Bloom, 2009).

Too soon; too late...

Whenever something extraordinary happens ... and affects us, it always comes *too early*... Vice versa, our response comes always *too late*, .... (Waldenfels, 2016, p. 22)

A skilled dancing partner floats in the dance,[7] one step behind and one step ahead of the person with whom she is dancing. This dance to the relational music, however, has a particular balance between the partners. We are never quite in synch with our patients just as no two persons can ever be. The temporal sequence of contacting contextualizes a too soon and too late, which shapes responsive intentionality of contacting of the psychotherapeutic field. Our sense of the emerging figure affects us almost an instant prior to our patient's awareness.

That is, we are responsive with awareness of the esthetic of the field. We are affected by the immediacy of the felt sense of the situation that is prior to our knowing clinical response. We knowingly respond to a developing figure of contacting with our clinical practical-wisdom, *phronesis*.

The emerging figure of contacting begins as its *prius*, a pre-given prior to the id of the situation (Robine, 2011, p. 215, 2015) a still hidden day in the atmosphere of the night just before the edge of dawn. We are a moment too soon when our responsivity joins the *prius* of the emerging figure of awareness; I sense without knowing; I initiate a gesture without deliberating. I am too late when I choose to reply to what has now passed and, by this fulfilled relational exchange, we are moving along with a new figure.

In terms of the structure of the contact-boundary, then, the time-lag in responsive intentionality establishes an asynchronous relationship, in terms of time, and an asymmetrical relationship, in terms of space. Instead of the mutuality of traditional dialogue, Waldenfels focuses on the asymmetry and asynchrony of *quasi*-dialogue.

> Going hand in hand with the temporal deferment of demand and response [intrinsic in responsive intentionality] is an unavoidable asymmetry that *throws out of balance the traditional dialogue*... As Levinas shows, this asymmetry does not depend upon the fact that in an ongoing dialogue rules are distributed unequally, rather asymmetry depends upon the facts that *demand and response do not converge.* (*emphasis added*)
> (Waldenfels, 2003, p. 34)

"Too soon" and "too late" are not evaluations of clinical failures. They are, rather, descriptions of undisturbed responsive intentionality. "Too soon" and "too late" support the emerging figure. They welcome, support, and go along with the emerging figure. There is never an "on" or "in" time. We are always chasing the comet's tale of experience. When we think we caught that comet, we've fallen into the fallacy that we've finally understood something. This is the trap of certainty (Staemmler, 2000). Rather, we've trapped and stilled the flow of responsive intentionalities and the aesthetic of relational contacting. "I heard you saying...." Or "I understand..." freeze a dance. Responsive intentionality of contacting is a gesture of welcoming and including, supporting and inviting, beckoning and wondering.

## Conclusion

The hand I hold holds the hand it holds. This is the interleafing of responsivity and responding. Touch touching touch being touched. Relational intentionality for contacting taken further through a responsive phenomenology shows responsivity and the ability to respond as emergent functions of the contact-boundary of the organism/environment-lifeworld field. Responsive intentionality reveals that our relational sensibilities to the other, our openness, our availability, and our willingness to be responsive and to respond, are intrinsic in Gestalt therapy's relational perspective.

Emmanuel Levinas, the philosopher who developed ethics as a first philosophy where ethics is relatedness to the other (Critchley, 2002, p. 15) and where our non-indifference to the other's call is inescapable, wrote of responsivity and ethics. To him,

> ethics is lived in the embodied exposure to the other. It is because the self is sensible, that is to say, vulnerable, passive ... that it is worthy of ethics.... [The] ... deep structure of subjective experience ... is structured in a relation of responsibility, or, better, responsivity to the other...This deep structure is the other with the same, in spite of me, calling me to respond."
> (Critchley, 2002, p. 21)

This is not an ethics of right or wrong, but an ethics of non-indifference. The "deep structure of subjective experience" must be understood in terms of our organism/environment-lifeworld field and consequently as the deep structure of intersubjective relational experience. This is the ethical field. Responsive intentionality is emergent of this field.

Each turn of Gestalt therapy somewhat adds to our perspectives. This chapter suggests a turn to responsivity.

Gestalt therapy has more and more opened its eyes to different forms of clinical suffering and wider and wider fields of practice. Now suffering calls across wide populations, needs for social justice, and the planet in crisis. Responsive intentionality of contacting is not a response to these calls; it is a way of finding within Gestalt therapy support for our responses.

Our responsive intentionality of contacting is our "exposure to the other." The other does not stop at the consulting room door any more than the lifeworld starts and stops at that threshold. Gestalt therapy's contribution to responsive phenomenology, some of which I intended here, is a contribution to an engaged phenomenology of the contemporary lifeworld where it takes a good deal of courage to hope and to care in the face of growing authoritarianism, suffering and despair in a fragile, diseased world.

## Notes

1 …the ultimate task of phenomenology … is to understand its relationship to non-phenomenology. What resists phenomenology within us natural beings cannot remain outside phenomenology and should have its place within it (Merleau-Ponty, 1968, p. 178).

2 See Francesetti and Roubal regarding *atopon* as "out of place" in the experience of a pathological field (Francesetti & Roubal, 2020, p. 120). They refer to this as if a stranger knocking at the door: something meaningless, strange, embarrassing, and so on. In my model, this would be something lurking at the contact-boundary, prior to contacting, and not taken up in the sequence of contacting itself. As such, it would remain an uncanny premonition from the past, as it were.

3 This is important. There is nothing diaphanous about the contact-boundary. Just as phenomenology is not idealism but a philosophy about being-in-the-world in its concreteness, experience emergent of the contact-boundary is of a whole, which can be looked at from a variety of perspectives. This paper is from the perspective of the clinical phenomenology of gestalt therapy.

4 Originally, intentionality was a function of a transcendental subjectivity by which am I constituted its world. Now relational/responsive intentionality can be called a function of transcendental intersubjectivity, by which a world of intersubjectivity is constituted.

5 This is a compressed clinical vignette. It also shows a gestalt phenomenological reduction involving the gestalt epoché and gestalt reduction explained in more detail elsewhere (Bloom, 2009).

6 See Husserl and Merleau-Ponty.

7 See Spagnuolo Lobb (2017) for a discussion of the dance of therapy.

# References

Bloom, D. (2009). One good turn deserves another … and another … and another: personal reflections. *Gestalt Review*, *15*(3), 296–311.

Bloom, D. (2013). Situated ethics and the ethical world of Gestalt therapy. In G. Francesetti, M. Gecele, & J. Roubal (Eds.), *Gestalt therapy in clinical practice: From psychotherapy to the aesthetics of contact* (pp. 131–145). FrancoAngeli.

Bloom, D. (2016). The Relational function of self: Self function in the most human plane. In J.-M. Jean-Marie Robine (Ed.), *Self, a polyphony of contemporary Gestalt therapists*. L'Exprimerie.

Bloom, D. (2018). Evil: The sight that cannot be seen: The speaking that cannot be said. In M. Spagnuolo Lobb & et al. (Eds.), *The aesthetic of otherness: Meeting at the boundary in a desensitized world*. Istituto di Gestalt HCCC Italy.

Bloom, D. (2019a). From sentience to sapience: The awareness-consciousness continuum and the lifeworld. *Gestalt Review*, *23*(1), 18–43

Bloom, D. (2019b). Gestalt therapy and phenomenology: The intersection of parallel lines. In P. Brownell (Ed.), *Handbook for theory, research, and practice in Gestalt therapy (2nd Edition)* (pp. 183–202). Cambridge Scholars Publishing.

Bloom, D. (2019c). Neither from the "inside" looking "out" nor from the "outside" looking "in." In G. Francesetti & T. Griffero (Eds.), *Psychopathology and atmospheres, neither inside nor outside* (pp. 178–190). Cambridge Scholars Publishing.

Bloom, D. (2020). Intentionality: The fabric of relationality. *The Humanistic Psychologist*, *48*(4), 389–396.

Critchley, S. (2002). Introduction. In *the Cambridge companion to Levinas*. Cambridge University Press.

Drummond, J. J. (2010). *The a to z of Husserl's philosophy*. Scarecrow Press.

Faulkner, W. (1951). *Requiem for a nun—Wikipedia*. Retrieved February 25, 2021, from https://en.wikipedia.org/wiki/Requiem_for_a_Nun

Francesetti, G. (2015a). From individual symptoms to psychopathological fields. Towards a field perspective on clinical suffering. *British Gestalt Journal*, *24*(1), 5–19.

Francesetti, G. (2015b). Pain and beauty: From psychopathology to the aesthetics of contact. *British Gestalt Journal*, *21*(2), 4–18.

Francesetti, G., & Griffero, T. Eds. (2019). *Psychopathology and atmospheres, neither inside nor outside*. Cambridge Scholars Publishing.

Francesetti, G., & Roubal, J. (2020). Field theory in contemporary Gestalt therapy, Part 1: Modulating the therapist's presence in clinical practice. *Gestalt Review*, *24*(2), 113–136.

Friesen, N. (2014). Waldenfels' responsive phenomenology of the alien: An introduction. *Phenomenology & Practice*, *7*(14), 69–77.

Gadamer, H.-G. (1976). The phenomenological movement. In *Philosophical hermeneutics* (pp. 130–181). University of California Press.

Harrington, A. (1996). *Reenchanted science: Holism in German culture from Wilhelm II to Hitler*. Princeton University Press.

Heidegger, M. (1962). *Being and time* (J. Macquarrie & E. Robinson, trans.). Harper & Row.

Husserl, E. (1970). *The crisis of the European sciences and transcendental phenomenology*. Northwestern University Press.

Husserl, E. (1989). *Ideas pertaining to a pure phenomenology and to a phenomenological philosophy, Second Book* (R. Rojcewicz & A. Schuwer, Trans.). Kluwer Academic Publishers.

Hycner, R. (1985). Dialogical Gestalt therapy: An initial proposal. *The Gestalt Journal, 8*(1), 23–49.

Jacobs, L. (2019). Relationality and relational process in Gestalt therapy. In *Handbook for theory, research and practice and Gestalt therapy (Second Edition).* (pp. 203–219). Cambridge Scholars Publishing.

Jacobs, L., & Hycner, R. (2009). *Relational approaches in gestalt therapy.* New York: Routledge, Taylor & Francis Group.

Landes, D. A. (2013). *The Merleau-Ponty dictionary.* Bloomsbury.

Luft, S. (2011). Facticity and historicity as constituents of the lifeworld in Husserl's late philosophy. In *Subjectivity and lifeworld in transcendental phenomenology* (pp. 103–125). Northwest University Press.

Merleau-Ponty, M. (1968). *The visible and the invisible: Followed by working notes.* Northwestern University Press.

Moran, D., & Cohen, J. D. (2012). *The Husserl dictionary.* Continuum.

Orange, D. M. (2011). *The suffering stranger: Hermeneutics for everyday clinical practice.* Routledge/Taylor & Francis Group.

Orange, D. M. (2018). My Other's keeper: resources for the ethical turn in psychotherapy. In M. Spagnuolo Lobb (Ed.), *The Aesthetic of Otherness, meeting at the boundary in a desensitized world* (pp. 19–32). Istituto di Gestalt HCCC Italy.

Parent, D.J. (1996). Introduction to the American Edition. In Waldenfels, B. (Ed.), *Order in the twilight* (pp. xvii–xxvi). Ohio University Press.

Perls, F., Hefferline, R., Hefferline, R., & Goodman, P. (1951). *Gestalt therapy: Excitement and growth in the human personality.* Julian Press.

Philippson, P. (2009). *The emergent self.* Karnac Books.

Ratcliffe, M. (2015). *Experiences of depression: A study in phenomenology (First Edition).* Oxford University Press.

Robine, J.-M., (2011). From field to situation. *On the Occasion of the Other* (pp. 103–121). Gestalt Journal Press.

Robine, J.-M. (2015). Contact at the source of experience. In *Social change begins with two* (pp. 59–68). Istituto di Gestalt HCCC Italy.

Schalow, F., & Denker, A. (2010). *Historical dictionary of Heidegger's philosophy (Second Edition).* Scarecrow Press.

Spagnuolo Lobb, M., & Amendt-Lyon, N. (2003). *Creative license: The art of Gestalt therapy.* Springer-Verlag.

Spagnuolo Lobb, M. (2014). *The now-for-next in psychotherapy: Gestalt therapy recounted in post-modern society.* Istituto di Gestalt HCCC Italy.

Spagnuolo Lobb, M. (2017). From losses of ego functions to the dance steps between psychotherapist and client. Phenomenology and aesthetics of contact in the psychotherapeutic field. *British Gestalt Journal, 26*(1), 28–37.

Spagnuolo Lobb, M. (2018). Aesthetic relational knowledge of the field: A revised concept of awareness in Gestalt therapy and contemporary psychiatry. *Gestalt Review, 22*(1), 50–68.

Staemmler, F. (2000). Like a fish in water: Gestalt therapy in times of uncertainty. *Gestalt Review, 4*(3), 205–218.

Waldenfels, B. (1996). *Order in the twilight*. Athens, OH: Ohio University Press.

Waldenfels, B. (2003). From intentionality to responsivity. In *Phenomenology today: The Schuwer SPEP Lectures, 1998–2002* (pp. 23–35). The Simon Silverman Phenomenology Center, Duquesne University.

Waldenfels, B. (2011). *Phenomenology of the alien: Basic concepts*. Northwestern University Press.

Waldenfels, B. (2016). Responsive love. *Primerjalna Književnost, 39*(1), 15–29.

Waldenfels, B. (2020). Responsivity and co-responsivity from a phenomenological view. *Studia Phaenomenologica, 20*, 341–355.

Yontef, G. (1993). *Awareness dialogue & process – essays on Gestalt therapy*. The Gestalt Journal Press.

# Chapter 6

# The Gifts and Risks in Relational Empathy: An Historical Perspective

*Jack Aylward*

The universality of an individual's desire for meaningful interpersonal contact was elegantly stated by author Jack Kerouac (1972), in perceiving "relationship as the diamond upon which existence rests" (Johnson, 2012, p. 236). Yet, applying such definition to the practice of psychotherapy may initially be perceived as being somewhat paradoxical. After all, to anyone seeking psychotherapy, it would seem somewhat intuitively obvious that an engagement in what would be considered a mutual joint effort of emotional problem solving would instinctively require some form of co-created intimacy manifested through an emotional connection between a therapist and a client. Historically, however, clinical empathy and its various mutations within the therapeutic encounter has a somewhat mixed and variable history with respect to its perceived effectiveness. In fact, some of the streams of data amassed throughout the past several decades would suggest a somewhat Hegelian dialectic process in which a particular thesis was proposed, eventually giving rise to a certain antithesis, with the resultant tension eventually resolved through a mutually agreed upon synthesis in support of such evidence.

## A Beginning Thesis

During the early years of psychoanalysis, little attention was given to any specific form of interpersonal machinations between therapist and patient other than what was more formally described as a projective process-related primarily to healing unresolved early childhood difficulties. Eye contact was minimal in that the therapist sat behind the couch-prone client, the former remaining mostly quiet and the latter being encouraged to speak freely as to whatever was on her or his mind. Anything spoken, while spontaneous, was very rarely relationally person-to-person communication, but instead centered around specific earlier unfinished developmental variables requiring resolution, a goal primarily diagnostically determined by the analyst. It must also be kept in mind that those early psychoanalytic years existed amid the sexually repressive climate of the Victorian age in which specific expectations

DOI: 10.4324/9781003255772-8

governing the social behaviors of men and women reigned. The therapeutic work done during those times by those pioneering analysts gave a great deal of validity and courage to the mental health profession, particularly with respect to working therapeutically with the unconscious and all of its variations and modifications during an era of highly repressive social and personal realities and expectations.

Some of those more daring individuals, such as Wilhelm Reich, took the practice of psychoanalysis to a different level in introducing the human body into the treatment room, which in addition to other hands-on treatment interventions and experiential theoretical formulation, eventually did not serve him well in the long run. However, his willingness to risk experimentation with novel forms of treatment modalities served as a beacon of courage for many of those who followed in his footsteps. Until that point, however, the basic psychoanalytic process for the most part centered on the structure of the work along with the "analyst" and the "analysand."

As the new "talking cure" gained medical credibility as a method for dealing with the treatment of those manifesting varying degrees of psychological pathology, psychoanalysis became the "treatment du jour" throughout the European continent. Eventually, other schools of psychoanalytic training emerged, many of which offered subtle, yet interesting variations on some of the major themes of classic psychoanalytic theory. Yet, it was the structure of the therapeutic practice itself that remained the primary concern. In outlining the history of psychotherapeutic thinking and practice it is helpful to remind the Gestalt community that the roots of Gestalt therapy were born from these creative mosaics of those earlier analytic speculations.

It was in Perls' work *Ego, Hunger, and Aggression* (1969), that marked his initial break from psychoanalysis in which he made his case for the importance of aggression as "a process mainly dependent on the destructive tendency of which should have its natural biological outlet in the use of the teeth (p. 81). And, it was this bit of theoretical difference that marked his initial break from psychoanalytic thinking concerning an individual's drive in maintaining a healthy balance between itself and the environment in the search for personal gratification. . Such a sentiment was alluded to in a more expanded manner in the Perls, Hefferline, & Goodman text *Gestalt Therapy: Excitement and Growth in the Human Personality* (1951), by again re-stating the idea that methods of aggressive engagements are: ...essential to the growth of the organism/environmental field; given rational objects, they are always "healthy" and in any case they are irreducible without loss of valuable parts of the personality especially self-confidence, feeling, and creativity (p. 340). Fritz wrote his original revisions on psychoanalytic theory in 1947, a position paper that would place him among such leaders of the second generation of practitioners as Carl Jung, Alfred Adler, and other revisionist psychoanalysts. Despite the accumulation of a variety of theoretical variances made to some of psychoanalysis's major underlying theoretical issues, patient/therapist interpersonal dynamics were not among them. In a later article by Kitzler and Lay, Bread from Stones (1984), the authors hint more directly on the importance of relational dynamics between therapist and client in conjunction with creative aggression, a dynamic without which serious impediments can occur in the therapeutic relationship, and that "the problem consequently seems to be a lack of aggressive connection within the patient-therapist field (p. 40). Before the onset of World War II, a psychoanalytic practice continued to set the standard in most psychotherapeutic circles. It was not until after WWII that many analytic practitioners fled Europe for safer ground given the devastation to human life and property resulting from the carnage that included the death of 72,000,000 human beings. After escaping to Denmark, Fritz and Laura Perls settled in South Africa for a few years before emigrating to the United States. And they arrived at a time that would eventually begin to sow the seeds for what we now refer to as Gestalt therapy given the cultural revolution that would affect both the practice of Gestalt therapy as well as the history of the American culture itself.

## The Antithesis

One of the many challenges facing psychotherapists who survived the wounds of the World War's demonic conflagration had to do with the search for techniques and clinical interventions that could in some way partially heal some of the war wounds incurred by many of their clients. Given the presence of the clinical residuals of unprecedented horror, people were looking for ways and means whereby some level of emotional integration could be achieved in order to feel somewhat safe while continuing to exist in a world for which they had little personal history or reference. The issues became more existential than clinical in nature, a transformation that led to the search for a loving and supportive community capable of being integrated into the therapeutic experience.

Many practitioners within the therapeutic community answered this clarion call as the doors for new and more comprehensive treatment modalities flew wide open. Compassionate human contact was a bottom-line objective in the experimentation that developed in the years following the war. While individual therapists experimented with new and different methods of emotional contact with their clients as a way of rendering the therapeutic relationship more "personal" in both form and nature, others began testing a variety of group formats that became quite popular given the aura of community involved. And, it was during these experimental and tenuous years that Gestalt therapy found a home both within the radical players in the major therapeutic schools of that era as well as the cultural mainstream of post-war America.

It was an unprecedented time of psychotherapeutic experimentation, as the ambiguity and the "hit and miss" techniques involved would often lead to both innovative yet at times unfortunate consequences. As an example, the psychiatrist Marty Shepard, while searching for methods and modalities for strengthening client/therapist intimacy authored *The Love Treatment* (1972), a book in which he proposed that sexual contact between therapist and client, in some cases, may be therapeutically beneficial. Primarily trained in psychoanalysis and then studying for a while with Fritz Perls, Shepard later wrote the 1975 book: *Fritz: An Intimate Portrait of Fritz Perls and Gestalt Therapy*. When taken in the time context of the prevalent radical atmosphere of what has since been labeled the Aquarian Age, such books were not necessarily frivolous anomalies, but rather represented some of the vigorous attempts being made in a world experienced by many as being primarily dysfunctional and possibly dangerous.

It was also in those early years of the Aquarian Age that *Gestalt Therapy: Excitement and Growth in the Human Personality* (PHG) hit the bookstores. Published in 1951, it was then, and in many ways continues now to be the theoretical bedrock as to how we think and work as Gestalt therapists. More importantly, the mid-50s through the 60s were the heydays of Paul Goodman, one of three authors of PHG whose later book *Growing Up Absurd* (1960), became a vital resource for those seeking to make major inroads into a variety of social and educational arenas. Goodman was also a peace and anti-war activist who viewed community as an essential ground for human enlightenment, a philosophy, and energy he also vigorously applied in his intimate therapeutic contacts with his clients, a passion also evident in the high spirited social nature he exhibited as an author, poet, and philosopher. As a practitioner his relationships with patients were highly relational, multiple, and varied, often encouraging them to relate to him in a variety of personal roles, most of which were direct and upfront encounters, which for him simulated a form of community healing, not only for the client but for himself as well. Given such intensity, he would occasionally become involved in what today would be classified as "dual relationships" that at times were both unorthodox and possibly unethical. In assessing such, it is important to remember that these were very early experimental forays during difficult and unchartered times, yet eventually served as an early harbinger for those later therapists searching for a sense of intimacy and community within the dyadic nature of the therapeutic experience.

As social and political foment increased during those years, many researchers in the academic psychological communities began to look more intensely into questions concerning, not only the nature and purpose of psychotherapy per se but also what types of therapist-patient interpersonal styles garnered the most success rates.

The beginning research seemed to be fairly unanimous in showing that, for the most part, therapeutic success was not necessarily dependent on the academic abilities or the certifications awarded to the therapist. Instead, it was becoming increasingly clear that it had more to do with the ability of the therapist to engage on a more personal level with the client that seemed to provide the main support in successful outcomes measured by both the client and professional observers (Gendlin & Rychlak, 1970; Herron, 1975). After reviewing the data, and in undertaking an extended review of various psychotherapeutic models and practices, a group of researchers began to re-examine the earlier work of Carl Rogers (1951) who in his book aptly entitled Client-Centered Therapy proclaimed that client success rates were correlated more to what he referred to as the characteristics of "the therapist as a person" than to either the skill of therapist, the problems of the client, or the brand of therapy administered. More specifically, he referred to the "genuineness" of a therapist's presentation in combination with a client's perception of the therapist's implicit respect for his or her worth and dignity, variables that led to the creation of an aura of egalitarian participation and eventually to optimal therapeutic outcome. For Rogers, the creation of such interpersonal variables allowed both the client and the therapist to feel "more real with each other," thus enabling each to experience the feelings that play out in the space between them while establishing a sense of participatory intimate connection. And, for Rogers, the emotional glue holding all of that relational space together was "empathy" – an interpersonal energy he deemed as the importance of therapeutic empathy has seemed to have stood the test of time and continues to influence therapeutic strategies both within and across many psychotherapeutic modalities as well as being more prevalent in the more general social discourse. For instance, in a recent article in the New York Review of Books (9/2020) journalist Fintan O'Toole noted in his review of the Democratic National Convention, that Michelle Obama used the term "empathy" five times in an eighteen-minute presentation!

It did not take long for the research to verify the importance of relational bonding as a major factor in the quest for emotional healing. Qualitative factors along with quantitative data supported prior assumptions on the positive impact that empathy, presence, and genuineness have within the therapeutic relationship. As a result, it has been frequently recommended that therapists, when working with their particular brand of therapy, simultaneously be mindful of the quality of empathy in their clinical relationships not only in terms of the therapeutic process, but as a tool for forging connections with clients that will be able to sustain them in dealing with people in general long after the therapy ends.

One of the major pioneer researchers in this area was Robert Carkhuff, PhD, who along with Bernard Berenson, authored the book, *Beyond Counseling and Therapy* (1968), a tome that did much to shift the practice of psychotherapy from an abstract theoretical procedure to one of a more emotionally operational nature. Often referred to as the "father of the science of human relating," Carkhuff was able to broaden the boundaries of therapy into larger person-to-person parameters while still maintaining the ability to apply quantitative measures to human relationships. Subsequent research continued to reinforce such conclusions in finding little correlation between therapist effectiveness based on one's academic background or formal training in a specific field of therapeutic orientation (Truax & Carkhuff, 1967). In addition, it was found that "lay" therapists, with specific training in empathic communication, did as well as the more seasoned therapists on measures of client satisfaction (Gendlin & Rychlak, 1970; Herron, 1975). A more extensive analysis of similar studies concluded that outcomes deemed to be low in relational empathy, were particularly problematic based on the researchers' conclusion that "two out of three of a practicing therapist's colleagues he can be quite certain, are ineffective or harmful" (Truax & Carkhuff, 1967, p. 34).

Many of those in the early phases of the Gestalt movement also adopted some of these attitudes in a less formal academic sense by encouraging the spirit of empathic connection in their individual practices. They looked to more literary resources, such as Martin Buber's *I and Thou*, Ram Dass's *Be Here Now* (1971), and Barry Stevens' *Don't Push the River* (1970) marked the culmination of both her three-month training with Fritz Perls at Esalen in 1969 as well as her collaboration with Carl Rogers in their co-authored book *Person-to-Person: The Problems of Being* (1967). In both books, Stevens integrates the empathic principles of client-centered therapy with many of the theoretical philosophies and practices of Gestalt therapy in attempts to define what it is that makes us real to others that plays out in the space between therapist and client, especially those that define and support a feeling of participatory intimacy. According to Stevens and Rogers (1967):

When a person comes to a therapist, he has a purpose. When the therapist receives the other person, he has a purpose. But when both get into reality together, without facades, the purpose gets lost, and all that is known is something is happening that happens of itself, and the noticing of this happening, in you, in me (p. 113).

## The Intimacy of Aggression

I decided to devote a special place for the consideration of the idea of "intimate aggression," primarily to point out the therapeutic importance Gestalt therapy has always placed on this vital human energy and its role within the therapeutic process. Historically, it was Fritz Perls, who during his re-evaluation of psychoanalytic theory, considered "dental aggression" as a more primal and important developmental phenomenon in influencing the way in which an infant learned to cope with her or his surroundings. And, it was his book, *Ego, Hunger, and Aggression* (1969) that eventually pulled Fritz away from his psychoanalytical roots, and into the beginnings of Gestalt therapy.

In the 1951 PHG book, Paul Goodman added material to the developmental significance of aggression in human behavior, not only in childhood but also as an important adult energy, one capable of positive self-regulative potential in a patient's capacity to deal with a variety of political and social restrictions and pathologies. In his book Nature Heals (1977) he agrees with Fritz's take on the developmental aspects of aggression, yet takes it a few steps further by differentiating between what he perceives as "natural" aggression from its more "unnatural" manifestations, the latter being determined more by restrictive social control or as a method of gaining approval from others rather than being employed as a natural form of energy Goodman once described as a "sympathetic passion with desire at its heart."

For Goodman, aggression in its more natural formations was an essential human element and therefore therapeutically useful in "the destruction of habits or second nature in the interests of rediscovering the primary experience of birth, infantile anxiety, grief, and mourning for death, simple sexuality" (1977, p. 24), as well as a natural aspect of human behavior intimately related to the well-being of the individual.

When teaching at Black Mountain College during the summer of 1958, and working in connection with other artists and intellectuals, Goodman was described by the artist Robert Motherwell as having the ability to "uncover structures found in the interactions of the body-mind and the external world, and the body-mind is active and aggressive" (p. 36). Goodman resonated with these impressions given his belief that "annihilating, destroying, initiative, and anger are essential to growth in the organism/environmental field" and also that "the destructive appetite is warm and pleasurable" (1977, pp. 156–157).

More importantly, he valued aggressive energy as being a highly relational therapeutic concept, and therefore of potential benefit within the psychotherapeutic encounter. When successfully integrated into the therapy, the role of the therapist begins to shift from a more-or-less invisible authority to a participant, primarily through the dynamic and relational interaction and eventually marked by a strong and aggressive coordinated effort on the behalf of both therapist and patient in successfully integrating whatever it was that seemed interesting and nurturing. Or to hear it from Goodman himself:

> For consider that if the association of the two persons will in fact be deeply profitable to them, then the destruction of the incompatible existing forms they have come with is a motion toward their more intrinsic selves – that will be actualized in the coming new figure; in this release of the more intrinsic, bound energy is liberated and this will transfer to the liberating agent as love. The process of mutual destruction is probably the chief proving ground of profound compatibility (1977, pp. 157–158).

Viewing aggression, not only as an important therapeutic variable, but as a dynamic potential in intimate relational bonding between a therapist and a client, remains one of Gestalt therapy's important concepts, one that, unfortunately, has received little clinical attention, even by Gestalt therapists themselves, or when approached, is often summarily dismissed or ignored.

In the larger therapeutic community, aggression is often viewed as almost sinful, a conception derived from a lack of differentiation of Gestalt's take on aggression from more dysfunctional emotions such as "rage," "hostility," or "fury," all of which are deemed to represent psychological flaws in need of "management" or somehow totally eliminated. Even in small doses, as when presented as "microaggressions," it is most often accompanied by negative connotations. In the various Gestalt communities, I often find a sense of discomfort in those attempting to atone for some of the "aggressive" therapeutic styles of some of our founders, including a touch of embarrassment to Fritz's interventions in the classic Gloria film.

It is proposed here that a more comprehensive understanding of Gestalt therapy's underlying theoretical tenets would clearly suggest that aggression, being more of a "de-structuring" energy and therefore a creative one, as opposed to a "destructive" one, that when applied therapeutically, allows several relational possibilities that can add to therapeutic richness commensurate within the quest for organismic, self-regulative growth, and creative adjustment.

### The Integration

What these various academic and therapeutic communities were searching for during those years of experimentation was, among other things, the development of a more comprehensive understanding of what it was, both clinically and personally, on the part of both the therapist and the client that could make therapy work more effectively. In general, therapists of every ilk and orientation seemed to be seeking clinical evidence for whatever it was that supported the more effective therapeutic outcome. One particular emphasis under exploration had to do with the measurement, not only clinical data, but the development of research tools capable of assessing the more qualitative aspects relative to various interpersonal dynamics going on between the therapist and the client, that may not only support the clinical work but in addition, would be able to somehow strengthen the cohesiveness and intimacy of client/therapist contact functioning.

Clients' subjective reports of their experiences, it indeed seemed to be looking for the same thing. Reactions such as: "I really felt she cared about me, not just as a patient, but as a person," or "His interest in how I was doing was just the motivation I needed to move on," were common responses to treatment inquiries, again independent of the particular therapeutic approach involved.

As this research expanded and coefficients of correlation strengthened, therapists of all theoretical persuasions began looking, not only at the data, but at each other in their attempts to find common denominators as to what personal qualities and attitudes seemed effective enough to strengthen their skills as therapeutic practitioners. Up until this point, therapeutic approaches were known more for their differences rather than their similarities. In Gestalt terminology, what emerged was a "foreground/background" shift in which the therapeutic techniques employed (usually foreground) receded to background while client/therapist intimacy (usually backround), became a more leading and dominant force. Given this newly found conviviality, therapists began to feel more comfortable in sharing ideas and interventions with colleagues of different therapeutic schools, resulting in a lot of professional crossbreeding, a process that enriched therapeutic effectiveness for a wide range of theoretical orientations. Be they behavioral, humanistic, analytic, or holistic in spirit they all seemed to morph into a professional agreement that as noted in the song popularized by the 1920s bandleader Jimmie Lunceford:: "It Ain't What You Do, It's the Way That You Do It!"

In addition, it was discovered by others that the eventual strength of relational contact seems to form during the initial meetings between a client and a therapist. Most often, this is a somewhat "formal" engagement given the usually assumed vertical structure one would anticipate in an introduction in which the "client" (the one in need of help) and the "therapist" (the one assumed to have the answers) sit face-to-face for the first time. Much productive groundwork can be established during this phase of initial contact that could set the therapeutic stage in forming a more horizontal, emotional platform of mutual support for more intimate professional and personal self-revelation as well as other co-creative relational possibilities.

We also need to be mindful of the fact that, in many respects, psychotherapy is a business; one requiring bureaucratic details such as licensing, financial contracts, and governmental and/or professional matters concerning confidentiality and other legal mandates proscribed by civil law, professional standards or both. Getting such matters resolved in the early therapeutic phases can open the door for higher levels of emotional intimacy, especially for the client whose information about the therapist typically is limited to educational level, license number, and professional title. While self-disclosure requires cautious therapeutic assessment, the therapist can begin by asking clients if there is anything they would like to know about him or her in a very open-ended and sincere fashion. Three areas I usually confront upfront are: What shall I call you? – such an inquiry is relevant to both the therapist and the client and one that can influence a transformation from top-down-power relationships to ones encouraging greater egalitarian options for both parties. Even when clients prefer the more formal form of address, equality of contact is best served under more casual and personal interactions. The title "doctor" for instance, almost assumes a level of hierarchy that may have a negative impact on subsequent client spontaneity and lead to more questioning as opposed to the freewheeling dialogue given an initial assumption of unexplored expertise projected by the client onto the therapist. Of course, Gestalt therapists have the advantage here in terms of using a wider range of experimental opportunities in experiments designed to "even the odds" in this type of communication pattern. The importance of this theme was driven home to me once by one of my trainers who once advised that: "If they call you doctor after the third session – refer them!"

What is my diagnosis? More than most therapeutic inquiry, this area of responsibility poses many questions regarding who has the answers and who has the problems, and, more importantly, how serious are the problems, and what can be done about them? This is particularly problematic for Gestalt practitioners given that Gestalt therapy typology is one of process, not of a person. *Or as Joel Latner* (1986) reminded us that when making a diagnosis, we believe that we put our finger on the problem when in reality what we have done is to "put our fingering on the fingering," (p. 175). Talking over all of these requirements with the client can be beneficial to both parties – for the therapist in order to be able to express her or his clinical concerns and for the client to be encouraged to include some honest, subjective, and helpful insight and awareness in a collaborative relationship. Often, I will give the diagnostic manual to a client for a week or two before asking for his or her impression. Most often, I find that there is satisfaction expressed about being able to find a clinical description of a particular diagnosis that a client may discover, and usually with a sense of some satisfaction expressed over not being the only person with that particular problem! The resultant confluence of camaraderie and client autonomy that results can be a major contribution to the overall therapeutic effort.

### Therapist – Client Self-disclosure

How much personal information is shared between therapist and client will vary given the particular dyadic nature of the encounter. Overall, such self-revelation can be best achieved if done spontaneously and genuinely rather than as an intentional clinical\or proscribed intervention style. The interpersonal Gestalt that forms will be unique to any particular situation in that it combines two independent personality styles that when morphing into a larger whole qualitatively transcends the sum of each of the two entities involved. In addition, the richness of the dyadic therapist/client Gestalt created, independent of any individual differences, can be further strengthened within a therapeutic atmosphere of mutual respect, empathic concern, and egalitarianism.

Historically, Gestalt therapy embodies many of these qualities in both in its theory and in its practice. For instance, Gestalt holds to the notion of organismic self-regulation – the belief in the individual's innate capacity to deal with life's problems in a natural and organic manner, a process best achieved when combined with adequate environmental support. Thus, rather than seeking "cure," in the more traditional clinical sense, the Gestalt therapist restores what is already there in nature in some form or another. Even when dealing more directly with clinical "symptoms," it is important to avoid labels and diagnostic titles such as "neurotic," or "personality disorder," or other clinical determinations that may take away from the psychological strength and mutuality of the client/therapist relationship. As such, it is important to remember that in Gestalt's terminology, symptoms are viewed as "creative adjustments" – those maneuvers that insure the integrity of the individual in using whatever creative options are available in order to maintain as much personal integrity as possible when dealing with problems. The artistic flair and the creativity used are best shared by a mutual type of admiration by both therapist and client in appreciating the ingenious gestures employed under such difficult circumstances.

## Toward an Expanding Relational Field

As we look back at the history of psychotherapy, as both art and science, and how it has evolved over the last century or so, it seems that the general field has been marked by many modifications, elaborations, integrations, as well as achieving a good dose of social relevance. On one level, it seems to have shifted from a more autocratic to a more client-centered modality with many of the more strictly "doctor/patient" models on the wane as well as a move toward increased community acceptance and, at times, more direct social involvement. Given our dynamically radical approach that encourages us to take into account the issues presented by those seeking our help, we also take into account, issues of the greater field, that include, but are not limited to, sociopolitical matters that present challenges to many in today's world.

These particular "gifts of Gestalt" have been noted by others in the psychological community. Social critic Roszac (1992) for instance, once described Gestalt as one of the few therapeutic approaches that is ecological in both spirit and application and therefore adequately equipped to deal, not only with the individual as "a patient" but also in a manner that allows for similar therapeutic strength in dealing with concerns of the environment and dysfunctional connections between people attempting to cope with adverse political, social, and community problems. A major contributing strength in that regard can be found in Gestalt therapy's definition of "self-formation" in which self-functioning is conceived as an ongoing, evolving dynamic partially formed "of" the surrounding field, rather than being more passively conceived as being merely "at" the boundary between the person and the world. For to be "at" that boundary suggests an identity formation separate and apart from any direct environmental influence. In contrast, to be "of" that boundary suggests that self-functioning is partially formed by the environment and therefore an integral part of self-formation. This then would suggest that matters of the social or political field are as much a part of who we are at any given point in time and therefore grist for therapeutic intervention. Incorporating such material into the therapy both broadens and widens Gestalt's scope of influence, thereby adding to the overall therapeutic impact

There are some therapists within the Gestalt community who feel that politics and social issues do not belong in the therapy per se, and that is their prerogative. However, to include these issues into the therapy is consistent with Gestalt's theoretical definition of self-function. To me it represents the "elephant in the treatment room," – it's always there in front of us. The issue is to ignore it or to work with it when appropriate.

Given the difficult conditions facing much of the world today, it may be time to re-institute the therapeutic gifts provided to us as Gestalt therapists in terms of re-appreciating the theoretical possibilities of applying the rudiments of our relational contact skills, not just in matters of clinical application, but also to various environmental concerns and social dysfunction. And more importantly, to attempt to integrate such material into our own personal sense of well-being and be willing to share such with the people we see in our practices. Gestalt's potential for social inclusivity remains permanently imbedded in the Perls, Hefferline, and Goodman text, particularly given the radical sociopolitical contributions of Paul Goodman. In some ways, it remains unfortunate that such ideas and clinical insights have been overlooked even by members of our own community. Given the benefits provided to us by our rich therapeutic heritage, we have the clinical power to both maintain and expand our relational connections with those we see, as well as the unique capacity to extend such into matters of the community by relating more empathically, fervently, and relationally to the ecological, political, and social issues that surround us and under which we all, both therapists and patients, strive to live and prosper.

In looking back at the ingenuity of Sigmund Freud, Paul Goodman (1977) wondered as to how Freud himself would have predicted the future of psychotherapy: It would become increasingly evident to him, would it not, that "cure" could not depend merely on talk, revival of affect and reconsideration, but "must pass over into practical behavior, and therefore must involve a change of the social rules so as to make such behavior possible" (p. 74).

## References

Buber, M. (1958). *I and Thou*. New York: Scribner & Sons. (Original translation, 1939).

Carkhuff, R. R. & Berenson, B. G. (1968). *Beyond Counseling and Psychotherapy*. New York: Holt, Rinehart & Winston.

Dass, R. (1971). *Be Here Now*, New Mexico: The Lama Foundation.

Duberman, M. (1972). *Black Mountain: An Exploration of Community*. New York: E.P. Dalton Press.

Gendlin, E. T. & Rychlak, T. F. (1970). Psychotherapeutic Processes. *Annual Review of Psychology, 21*, 155–190.

Goodman, P. (1960). *Growing Up Absurd*. New York: Random House.

Goodman, P. (1977). *Nature Heals*. New York: Free Life Editions.

Herron, W. G. (1975). Further Thoughts on Psychotherapeutic De-professionalization. *Journal of Humanistic Psychology, 15*, 65–73.

Johnson, J. (2012). *The Voice is All*. New York: Penguin Group.

Kitzler, R. & Lay, J. (1984). Bread From Stones. In *Psychotherapy and the Abrasive Patient*. (E. M. Stone, Ed.) (pp. 39–44). New York: The Haworth Press, Inc.

Latner, J. (1986). *The Gestalt Therapy Book*. Gouldsboro, ME: Gestalt Journal Press.

Motherwell, R. (1992). *The Collected Writings of Robert Motherwell*. (S. Terenzca, ed.). New York: Oxford University Press.

O' Toole, F. (9/21/2020). Night and Day. In *The New York Review of Books*. pp. 37–38. New York, NY.

Perls, F. P., Hefferline, R. & Goodman, P. (1951). *Gestalt Therapy: Excitement and Growth in the Human Personality*. New York: The Julian Press.

Perls, F. (1969). *Ego, Hunger, and Aggression*. New York: Random House.

Rogers, C. (1951). *Client Centered Therapy*. Boston: Houghton Mifflin.

Rogers, C. (1962). The Interpersonal Relationship: The Core of Guidance. *Harvard Educational Review, 32*, 416–429.

Roszac, T. (1992). *The Voice of the Earth*. New York: Simon & Schuster.

Shepard, M. (1972). *The Love Treatment: Intimacy Between Patients and Psychotherapists*. New York: Wyden Books.

Shepard, M. (1975). *Fritz: An Intimate Portrait of Fritz Perls and Gestalt Therapy*. Toronto: Clarke, Irwin & Company.

Stevens, B. & Rogers, C. (1967). *Person to Person: The Problems of Being Human*. Moab, Utah: Real People Press.

Stevens, B. (1970). *Don't Push the River*. Moab, Utah: Real People Press.

Truax, C. B. & Carkhuff, R. R. (1967). Towards Effective Psychotherapy. *Annual Review of Psychology, 21*, 170–171.

Truax, C. B. & Mitchell, K. M. (1970). Research on Certain Therapist Interpersonal Skills in Relation to Process and Outcome. In *Handbook of Psychotherapy and Behavioral Change*. New York: John Wiley.

# Chapter 7

# Living in a World of Meaning

*Friedemann Schulz*[1]

A few years ago I participated in a study group that set off a transformational process that is still reverberating for me to this day. At the time, our group[2] was studying various philosophical threads and we had begun to consider phenomenology, specifically some of its aspects written about by Maurice Merleau-Ponty and his former teacher Martin Heidegger. The particular topic that was so startling for me was their claim that the scientific accomplishment of the western world is only one specific way of knowing (Macann, 1993, pp. 72–73, 161–162). They considered this kind of knowledge merely as one aspect within a wider realm of a phenomenal reality, namely that of human experiencing (Carr, 2012, pp. 489–491, 497–501; Safranski, 1998, pp. 96–97, 150–151).[3]

I grew up as part of the first post-WWII generation in a small village in a rural region of what was at the time known as West Germany. Culturally speaking, what was considered real in our community was informed by the norms of the Christian beliefs that were intertwined within the traditions of the village that I grew up in, as well as the authority of the scientific knowledge that we were exposed to through our educational systems. As it was for many of my generations, my religious faith began to waver during my teenage years, but my confidence in the physical sciences only grew over time. In fact, it became indistinguishable from what I, and perhaps many of my contemporaries, considered to be reality. In other words, the physical sciences seemed to be windows to the reality that not only included but actually went beyond what human beings are able to experience. In part, this is because the scientific findings disclose aspects of nature that are hidden from human view, which can make the ordinary human experience feel minute and insufficient. But Heidegger and his fellow philosophers challenged this worldview in a profound way. What made me prick up my ears was that he, and nearly all phenomenologists since then, made the point that it is human experiencing that *is* the reality that we live in as human beings (Hersch, 2003, pp. 49–54; Spinelli, 2005, pp. 7–11).

The philosopher Charles Taylor wrote: "Human beings are constituted in conversation" (as cited in Gergen, 2009, p. 45), which refers to the notion

DOI: 10.4324/9781003255772-9

that human beings are not isolated, free-floating objects, but that human existence is fundamentally an interpersonal process (DeYoung, 2015, p. 170). As persons, we exist within our many varied and changing relationships and their material and social contexts. All of us have unique and individual experiences, but human experience in itself is a product of relationality. It is our embeddedness within our relational networks, that is, our manifold cultural contexts, that makes the world intelligible and accessible to us (Buber, 1970, p. 62; Gergen, 2009, pp. 32, 39; Stolorow et al., 2002, pp. 9, 34, 84–85). These contexts include concepts and narratives such as the atom, the unconscious, God, one's identity, or what it takes to be a good person, which we live by and live within (Wheeler, 2000, pp. 318–371).

These stories, at least for a time, become our "intelligible realities" (McNamee & Gergen, 1999, pp. 10–27) – but they can and do change. Over time, they acquire various meanings and thus create new veracities. As therapists, we too have our own intelligible realities – stories that we lean on to give us guidance in our work. Important aspects of these narratives include the psychotherapeutic theories that provide us with a sense of direction for our therapeutic task. For instance, in what is at times referred to as "classical Gestalt therapy" (Wegscheider, 2020, pp. 113–131, 139), an important focus was the differentiation between the individual and his or her environment (Lee, 2004, p. 6; Perls, 1973, pp. 109–114). This conception shaped Gestalt therapists' views on healthy maturation, which often led to an emphasis on helping a client move from environmental support to self-support. From an individualistic, one-person-psychology perspective, it made sense to focus on the autonomy and independence of an individual (Robine, 2011, pp. 29–64; Staemmler, 2017, p. 13), but from a more relational point of view, this focus does not fit the contemporary understanding of phenomenal field theory or dialogic theory.[4] From a relational Gestalt therapy perspective, self-support derives from environmental support, and self-sufficiency is no longer considered the end goal for a mature individual. The focus in present-day Gestalt therapy theory has turned to the interdependence of human existence and toward how people co-construct each other's experience (Jacobs, 2016, p. 253; Lee, 2004, p. 6).[5]

Over time, our stories and theories evolve and the notion that relationships are as real as the physical objects in our world has led to a greater emphasis on the relational aspects of Gestalt therapy. For example, the relational perspective maintains that a person's identity and in particular their sense of self is formed within their various relationships (McNamee & Gergen 1999; Robine, 2016; Staemmler, 2017; Wegscheider, 2020). This means that relationships are processes within which our experiential worlds are created and transformed, which is, of course, the crux of the psychotherapeutic endeavor.

As a result of this change in perspective, Martin Buber's dialogic theory took on a more central position in the practice of Gestalt therapy within the last 40 years (Hycner & Jacobs, 1995; Jacobs & Hycner, 2009; Staemmler, 2017; Wegscheider, 2020; Yontef, 1993). Buber's method has been discussed in detail in numerous sources (Buber, 1999; Friedman, 1955; Jacobs, 1989; Jacobs & Hycner, 2009; Yontef & Jacobs, 2007). Here, I will concentrate on Buber's concept of "the between," and on its importance as one of the transformational aspects of the psychotherapeutic process.

## The Between and the Process of Transformation

"the phonetic event fraught with meaning, whose meaning is to be found neither in one of the two partners nor in both together, but only in their dialogue itself, in this 'between' which they live together"

(Buber, 1999, p. 75)

People cannot be known in the same way as things or objects, but in order to understand another person, we need to engage with each other. When we participate in an engaged dialogic relationship, we take part in a reality of something that is part of oneself and part of what is not oneself. As an aspect of dialogue, "the between," does not imply a physical location, but refers to the notion that what emerges through dialogue is not owned by either of the dialogic partners. Martin Buber wrote, "All reality is an activity that I am part of without being able to make it my own" (as cited in Staemmler, 2017, p. 112 – all translations my own). Furthermore, the body's tactile experience often occurs ahead of the thinking process and cannot be fully captured through language.[6] This means, that one starts to create meaning before being able to articulate it, underscoring that important aspects of a dialogic engagement cannot easily be heard, seen, or thought. Our bodies have their own ways of communicating with their human and non-human environments, a process that sociologists call affectivity (Clough, 2008; Cromby, 2005, pp. 117–123; Cromby & Willis, 2016). Affectivity refers to human processes that are mostly unarticulated and that operate on the level of automatic, pre-conscious bodily reactions, responses, and resonances.[7] But this yet-unformulated experience impacts and influences us (Stern, 2010, p. iiix), which implies that we develop an "implicit relational knowing" (DeYoung, 2015, p. 67), prior to any cognitive assignment of meaning (Robine, 2016, pp. 216–217).[8] The body is thus an ambiguous bridge between self and the other, and there is no absolute distinction between a person and his or her natural and social environment (Gregg & Seigworth, 2010; De Jaegher, 2015).

Emotions can be seen as a hybrid process between the yet-unformulated and the conscious experience, which is one of the reasons why they play such an important role in Gestalt therapy. Emotions are experienced before they are put into words, which makes them an important channel to connect the unformulated to the articulable. A person's emotional experience often reveals the meaning that an event or situation holds for them and accordingly, the exploration of that experience is a crucial aspect of the psychotherapeutic meaning-making process (Orange, 2010, p. 2).

> *My client teared up in the middle of the session. We had been discussing the anxiety he felt about an upcoming stressful work situation. "I don't even know why I am crying," he said, and for a while we just sat together. Eventually I told him that his situation seemed like a "double exposure" to me, in that his historical theme of being left alone by his family had become connected to the current stressor of imagining a lack of support during his meeting with his project partners. He agreed that his reactions to his current situation felt emotionally close to his feelings as a boy, which he expressed as, "Nobody wanted to be with me," and, "I was convinced that I was just not good enough for them!"[9]*

This sense of sadness and shame had already been in the background for him during much of the current, but also some of our prior sessions. The bodily reaction of crying became a catalyst for his emerging awareness of feeling bereft and sad. The articulation of these specific feelings occurred when I helped him create a connection between his boyhood experiences and the strength of his current emotions.[10] To reiterate, "the between" is part of our unformulated experience as well as what we are aware of as conscious meaning. It is an indeterminate mid- or meeting-point between us and our social contacts and includes the therapist-client relationship.[11]

"The between" does not operate within us, but involves all partners of the dialogue. For example, before any words are spoken, our clients experience our tone of voice, gestures, efforts to understand them, confusions, reactions, emerging insights, as well as our interest and sense of care – in short our presence, if they are aware of it or not. This means that they are not only confronted and influenced by our ideas and ways of conceptualizing – when, for instance, we are establishing links between their current experience and their relational histories – they also see us reacting to our understanding of their situations and they can sense our intellectual, emotional, and embodied participation in their struggles.

> *Many years ago, as a member of a Gestalt therapy training group, I talked about a situation in my family of origin. I had come home after a long absence and as I sat down with my parents and a couple of my siblings, the TV was left on. As was usual in our family, the whole group sat in a semi-circle and everyone's faces were turned towards the TV. I finally got up and switched off the TV, saying, "I am here now!" There was confusion in my father's eyes, and later an older brother criticized me because he felt that I had embarrassed my parents. As I was telling this story in my training group, I was aware of the hurt and*

*disappointment I had felt then, but the outrage I saw in the eyes of some of my peers increased those feelings, changing my sense of what the experience meant to me.*

This unarticulated aspect of the psychotherapeutic dialogue cannot be addressed directly at first, but is attended to through the attitude that the therapist brings to the therapeutic situation. For instance, we cannot will ourselves to like a particular client, but we can adopt the practice of interest, openness, and care. I have found that these practices always lead to a greater sense of appreciation and often even affection for my dialogic partners. Donna Orange once wrote "...understanding is application" (2011, p. 26), and, I would like to add, the attitude with which we therapists approach our clients is application as well.

On the other hand, sorting through the various meanings being communicated between therapist and client during their conversations comprises one of the more conscious aspect of "the between." In therapy, the dialogic process illuminates to both partners how events and oneself can be experienced differently by the other, through the nuanced, articulations of each participant. New understandings between client and therapist will develop and these novel constructions are useful until other aspects emerge, and consequently the prior grasp of what was understood changes again. Over time, the meaning worlds of both partners in the dialogue are subtly transformed (McNamee & Gergen 1999, p. 14).[12]

The dialogic back-and-forth between client and therapist does not necessarily create harmony or agreement. In fact, the differences that emerge in an engaged dialogue are an important challenge to both the client's and the therapist's habitual ways of making sense of their perceptions. All of us have unique and thus different meaning worlds, and the same words spoken by different people never mean exactly the same thing. Understandings always stay preliminary, and their efficacy does not depend on their sustained reliability, but instead on their ability to support the next step in the dialogic process. For instance, the ruptures that inevitably occur during a prolonged dialogic effort need to be attended to and understood in order for all parties to feel supported enough to "stick with" the therapeutic process. According to Staemmler, misunderstandings are part of communication and these non-optimal interactions have their own worth. Furthermore, conflicting meanings are an inevitable outcome of social engagement, because they arise from the unique personal and cultural histories of the dialogic partners. What is important is how we deal with these communitive rifts (Staemmler, 2017, p. 39).

*In my early years as a therapist, I worked in a psychiatric office and led drop-in groups for psychiatric patients. On one occasion, a new group member managed to antagonize and offend almost everyone else in the group. This continued for the next couple of weeks and I realized that I needed to find an alternative for her. I eventually told her that I needed to take her out of the group, but offered her individual sessions as an alternative. She took my offer and the following week I braced myself for our first meeting. We did have our arguments and spats along the way, but what ensued was a very different experience from what I had foreseen. In this one-on-one setting she was able to take in some of what I had to say and I too was able to make more of an effort to understand her ways of thinking, feeling, struggling and reacting. After a few sessions we started to feel more relaxed with each other and I think that both of us were surprised that over time we gained a sense of trust, even closeness. Because of the limits of her insurance coverage we were only able to continue with her therapy for six months, but when we said good bye, both of us had tears in our eyes.*

The philosopher Levinas warned that there always will be a limit to our ability to understand another person. In fact, he feared that our wish to understand the other, in particular when employed in the service of creating harmony, could contribute to a kind of same-making. Levinas considered this a violation of the other, which he called "totalizing." Totalizing limits our understanding of our dialogic partners to what is already known to us (Staemmler, 2017, pp. 112–117),[13] especially since we are prone to interpret our current experience on the basis of our prior understandings. Specifically, we might miss feelings, ways of thinking, attitudes, perspectives, leanings, and sensory experiences that vary from our own. Moreover, it can be very painful and thus difficult to be open to a client's seeming self-sabotage or self-rejection. However, it helps to keep in mind that these tendencies were originally formed in the service of giving the client a chance to stay in connection with an important person in their lives, and that a continual, authentic relationship with the therapist can serve as an emotional corrective experience.

*A young woman suffered from very low self-esteem and her narratives in therapy were filled with her experiences of shame and self-loathing. At times, I tried to draw attention to aspects of what she described about her life that seemed positive or successful to me. In retrospect, I would say that I did so in the hope of making her feel better, and myself as well. But she did not show much of a reaction to my comments. During one session I pointed this out and said that it seemed to me as if what I said to her actually increased the distance between us. She agreed with my sense of greater distance, but the reason that she did not react well to my comments was not because she disagreed with my perspective. She actually appreciated that I could see some of her successful social negotiations. "But," she said, "I am afraid that you think that I am getting well." I was perplexed and asked, "What's wrong with getting well?!" She replied, "If you start thinking that I am OK, I am afraid you'll tell me that we need to end therapy soon!" I had no idea that this had been on her mind, but was glad that she told me about her trepidations. In consequence, our conversation changed directions and we began to discuss what it was like for her to be in therapy, and that she felt "too needy" at times, but also resentful for being "too dependent." This opened a whole new territory in our talks. It was our muddling through these issues that eventually helped us to become more at ease with each other and to deepen our relationship.*

As the dialogue continues in therapy, each person is confronted with alternative or newly emerging meanings. In that process, not only one's perception of events, but also the relationship within which the dialogue takes place, changes over time: "it is out of relationships that we develop meaning, rationalities, the sense of value, moral interest, motivation, and so on" (McNamee & Gergen 1999, p. 10). What changes in this process are the meanings that each of the partners ascribes to events, memories, or their current focus of exploration (Candiotto, 2019). Whether experienced as a sudden breakthrough or as a gradual shift of meaning, these changes are transformational (Staemmler, 2009, pp. 340–341), because new understandings, big or small, alter one's sense of the world and of oneself within it.[14] Moreover, a newly emerging meaning cannot completely revert back to a previous one and will in turn also influence interactions in relationships outside of the therapeutic context.[15]

One will, of course, have similar experiences as before, such as feeling anxious or feeling shame. But clients that have gone through a sustained dialogic process will have more nuanced options in how to relate to these painful experiences. For instance, a new understanding of their emotions does not prevent a client from experiencing shame at times, and that experience will feel as "rotten" as it ever did before. At the same time, this experience of shame is now felt within an altered mindset and thus a new context is created for its emergence. The client might now be able to identify it as something that has a history and may even be able to trace it in terms of its triggers and background. They might not feel quite as alone with this feeling anymore, due to their experiences in which others were accepting of their struggle. Therefore, they may be able to identify the shame-producing experience as something that is painful but transitory, or as a painful memory that no longer defines who they are – at least not completely.

*A client of mine, a therapist herself, who regularly experienced shame attacks, came to our session one day with this story: a couple of days earlier she had felt terrible over a session she had had with a client of hers. "I could hardly drive, I was so upset," she said, referring to her shame reaction. But a short while later, as she was walking from her car to her apartment, she thought more clearly about what had happened between her and her client. As she went over it in her mind, she was able to parse out some of the things she had felt had gone wrong, and she realized that those moments had only been a minor aspect of the session, which had otherwise gone quite well. This reflection helped her regain a sense of calm, and, as she said, "I was even able to sleep." I responded, "The way you dealt with this experience seems very similar to talks you and I have had in our sessions." "Yes," she said, "But this time I didn't have to push it back until I came to see you!" We both felt a sense of celebration.*

To summarize, the change brought about by a dialogic engagement is transformational because a new understanding leads to new ways of experiencing ourselves and the world around us. Eventually, we integrate these new meanings and they become part of the fabric of who we are – they become our new intelligible realities. What this means is that the psychotherapeutic dialogue is not just a way of increasing the client's intellectual awareness, but that dialogue in the Buberian sense (Friedman, 1991, pp. vii–xi) is also a method of altering one's way of being in a relationship with oneself and with others: "In the same way that personal identity is realized within relationships, so can forms of relatedness themselves be constructed" (McNamee & Gergen, 1999, p. 21).

To conclude, I will organize this transformative process into three steps:

### The Loss of Original Meaning[16]

Being exposed to alternative interpretations of one's experiences through the dialogic process transforms habitual meaning that originated within other, prior contexts, such as one's family of origin. Growing up within our specific relational situations, family, school, neighborhood, etc., we learned to function in a certain way. In other words, our thinking, sensing, feeling, and behaving are products of these cultural field conditions. For instance, we learned a language and became able to communicate with words. But along the way, we also acquired innumerous cultural understandings about what is acceptable or useful within various settings: how to behave, how to think of oneself and one's circumstance, and so forth. These cultural learnings help us function within countless interpersonal situations and they are filled with stories that make up our experiential worlds. For example, in order to adapt to growing up in a neglectful household, one might have constructed a meaning of that experience as: "I am not as important a person as most other people." This may have created a perspective in which other people's needs became habitually more figural than one's own. Within a psychotherapeutic context, this notion then is challenged, simply by the attention of the therapist to the client's experience in their person-to-person interactions – first implicitly, but eventually also through the articulated dialogue.

### Through Dialogue, a Subtle Shift Occurs in How Language Is Used and What Is Meant by It

Continuing with our example, the client first experiences his therapist's attentiveness as different from what he is accustomed to on a level that is yet unformulated. The therapist's interest might make him feel uncomfortable, even feel intruded upon, and he might say, "I feel as if I am under a microscope, when you are *so* interested in every detail of my life." His therapist will likely want to explore this further and together they might eventually be able to shed some light on his reactions. This could in turn lead them to create linkages to the historical milieu in which he grew up. For instance, they might find that his enduring relational theme of not feeling as important as others leads him to habitually reject interest that is focused on him.[17] A situation in which he shields himself from the shameful desire of wanting to be seen by others, while at the same time this deprives him of what he has yearned for all his life. As the dialogue continues and the client grows more resilient and more responsive to the therapist's interest and her questions, he might eventually feel less threatened and his interpretation of the therapeutic situation might shift from being experienced as "making much ado about nothing," to instead feeling exciting and stimulating, even though at times it might also be scary and challenging. At this point, the old, habitual ways of making meaning and the new experiences emerging within the therapeutic environment might both be present, which could lead to the client feeling confused and even more vulnerable than at the start of the process. He might also feel that the newly articulated story only takes place in the therapeutic relationship and is not related to his interactions with the rest of his social world.

### The Word-meaning Changes for Future Use[18]

But eventually, what is experienced and talked about in therapy becomes *the* story, a new way of experiencing oneself in the world. The old story-lines still exist as a way of relating to how "I used to experience myself in this or that situation." Furthermore, at times we fall back into anxious or depressed moods, shame pockets, or behaviors that seem to come from a different era. It might be disappointing to learn that "these old worn-out clothes are still in my closet," but they are no longer perceived as the whole story. For better or worse, once we experience and eventually integrate something new, we cannot go back to how we previously saw the world, and ourselves in it.[19] We, and the world we inhabit, have changed along the way. In fact, one of the main premises of psychotherapy is that through the dialogic process, the partners can influence the direction that this transformation will take.

## Notes

1 A big thank you to my daughter Adrina Schulz for her fantastic editing work and to Peter Cole, the editor of this volume, for starting the book-project in the first place and for his encouraging support throughout.

2 The study group consisted of the faculty members of the Pacific Gestalt Institute.

3 Merleau-Ponty: "The physicist's atom will always appear more real than the historical and qualitative face of the world, the physico-chemical processes more real than the organic forms, the psychological atoms of empiricism more real than perceived phenomena, the intellectual atoms represented by the 'significations' of the Vienna Circle more real than consciousness, as long as the attempt is made to build up the shape of the world (life, perceptions, mind) instead of recognizing, as the source which stares us in the face and as the ultimate court of appeal in our knowledge of these things, our *experience* of them." (As cited in Cerbone, 2012, p. 19. Italics in the original).

4 A contextual and relational foundation was already articulated in the earlier writings of Perls et al., (1951), but the dialogic theory, in particular, was only later explicated further (Hycner, 1991; Hycner & Jacobs, 1995; Yontef, 1993).

5 "Individuation is only the indispensable personal stamp of all realization of human existence. The self as such is not ultimately the essential, but the meaning of human existence given in creation again and again fulfills itself as self. The help that men give each other in becoming a self leads the life between men to its height" (Buber, 1999, p. 85).

6 As the philosopher Levinas pointed out, "knowledge is always late" (Tallon, 2004, p. 51).

7 In the gestalt therapy literature this is at times referred to as the "Id of the situation" (Botelho Alvim, 2015, pp. 317–337; Wollants, 2012, pp. 51–52).

8 It is important to note that Buber's conception of dialogue does not just imply a verbal exchange, and that his concept of "the between" includes this liminal experience (Friedman, 1955, p. 101).

9 To protect the identities of the actual individuals I changed some of the details in these vignettes, unless they allowed me to tell the story as it appears.

10 "In psychotherapy, the symbol is most powerful when its meaningfulness arises out of experiences which exist first for their own sake and *then* project themselves into a natural and evident meaningfulness which helps tie experiences together" (Polster & Polster, 1973, pp. 16/17, italics in the original).

11 Buber: "The between is not an auxiliary construction, but a real place and carrier of interpersonal happenings; it has not received particular attention, because in comparison to the individual soul and the environment it does not display a simple continuity, but reconstructs itself anew according to the particular interhuman meeting." (Wegscheider, 2020, pp. 79–80).

12 "Buber refers to 'genuine and unreserved communication as a characteristic of dialogic presence. Fully present people share meaning with each other. For the therapist it means sharing meaning with the patient. Full meaning includes despair, love, spirituality, anger, joy, humor, sensuality. In the dialogic relationship the therapist is present as a person, and does not keep himself or herself in reserve as in the analytic stance nor function primarily as a technician" (Yontef, 1993, p. 35).

13 In 2009 Frank Staemmler wrote a book with the title "Das Geheimnis des Anderen" (The mystery of the other) in order to emphasize Levina's point (Staemmler, Personal communication, 2012). The title of the same book in English is "Empathy in Psychotherapy."

14 Of course, there will never be a final meaning of a memory or a situation, just as there will never be a final identity of oneself (McNamee & Gergen, 1999, p. 26).

15 Lee writes: "the more flexible a person's ability in relational contexts is, the greater the ability to find satisfying solutions to novel situations" (2004, pp. 16–17).

16 I took this structure from McNamee & Gergen, but I expanded upon it (McNamee & Gergen, 1999, pp. 25–26).

17 "I have built my understanding of repetitive modes of engagement that occur between therapist and client on an aspect of personality function that I refer to as 'enduring relational themes'" (Jacobs, 2017, p. 9).

18 Gergen writes, "the meaning of most words is polysemous, carrying the semantic traces of many contexts of usage" (Gergen, 2009, p. 43, footnote).

19 "They have a new awareness of self as a thinking/feeling/choosing person, and a new felt sense of meaningful personal narrative" (DeYoung, 2015, p. 39).

## References

Botelho Alvim, M. (2015). The Id of the situation as common ground of experience. In J. M. Robine (Ed.), *Self: A polyphony of contemporary Gestalt therapists* (pp. 317–337). St Romain la Virvee, France: Editions L'Exprimerie.

Buber, M. (1970). *I and thou* (W. Kaufmann, Trans.). New York, NY: Touchstone.

Buber, M. (1999). Elements of the interhuman. In J. Buber-Agassi (Ed.), *Martin Buber on psychology and psychotherapy: Essays, letters, and dialogue* (pp. 72–89). Syracuse, NY: Syracuse University Press.

Candiotto, L. (2019). Emotions in-between: The affective dimension of participatory sense-making. In L. Candiotto (Ed.), *The value of emotions for knowledge* (pp. 235–260). Cham, Switzerland: Palgrave Macmillan.

Carr, D. (2012). Experience and history. In D. Zahavi (Ed.), *The Oxford handbook of contemporary phenomenology* (pp. 483–502). New York, NY: Oxford University Press.

Cerbone, D. (2012). Phenomenological method: Reflection, introspection, and skepticism. In D. Zahavi (Ed.), *The Oxford handbook of contemporary phenomenology* (pp. 7–25). New York, NY: Oxford University Press.

Clough, P. (2008). The affective turn. *Theory, Culture & Society, 25*(1), 1–22.

Cromby, J. (2005). *Feeling bodies: Embodying psychology*. London, England: PalgraveMacmillan.

Cromby, J. & Willis, E. H. (2016). Affect – or Feeling (after Leys)?. *Theory & Psychology, 26*(4), 476–495.

DeYoung, P. A. (2015). *Understanding and treating chronic shame: A relational/ neurobiological approach*. New York, NY: Routledge.

Friedman, M. (1955). *Martin Buber: The life of dialogue* (4th ed.). New York, NY: Routledge.

Friedman, M. (1991). Preface. In R. Hycner, *Between person and person: Towards a dialogical psychotherapy*. Highland, NY: The Gestalt Journal Press.

Gergen, K. J. (2009). *Relational being: Beyond self and community*. New York, NY: Oxford University Press.

Gregg, M. & Seigworth, G. (Eds.). (2010). *The affect theory reader*. Durham, NC: Duke University Press.

Hersch, E. (2003). *From philosophy to psychotherapy: A phenomenological model for psychology, psychiatry, and psychoanalysis*. Toronto, Canada: University of Toronto Press.

Hycner, R. (1991). *Between person and person: Towards a dialogical psychotherapy*. Highland, NY: The Gestalt Journal Press.

Hycner, R., & Jacobs, L. (1995). *The healing relationship in Gestalt therapy: A dialogic/self psychology approach*. Highland, NY: The Gestalt Journal Press.

Jacobs, L. (1989). Dialogue in Gestalt theory and therapy. *The Gestalt Journal, XII* (1), 25–67.

Jacobs, L. (2016). Meaningfulness, directionality and sense of self. In J. M. Robine (Ed.), *Self: A polyphony of contemporary Gestalt therapists* (pp. 251–260). St Romain la Virvee, France: Editions L'Exprimerie.

Jacobs, L. (2017). Hopes, fears, and enduring relational themes. *British Gestalt Journal, 26*(1), 7–16.

Jacobs, L. & Hycner, R. (Eds.). (2009). *Relational approaches in Gestalt therapy*. New York, NY: Routledge, Taylor and Francis.

Jaegher, H. (2015). How we affect each other. *Journal of Consciousness Studies, 22*(1–2), 112–132.

Lee, R. G. (2004). Ethics: A Gestalt of values the values of Gestalt a next step. In R. G. Lee (Ed.), *The values of connection: A relational approach to ethics* (pp. 3–33). Hilldale, NJ: The Analytic Press.

Macann, C. (1993). *Four phenomenological philosophers: Husserl, Heidegger, Sartre, Merleau- Ponty*. New York, NY: Routledge.

McNamee, S. & Gergen, K. (Eds.). (1999). *Relational responsibility: Resources for sustainable dialogue*. Thousand Oaks, CA: Sage Publications, Inc.

Orange, D. (2010). *Thinking for Clinicians: Philosophical resources for contemporary psychoanalysis and the humanistic psychotherapies*. New York, NY: Routledge.

Orange, D. (2011). *The suffering stranger: Hermeneutics for everyday clinical practice*. New York, NY: Routledge.

Perls, F., Hefferline, R. & Goodman, P. (1951/1991). *Gestalt therapy: Excitement and growth in the human personality*. Gouldsboro, ME: The Gestalt Journal Press.

Perls, F. (1973). *The Gestalt approach & Eye witness to therapy: Perls' last and most comprehensive work*. USA: Science and Behavior Books.

Polster, E. & Polster M. (1973). *Gestalt therapy integrated: Contours of theory and practice*. New York, NY: Vintage Books.

Robine, J. M. (2011). *On the occasion of another*. Gouldsboro, ME: The Gestalt Journal Press.

Robine, J. M. (2016). (Ed.). *Self: A polyphony of contemporary Gestalt therapists*. St Romain la Virvee, France: Editions L'Exprimerie.

Safranski, R. (1998). *Martin Heidegger: Between good and evil*. Cambridge, MA: Harvard University Press.

Staemmler, F. M. (2009). *Aggression, time, and understanding: Contributions to the evolution of Gestalt therapy*. Santa Cruz, CA: The Gestalt Press.

Staemmler, F. M. (2017). *Relationalität in der Gestalttherapie: Kontakt und verbundenheit*. Gevelsberg, Germany: Verlag Andreas Kohlhage.

Stern, D. B. (2010). *Partners in thought: Working with unformulated experience, Dissociation, and enactment*. New York, NY: Routledge.

Stolorow, R., Atwood, G., & Orange, D. (2002). *Worlds of experience: Interweaving philosophical and clinical dimensions in psychoanalysis*. New York, NY: Basic Books.

Spinelli, E. (2005). *The interpreted world: An introduction to phenomenological psychology* (2nd ed.). Thousand Oaks, CA: Sage Publications.

Tallon, A. (2004). Affection and the transcendental dialogical personalism of Buber and Levinas. In P. Atterton, M. Calarco & M. Friedman (Eds.), *Levinas & Buber: Dialogue & difference* (pp. 49–64). Pittsburgh, PA: Duquesne University Press.

Wegscheider, H. (2020). *Dialog und intersubjektivität in der Gestalttherapie: Von der jüdischen tradition und der dialogphilosophie zu relationalen entwicklungen in psychoanalyse und Gestalttherapie*. Gevelsberg, Germany: Verlag Andreas Kohlhage.

Wheeler, G. (2000). *Beyond individualism: Toward a new understanding of self, relationship, & experience*. Hillsdale, NJ: The Analytic Press.

Wollants, G. (2008/2012). *Gestalt therapy: Therapy of the situation*. Thousand Oaks, CA: Sage Publications.

Yontef, G. (1993). *Awareness, dialogue & process*. Highland, NY: The Gestalt Journal Press.

Yontef, G. & Jacobs, L. (2007). Gestalt therapy. In R. Corsini & D. Wedding (Eds.), *Current psychotherapies*, (8th ed., pp. 328–367). Belmont, CA: Brooks/Cole Thompson Learning.

# Applications of the Relational Gestalt Perspective

# Chapter 8

# A Classical Beginning and a Relational Turn: A Gestalt Therapy Case Study

*Charles E. Bowman and C. Ann Bowman*

> *'When I use a word,' Humpty Dumpty said in rather a scornful tone, 'it means just what I choose it to mean–neither more nor less.' 'The question is,' said Alice, 'whether you can make words mean different things–that's all.' 'The question is,' said Humpty Dumpty, 'which is to be master–that's all'*
> *– Lewis Carroll in* Through a Looking Glass

Humpty Dumpty's private language characterizes a classical Gestalt therapy attitude in a stereotypic manner. It is reminiscent of Perls's "I do my thing and you do your thing" in that we are all free to express our-selves in individualistic ways. From this classical Gestalt therapy, per-spective meaning is subjective, highly individual, and it is up to the other to seek to understand. As Gestalt therapists, we cut our teeth on this "take responsibility" approach to Gestalt praxis. In fact, one of the basic principles of classical Gestalt therapy is that the client learns to accept responsibility for their experience in the present. The laissez-faire asser-tion of this axiom colored our early Gestalt training as we moved from environmental support to self-support in the name of maturation. This produced a polarity between apathy and empathy. Perhaps this current work on classical and contemporary Gestalt praxis is our attempt to in-tegrate those fragments from our training and complete an incomplete Gestalt.

Alice counters Humpty Dumpty with Wittgenstein's social approach to language and argues against the private meaning of language (Wittgenstein, 2009). As contemporary Gestalt therapists, we disagree with Humpty! Words *do* mean different things, but this meaning is co-created in dialogue. The question isn't which is to be master. The answer to the question, always, lies in seeking to understand and meeting in dialogue. In service to this answer, we utilize both a classical and a contemporary Gestalt therapy approach in our practice of Gestalt therapy – sequentially at times and concurrently at other times. However, in the final analysis, we rely on the contemporary model of Gestalt therapy to integrate the therapeutic work into our lives and the lives of our clients. The contemporary, or relational

DOI: 10.4324/9781003255772-11

model currently practiced by Gestalt therapists, relies not only on socially created linguistic definitions but upon co-created experience in general.

At first glance, this polarity of classical and contemporary Gestalt therapy exists between the concepts of organismic self-regulation and the further reaches of an embodied relational field. We have been Gestalt therapy students, practitioners, and trainers for decades. The development of an embodied relational approach to Gestalt therapy (see Clemmens, 2020) is the most dramatic advance in the praxis of Gestalt therapy during our time. This advance sprang from what psychoanalysts first dubbed "the relational turn" (see Stolorow et al., 1987; Mitchell, 1988) and what early Gestalt therapy innovators introduced as "relational Gestalt therapy" (see Jacobs, 1989, 1992; Yontef, 2002).

Our intention in this chapter is not only to demonstrate the fluid nature of these models of Gestalt therapy but also to show how contemporary (relational) Gestalt therapy rests upon the shoulders of classical Gestalt therapy. We prefer the broader label "contemporary" instead of "relational" Gestalt therapy and contrast it with the earlier, Perlsian approach, or "classical Gestalt therapy." We intend to highlight how both conceptions of Gestalt therapy contribute to the ongoing growth and trauma recovery of our client, "Claudia." Of course, the information presented here has been anonymized and the client's identity is held in confidence. Only one of us maintained a therapeutic relationship. The other provided clinical supervision and feedback over time.

In contemporary Gestalt therapy, as in relational psychoanalysis, the therapist is "able and willing to enter into the patient's suffering and share the painful history, able and willing to 'undergo the situation' with the other" (Orange, 1995, p. 5). By sharing their own internal experience of themselves as well as their awareness of what the client is doing and saying, the therapist invites the client to explore new internal and external awareness. Examining the shared phenomenological experience together becomes its own grand experiment. This journey shapes the ongoing relationship and expands the client's capacity to express experiences in new, fresh ways that differ from stale, habitual expressions.

*I started seeing Claudia in my Gestalt therapy practice in 2010. She was 35 years old and living a life of social isolation and exploitive work. She sought therapy for compulsive overeating, rapid weight gain, and excess "stress." She was interested in learning how to live without turning to food and presented a history of "yo-yo dieting" with multiple episodes of nearly 100-pound weight fluctuation and an insatiable demand for perfectionism in all aspects of her life. Early interventions included guiding her awareness to body sensation and supporting attempts to recognize and express emotions. These included asking her to "own" her experience using "I statements" or inquiring as to her somatic experience. For example, she stated, "I binge eat until it hurts. Why would anyone do that?" I gently invited her to state, "I binge eat until I hurt and don't know why I do that."*

In these early sessions, establishing first-person, direct expression provided a solid base for future dialogue. This is an example of a classical directed language experiment and it is also teaching "the rules and games of Gestalt therapy" (Levitsky & Perls, 1970, p. 140). This and other awareness experiments are foundational to a classical Gestalt therapy model.

*Although she grew up with an alcoholic father and family system, she maintained an idealized, bucolic recollection of childhood. This loving family was rife with alcohol abusing and alcoholic members and all maintained a fierce commitment to confluence in order to maintain the idealized pastoral fantasy of her family. As a result, Claudia had no support for knowing her own unique experience. In creatively adjusting to this family system, she demonstrated many traits of a bulimic teenager and young adult. She described herself as "big but active" in high school and a chronic over-achiever who accepted nothing but perfect marks throughout her academic career. She presented this history in a session after binge eating the night before – a pint ice cream, two slices of cake, a pint of macaroni and cheese, and a pint of milk.*

Essential to the therapy at this point was guiding Claudia in promoting self-awareness and relying less upon deflection or desensitization, as she had learned to do in her addictive family. In a classical stance, the client was asked repeatedly to pause, notice, identify and express her awareness of sensations, feelings, energy, and needs as she told her story. This was a novel way of communicating for Claudia, difficult and awkward since she preferred cognition and had learned to devalue her embodied experience.

Identifying and expressing immediate experience in a present-centered dialogue is the Gestalt therapy medium for healing, choice, and change in both classical and contemporary Gestalt therapy paradigms. With this commitment to dialogue, a contemporary Gestalt approach creates the relational sustenance that supports this ongoing, developing awareness of our experience in the here and now. This is essential for addiction and trauma recovery (Van der Kolk, 2015; Brownell, 2012). In addition to this availability for dialogue, the work of the therapist also includes expressions of validation, genuine interest, and the willingness to be impacted by the client. People need others to mirror and reflect back to them: "I see you seeing me."

Claudia also presents a classic Perlsian "top dog-underdog" adjustment (Perls, 1969b) with demands for unobtainable goals and impeccability on the one hand and the self-torture processes of browbeating and binge eating on the other. This pattern developed in adolescence and persisted throughout her life. Many of our early sessions were spent sharpening awareness of this polarity. In therapy, she grew in her capacity to notice the judgmental critic that lived in her sub-vocally. In addition to traditional empty chair work with the polarity – the spontaneity of which she found unbearable – we would examine homework as she kept a written script of a dialogue between those disparate parts. We also conducted the intrapsychic dialogue in fantasy. Initially, this work led to a greater awareness of her inner turmoil. Gradually, the inner turbulence began to lessen.

> *A devout Catholic, she was battling the church bureaucracy to annul a 4-year marriage that had been marred by deceit and lies of the highest caliber by a narcissistic husband. As she lapsed into depression in this process, I responded angrily about the unfairness of church doctrine and the abuse she had undergone in such a terrible marriage. Her response to me and to the church was alexithymic. When I shared my awareness of the small tear on her cheek, she responded with curiosity. She had no awareness of any anger in her life but wondered aloud if her tears replaced anger, frustration, and annoyance.*

Claudia's process of retroflecting described above dramatically stifled emotional awareness and expression. The long-term result of this retroflection included morbid obesity, body dysmorphia, and workaholism.

In this passage, we see the convergence of classical and contemporary Gestalt therapy. A key concept in Gestalt therapy theory is apparent regardless of the nature of one's Gestalt praxis. The concept is often taught as "the use of self as a therapeutic instrument" (see Polster & Polster, 1973) and is obvious from both perspectives. From the very beginnings of Gestalt therapy comes the idea of "concentration therapy" (Perls, 1947, 1969a) and a classical Gestalt therapy intervention – directed awareness. This involved the therapist sharing an observation, noticing the tear on her cheek. This was paired with the therapist's sharing their own internal awareness of anger toward the church, which lead to a fuller expression of her history of conflict avoidance. This powerful combination allowed Claudia to open to her own curiosity about her alexithymic adjustment. The therapist's sharing anger and awareness in this instance began the process of directing awareness to Claudia's emotions with a felt sense of support in the actual therapeutic experience.

> *Claudia had made several partner choices resulting in relationships with men who were chronic liars. Her blind trust in these men and her inability to express anger towards them were significant contributors to a life of self-loathing and obesity. She rationalized that being overweight meant she would be loved for who she was and not for her looks, thereby assuring a more honest relationship. The result? She hopelessly longed*

*for relationship. As we worked through the enactment of this fixed gestalt in the therapy, she slowly allowed herself to care about me. This presented many opportunities for dialogue around a major relational aspect of our work: learning to stay in contact with me, trusting her embodied response to me, and observing and trusting my intentions.*

Somewhere around the 30th session, the tenor of the treatment began a distinct shift into a dynamic, contemporary Gestalt therapy approach. This *relational turn* is marked by closer attention to the therapist-client relationship in the present, the available support offered by the therapist in the moment and the detailed attention to relational needs. These included needs for safety and security, validation and acceptance, confirmation, the need for self-definition, and the need to express and to receive love (Erskine, 1998; Erskine et al., 1999). The earlier attention-given sensation, awareness, polarity integration, and self-expression from the classical Gestalt approach provided a solid ground for an embodied relational approach within the dialogical relationship. The therapeutic relationship stood in sharp relief upon such fertile ground.

It's not been our experience that contemporary Gestalt therapy is a brief therapy. Certainly, Gestalt techniques have been used in the service of short-term therapy, but in contemporary applications this is not the case. The therapeutic relationship represents a way in which the client and therapist engage in an opportunity to remake a unique relational history. This allows the client to perceive themselves and the world differently, "... to feel more free and able to make her/his own contribution to relationships and hence to the world in which s/he lives" (Spagnuolo Lobb, 2009, p 114). This deliberate building of an intimate relationship proved the container for the next phase of the work.

*During our 35th session Claudia shared that she had been raped when she was 15 years old by her best friend John's older brother. John had betrayed her. He drove the three of them to a park, then got out of the car and locked her in with his brother while he raped her. This initial recall was very fuzzy, and details remained indistinct for many sessions afterward. What she did recall shortly after this earliest verbalizing of this experience was the young man forcing himself on top of her while she fought and desperately tried to pull open the lock on the car door. She remembered looking out the back window and seeing John watching the entire rape with no effort to intercede. Their eyes met and he turned away. She later realized the rape had been planned.*

*Claudia would later recall forcing her way out of the car and walking home in a daze, pulling herself together enough to walk past her family at the dinner table, feign normalcy, take a shower, and return for the end of the family dinner. Nobody noticed her trauma. Nobody asked. Nobody knew.*

*As Claudia shared this horrific memory, I sat with her, silent, teary-eyed, full of compassion. In the following session she reported having the insight that her family was supportive only during the good times and that the heartbreaking sides of life were routinely overlooked. The loneliness of this 15-year-old rape victim was tragic and persisted for the next 20 years. Working through this trauma in therapy waxed and waned.*

Some of the earliest writings about Gestalt therapy support the maxim, "nothing takes the place of knowing when to do nothing" (see Enright, 1970; Fagan, 1970). This lack of active intervention, being instead of doing, was key in Claudia's disclosing the rape. This afforded her the safe relational container and ultimately provided the ground for a number of additional insights about her own self-functioning, much improved self-care behavior, and a budding new ability to self-nurture. For instance, shortly after this session, she recognized that her weight-gain strategy for promoting honesty in relationships had not only failed but was a strategy for isolation.

*Just prior to the next session she dreamed of every one-night stand in which she had ever engaged. She awoke exhausted, feeling like the dream had lasted all night. She came into the session sad and full of regret that she had treated herself with such callous disregard. Most of this session was devoted to classically working through the dream, with Claudia eventually addressing herself as "the dreamer" in an empty chair. This brought her an awareness that she was seeking atonement and self-forgiveness.*

The palpable healing energy of this session rested not in the skill of the therapist walking her through the dreamwork technique but in the witnessing presence as she wept for herself. Perhaps the early Gestalt therapy writers mislabeled this as "doing nothing." Today we reframe this as a relational skill to be developed.

*We devoted much of the therapy over the next year to realizing the impact of the rape on her life, continuing to take a hard look at her self-judgements, addictive behaviors, and isolation. During this time, she would not discuss the rape itself, often claiming very poor recollection of the event.*

Miriam Taylor (2014) has noted that persons recovering from traumatic experiences often experience what is termed a narrow window of tolerance. In other words, the traumatized person becomes overwhelmed by the intensity of embodied emotional experiences that result from recalling memories. They are often unable to identify and express their experiences as was the case for Claudia.

Clients experiencing hyperarousal (heightened anxiety) need help with grounding, support, and awareness. Clients experiencing hypo arousal (which is also a result of heightened anxiety but manifests as shutting down awareness and energy) benefit from interventions that support awareness, finding their energy, and engagement in the process. To be effective, therapists must not only have an understanding of energy regulation, they also need a wide window of tolerance themselves. The therapist must be present as solid, believable, empathetic, attuned, and involved – a strong, dependable other (Taylor, 2014; Erskine et al., 1999). It is imperative that the therapist understand the idea of the window of tolerance and the need for relational involvement if a course of Gestalt therapy is to be effective in bringing about healing.

> *A failed relationship around session number 50 prompted Claudia's revisiting the rape in psychotherapy. This was significant not only as a triggering event but also because it was the first relationship in which she allowed herself to be vulnerable since her marriage. "I can't stop thinking about John," she said in a subdued and tearful whisper. In an attempt to lighten the conversation, she added – in a joking voice while glancing away, "... and to top it all off, this stabbing pain in my stomach is back!" I asked her to repeat the sentence "I have stabbing pain in my stomach" a number of times while maintaining eye contact. As she did this her voice became stronger and she reported a sense of power and determination not to let this latest breakup throw her into a depression. I suggested she focus on her stomach and encouraged her to be curious about this sensation.*

This attention to sensation, body, and movement to support emotional regulation and processing of memories is known as "bottom up intervention" in the literature on trauma recovery (Grabbe & Miller-Karas, 2018). In Gestalt therapy, this process is the foundation in which all embodied interventions begin. The awareness of our subtle, sensory, body-based feelings (interoception) is often "knocked out" in trauma survivors but it is necessary for developing the potential for self-agency (Van der Kolk, 2015). A somatic, or "bottom-up," approach teaches sensory awareness as the means for regulating and integrating emotions. This practice has been an integral component of Gestalt therapy from its very beginning.

> *As Claudia focused on the sensations in her stomach she spontaneously stated, "I feel like someone just punched me in the gut." Together we began designing an experiment to facilitate her expressing retroflected emotion. I suggested she address her now-lost lover in an empty chair with the sentence, "I'd like to punch you in the gut!" "You know I can't talk to an empty chair" she reminded me. Grading the experiment in the classical sense (Zinker, 1970) I suggested she first imagine saying this to a trusted*

*peer at work. Next I asked her to say it to me, encouraging her to repeat the sentence and get progressively louder. Although she did not get to a level of shouting, she could raise her voice and feel "energy." Next, I asked her to imagine shouting at both John and the rapist, "I'd like to punch you in the gut!" She stated that she could not do this and her energy and expression notably dampened – an example of hypo arousal noted above. (For a discussion of Perls' concept of dampening, see* Bowman, 2019). *I asked her to imagine both of us towering over them and shouting together. She smiled and stated the fantasy felt good and brought relief from her stomach pain. We closed the session with her strongly proclaiming on her way out the door, "I'd like to punch them in the gut!"*

As Claudia walked through the above experiment her stomach pain decreased. Throughout the next several sessions her pain would return episodically but never with the intensity she previously experienced. This marked integration of her somatic experience, memories, and thoughts along with accepting her need for my support. She lost ten pounds over the course of six weeks and refrained from binge eating. This behavior change has continued to this day.

*At session number 60 Claudia fully recalled the rape scene, complete with words and sounds, sensations and clear visual detail. She remembered the rapist's name, the make of the car, and the shape of the door lock as she frantically tried to grasp and open it. She recalled yelling for John through the car window and she remembered repeatedly yelling "STOP!" This time she vividly remembered walking home, through the house, past her family, and taking a shower. During this recollection I focused her attention to slow full breathing, my presence and witness, pacing and pausing. After crying together following this crisp recall, she commented abruptly that she realized I would be retiring someday. I heard this comment as an awareness of the relational vulnerability that she felt as a result of feeling connection and support with me. We talked about holding both – the vulnerability (uncertainty of life) as well as my commitment to her to continue our work as long as she needed.*

Another long series of sessions ensued, characterized by venting about daily stressors, problem-solving, and weight management – in one sense a commentary on the difficulty of daily life and in another sense a dampening with the pull toward homeostasis. Rather than the classical Gestalt therapy view of these session themes as deflection or denial, a more contemporary view portrays these sessions as integrative and self-regulatory – that is, self-regulation within the context of an environment. No longer is self-regulation seen as an activity of an organism. It is an activity of the field and of contact-in-relationship.

*Claudia called me in crisis early in 2016 and was frantic. An urgent call such as this had never happened in all the years of our therapy together. She was traveling for work and had a lucid nightmare of rape. She fought the perpetrator off by scratching, yelling, and gouging eyes. She awoke feeling it was real – to the point of checking the hotel room, getting very paranoid, and trying to call a friend. She apologized for calling me in the middle of the night. Much like the previous comment she had made about my retiring someday, I understood her reaching out to me in this instance not only as an urgent situation, but as another sign of (and test of) how safe she felt in our relationship. I responded with reassurance that I willingly accepted her call and was pleased she sought support in our relationship instead of resorting to the self-destructive behaviors she had relied upon in the past to calm herself down. Claudia was clearly growing in her ability to find support in her environment. When we next met, I reframed the dream as a healing dream in which she used aggression to break free. This dream marked another pivotal moment in therapy as Claudia experienced a remarkable increase in self-agency by fighting back. She was metaphorically able to "escape from the car." In this session she expressed to John in an empty chair, "why do you just stand there watching, why don't you do something!" She proclaimed this forcefully and with anger.*

Months followed in what this time seemed to be an avoidance of the work at hand. I took a risk and revisited the dream with a relational intervention. I began the session with a comment on this apparent stall, our lack of more serious dialogue, and an invitation to experiment.

*"I agree we are going nowhere. Maybe you should push me harder and not be so patient," she replied. "Do you want to try something different?" I asked, "Maybe an experiment will help move us forward." I suggested we once again revisit the rape scene and she hesitantly agreed. After initially reviewing the scene in the present, reminiscent of beginning a classical dreamwork session, I asked her to make the statement "why do you just stand there watching, why don't you do something" directly to John. She did so congruently and forcefully. Next, I asked her to imagine it was me standing outside the car and suggested she direct the same statement to me – "why do you just stand there watching, why don't you do something." She initially could not make that statement directly to me until I added some context. I proposed that her comment about my patience and her stuckness seemed a similar dynamic to her position in the car relative to John's watching and doing nothing. Further, I wondered aloud if she felt she was struggling on one side of the window wanting me to intervene, while I merely watched her struggling, just as John did in reality. She understood my comment. Still, she was not willing to put me in John's position in the scene.*

The suggestion of an experiment has relational implications, even if the experiment is neither accepted nor conducted. Over the next dozen sessions following this rejected experiment, we worked on the rape. We did so in an energizing new manner. We worked on the unfinished business of the rape, particularly the betrayal, simultaneously through the therapeutic relationship and through the original memory of the event. Often, the work would shuttle between asking Claudia to direct her expressions of anger toward me, and then toward John in the rape scene. She vacillated between retroflecting the anger, moving in and out of feeling she was not worth helping, feeling intense anger toward John, and a blind rage toward the rapist. Simultaneously, she expressed a newfound warmth and comfort with the therapeutic relationship – an indication of a growing ability to differentiate the current relationship from the transference relationship. Tracking all of this was no small task.

Fully six years after starting therapy Claudia gingerly began expressing anger. At first, anger was directed toward the church for their decision to deny the annulment, then toward the rapist and the betrayer, and eventually toward her parents for not recognizing that she had been through something immediately after the rape. By becoming more accepting of her feelings of anger, she also regained the experience of aggression, which is necessary to make contact with the world and to get what is needed from the world (Perls et al., 1994). Aggression helps us deconstruct and reconstruct attitudes, opinions, and perceptions. It is essential for creativity and growth. Women, in particular, are socialized to deny their experience of aggression and anger but by doing so their aliveness, spontaneity, momentum, and mobilization of energy for action is also denied (Bowman et al., 2011). Claudia began reclaiming her aggression in the dream mentioned previously, but by inviting a here and now relational experience such as expressing anger toward the therapist, the necessary conditions were created for the safe experiencing and reclaiming of her power. This is necessary for finishing the unfinished business. With practice in the "safe emergency" of the consulting room (see Perls et al., 1994), anger and aggression slowly became a known entity and a commodity for managing daily life. The client's felt sense of relationship provides both the security and the structure that allows for expression and assimilation of the anger and of the trauma.

> *A testament to her growth, Claudia now recognizes and expresses her anger and frustration to me, to the original perpetrators of the trauma, and to people currently in her life in honest and direct ways. She is participating in relationships without the retroflective, destructive behaviors that have hastened so many ruptures. For the last several years Claudia has progressed in her weight loss quest by meeting small goals – an ideal way to establish and maintain a healthy lifestyle. Feeling her own embodied needs within the therapeutic relationship has allowed a rebirth of sorts.*

## Conclusion

Lewis Carroll himself endorsed the "private" language of Humpty Dumpty which Wittgenstein opposed. Relational Gestalt therapy employs the same sort of exploration in the attempt to know the "private" experience of the client. In our experience of Gestalt therapy, words are perhaps the most valuable tool in understanding the client's experience – in combination, of course, with somatic experience, movement, inflection, and the swarm of nonverbal experiences before us in any encounter. Regarding words, the contemporary Gestalt therapist must hold meaning in a light and fluid manner, allowing the words of the client to mean "just what I choose it to mean–neither more nor less." It is in this therapeutic stance that contemporary and classical Gestalt therapy are most different. Here is the task of the Gestalt therapist according to Fritz Perls in 1970:

> We apply enough skillful frustration so that the patient is forced to find his own way, discover his own possibilities, his own potential, *and discover that what he expects from the therapist, he can do just as well himself* (italics in original).... And this is what we are again and again trying to do, to frustrate the person until he is face to face with his blocks, with his inhibitions, with his way of avoiding having eyes, having ears, having muscles, having authority, having security in himself. (pp. 40–41)

We are not challenging classical Gestalt therapy in terms of what is and what is not Gestalt therapy. We are shining the light in a different direction when we choose to focus on the support necessary to facilitate the clients contacting as opposed to the skillful frustration mentioned above. Gestalt therapy has always helped clients develop their own support (Perls, 1992). Classical Gestalt therapy bifurcates the support into self-support and environmental support. We are not advocating this bifurcation. Instead, we understand support in the fullness of the term and recognize that "not all support is gentle or even kind" (Jacobs, 2006, p. 10). Support can also be firm, confrontive, benign, or neutral, and qualities in between.

Margherita Spagnuolo Lobb (2009) also captures the spirit of contemporary Gestalt therapy support beautifully:

> "It is not the technique used by an expert or another person... But two people who together find possibilities of fulfilling interrupted intentionality. It is the dance that the therapist with all her/his knowledge and humanity, and the patient with all his/her pain and desire to get well, create in order to rebuild the ground on which the life of the relationship rests." (p. 115)

The contemporary notion of support was embraced by Claudia in the warm and contactful relationship that developed between us in the course of our work together. We often found ourselves, both of us, entangled in deep wounds, frustrating blocks in awareness, or at a significant loss for words. And, we climbed out of the morass together. Today, Claudia is able to express her gratitude for our work together and for me personally. It is the contemporary focus on support versus frustration that creates a field of gratitude, empathy, and healing.

## References

Bowman, C. A., Feinstein, G. & Graham, J. (2011). Women and aggression: A pre-conference workshop. In D. Bloom & P. Brownell (Eds.), *Continuity and Change: Gestalt Therapy Now* (pp. 72–85). New Castle upon Tyne, UK: Cambridge Scholars Press.

Bowman, C. E. (2019). Psychotherapy of awareness: A missing link in the evolution of Gestalt therapy. In J. Robine & C. Bowman (Eds.), *Psychopathology of Awareness: An Unfinished and Unpublished Manuscript with Commentaries by Contemporary Gestalt Therapists*. St. Romaine la Vireé, France: l'exprimerie.

Brownell, P. (2012). *Gestalt Therapy for Addictive and Self-medicating Behaviors*. New York: Springer Publishing Company.

Clemmens, M. (2020). *Embodied Relational Gestalt: Theories and Applications*. New York: Routledge.

Enright, J. (1970). An introduction to Gestalt techniques. In J. Fagan & I. Shepherd (Eds.), *Gestalt Therapy Now* (pp. 107–124). Palo Alto, CA: Science & Behavior Books.

Erskine, R. (1998). Attunement and involvement: Therapeutic responses to relational needs. *International Journal of Psychotherapy*, *3*, 235–244.

Erskine, R., Moursund, J. & Troutman, R. (1999). *Beyond Empathy: A Therapy of Contact-in Relationships*. New York: Routledge.

Fagan, J. (1970). The tasks of the therapist. In J. Fagan & I. Shepherd, *Gestalt Therapy Now* (pp. 88–106). Palo Alto, CA: Science & Behavior Books.

Grabbe, L. & Miller-Karas, E. (2018). The trauma resiliency model: A "bottom-up" intervention for trauma psychotherapy. *Journal of the American Psychiatric Nurses Association*, *24*(1), 76–84.

Jacobs, L. (1989). Dialogue in Gestalt theory and therapy. *Gestalt Journal*, *12*(1), 25–68.

Jacobs, L. (1992). Insights from psychoanalytic self-psychology and intersubjectivity theory for Gestalt therapists. *Gestalt Journal*, *15*(2), 25–60.

Jacobs, L. (2006). That which enables-support as complex and contextually emergent. *British Gestalt Journal*, *15*(2), 10.

Levitsky, A. & Perls, F. (1970). The rules and games of Gestalt therapy. In J. Fagan & I. Shepherd (Eds.), *Gestalt Therapy Now* (pp. 140–149). Palo Alto, CA: Science & Behavior Books.

Mitchell, A. (1988). *Relational Concepts in Psychoanalysis*. Cambridge, MA: Harvard University Press.

Orange, D. M. (1995). *Emotional Understanding: Studies in Psychoanalytic Epistemology*. New York: Guilford Press.

Perls, F. (1969a). *Ego, Hunger and Aggression.* New York: Random House. (Original work published 1947.)

Perls, F. (1969b). *Gestalt Therapy Verbatim.* Moab, UT: Real People Press.

Perls, L. (1992). *Living at the Boundary.* Gouldsboro, ME: Gestalt Journal Press.

Perls, F., Hefferline, R., & Goodman, P. (1994). *Gestalt Therapy: Excitement & Growth in the Human Personality.* New York: Gestalt Journal Press. (Original work published 1951.)

Polster, E. & Polster, M. (1973). *Gestalt Therapy Integrated: Contours of Theory and Practice.* New York: Random House.

Spagnuolo Lobb, M. (2009). The therapeutic relationship in Gestalt therapy. In L. Jacobs & R. Hycner (Eds.), *Relational Approaches in Gestalt Therapy* (pp. 111–130). Santa Cruz, CA: Gestalt Press.

Stolorow, R., Brandschaft, B., & Atwood, G. (1987). *Psychoanalytic Treatment: An Intersubjective Approach.* Hillsdale, NJ: The Analytic Press.

Taylor, M. (2014). *Trauma Therapy and Clinical Practice: Neuroscience, Gestalt and the Body.* Maidenhead, UK: McGraw-Hill Education.

Van der Kolk, B. (2015). *The Body Keeps the Score: Brain, Mind, and Body in the Healing of Trauma.* New York: Viking.

Wittgenstein, L. (2009). *Philosophical Investigations* (4th edition). P. Hacker & J. Schulte (Eds. & Trans.), Oxford: Wiley-Blackwell.

Yontef, G. (2002). The relational attitude in Gestalt therapy theory and practice. *International Gestalt Journal, 25*(1), 15–34.

Zinker, J. (1970). *Creative Process in Gestalt Therapy.* New York: Random House.

## Chapter 9

# When the World Changes in an Instant: Exploring "Cracks in the Continuity of Experience" [1]

*Michelle Seely*

*Adapted from a lecture given at the Pacific Gestalt Institute Winter Residential, March 2019, Ojai, California.*

A shift or sudden break in the flow of human experience is a common phenomenon. As we go along in our lives, these interruptions range from the intense but pleasant shifts of aha moments and feeling love-struck, to the more difficult experiences of being blindsided by panic, shame, or trauma. We are affected when the world is changed. The pleasant shifts leave us feeling more welcomed—our place in our world feels more established and safe, and the difficult shifts leave us outside a world of belonging.

This chapter is born of a jarring personal experience that occurred in the backseat of a taxi, an experience I initially identified as shame. Spending time in training on panic disorder with Gianni Francesetti caused me to reconsider my experience in the cab. Was it really a matter of shame, or could it have been panic? As I sat with this new possibility, what especially caught my attention was that precise moment of change when the world shifted, when there was "a crack in the continuity of experience" as Francesetti describes it (2018).

The "crack" happens so quickly—often between eye blinks—that most times we don't recall it or even think to go back to look at it once we are calm again. This chapter is a consideration of that moment, taking a closer look at that crack between a familiar *now*, and a surprising *next*.

## The Taxi Incident

When my long marriage ended with the revelation of an epic betrayal, I was 52 years old. I had not been on a date with anyone but my husband since my early 20s. New love seemed like a younger woman's prerogative. I felt too old. I'd been humiliated. I was grieving. I had zero interest in dating. So, I decided I would just let the "romantic love" chapter of my life come to a close. I was surprised when, some years later, the possibility of a relationship with an old boyfriend revealed romantic stirrings that had teenage energy in them. It was

DOI: 10.4324/9781003255772-12

exciting! Delightful! Compelling! It seemed that a longing-for-love had not hit its expiry date in me after all. And so, at the time of this story, some six years after my divorce, I found myself feeling optimistic about romance. Hope and a re-awakened desire for love were coloring the world.

On the particular evening of this story, I had plans to meet my friend Charmaine for dinner. I was feeling good. I had taken some time with my appearance. I had done my hair, put on make-up and a sexy top, I wore a leather jacket—not my everyday look. I wanted to be able to drink wine with Charmaine at dinner, so I took a cab to the restaurant. I sat in the backseat of the taxi, happy and relaxed until the moment I caught my own eye in the rearview mirror.

Right then the world changed.

Suddenly all I could see was loose skin hanging in folds on my neck, and deep craggy lines on my face. I looked frightening. In a flash, my joy and exuberance were replaced with horror. I was so fixated on my hideous appearance that nothing else registered. I was stricken. I was in suspension. I no longer felt like I was part of this world.

I felt an urgency to get home. A breath later, my head began to fill with critical self-talk that declared my happy mood to have been a joke. Actually, I was the joke. Why had I considered finding love? My mind was filled with negative thoughts: I was ridiculous, stupid, crazy, too old, too ugly, and on and on. The barrage continued for the rest of the 20-minute ride to the restaurant. By the time the taxi pulled up to the curb, I was fighting hard not to cry. My heart had turned to stone, my lungs were tight and could hardly expand. I was barely there—what felt like a hologram of *Michelle* exited the cab and walked into that bar. It felt like the rest of me was suspended over a chasm, or maybe was already dead. I felt vacant, eliminated.

If Charmaine hadn't been such a good friend, I would have gone straight home. Fortunately, I felt safe to tell her what was going on. She said something sweet like, "Oh, baby! You're nuts! You're beautiful. Come here!" Charmaine hugged me for a while, and I calmed a tiny bit with her touch, her warmth, and her insistence that I was wrong. Maybe it all wasn't as bad as it had seemed? I felt a little better, a little safer to stay out with her, and little more hopeful.

In an effort to show me how wrong I was, Charmaine took my picture with her phone and showed it to me. I could see that I looked fine. In fact, I looked good. It was a really nice photograph of me.

This was very confusing. Although my eyes could see that I was not hideous, my body was not convinced. I still felt so tight. The shame stories quieted down from a full torrent to a trickle, and then to a lingering threat. I took some deep breaths. Charmaine teased me gently and I could laugh a little with her about how convinced I'd been that I looked like an ancient lizard woman. This helped me to relax a bit, but I was still quite tense and shaken. I could still feel a residue of terror in every cell of my body.

## The Shame Spiral Aspect

While still in the cab I recognized the experience I was having as shame. Even before the critical thoughts began, I recognized shame in the strong pull to stop what I was doing and to give up and go home before I humiliated myself further. I knew the sinking, deadly-still dread that invaded my chest and belly as shame. Whether silent or invective-filled, in shame the familiar "trance of unworthiness" (Brach, 2004) engulfs me and cuts me off from the rest of the world.

Informed by Gestalt theory and practice, Buddhist psychology and practice, and the balm of the many supportive relationships I've enjoyed over the years, I have learned to meet and tend to shame experiences in the manner of "good self-parenting" (Yontef, 1993, pp. 521–524). This friendliness to my own experience is informed by and rests on the idea that the overwhelming sense of unworthiness (in all its forms) is an experience I am having, but is not the truth about me. Yontef points out that in shame "... self accusations are treated as fact rather than being a direct and insightful expression of the shame affect" (p. 491). Also in Yontef, the idea of shame as the early and enduring byproduct of a family culture where interactions do not support identification with forming figures, do not "favor contact and differences between people," but instead interrupt forming figures and leave one with "a negative reaction to one's self as a whole" (p. 492).

As Wheeler (2000) points out, in the West we tend to view people through an individualist lens rather than a relational lens, and, as a result, are taught and believe that our relational needs will fade away as we mature. When we do not outgrow our need for supportive others, we are judged, and we also judge ourselves negatively for needing people, and sometimes for needing anything at all.

For many of us, direct knowledge of our relational needs becomes hidden from our awareness—instead of knowing what we need, we are only aware of the shame that arises in us when we are not well met. Robine (2013) writes that "shame triggers off the feeling of a lack of harmony between one's experience of oneself and one's experience of the external world" (p. 245). We learn to make sense of the disharmony by implicitly agreeing that our needs are bad/we are bad and so the shame is deserved. Disharmony is a good way to describe what happened in the moment of the "crack," and how it rippled on afterward. The disharmony can feel mystifying and this confusion can dysregulate us. In trying to make sense of it so we can settle down, most of us get busy blaming ourselves or others for the lack of connection.

Once we can unhook shame from worthiness, we can see that the mere presence of shame does not signify defects in individuals who are experiencing it. This makes possible the radical option of interpreting "shame" sensations as simply the body's reaction to feeling unsafe or unwelcome in this relationship/situation/world. If we don't interpret the muscular contractions, the emptiness, and the disconnection we experience and are so quick to call shame, we can simply let them be what they are—the dreaded feelings of being too alone. "Unsafe" and "too alone" are synonymous in this context. So, shame points to unsafety or lack of support. Unmet desire is a common shame catalyst (Lee, 2004 p. 22; Robine, 2019). Desire is what makes us so vulnerable because it pulls us into the world and toward relationships. Thwarted desire becomes shame, and shame comes in to regulate our movement, steering us away from desires that could lead to unsafe or unsupported next moments or situations (Lee, 2004, 2013; Wheeler, 2000). Desire loves a risk, and it does not find uncertainty to be so scary; shame doesn't feel the same way. Shame steers us back home, away from the risk and potential chaos that our longing to be met and welcomed by another invites—it steers us back home where it is safer (and lonelier.)

The shame-based criticisms of self and other can also be considered "second arrow" behaviors. In Buddhist teaching, the second arrow refers to the optional suffering we engage in after the first unavoidable suffering hits us. In the teaching story, someone is shot with an arrow and it really hurts! Then, while they are suffering the first hurt, they pick up a second arrow and start stabbing themselves and saying things like, "Why am I so unlucky?"; "Why did I walk here, I should have known better!"; "Everyone hates me"; and so on. Second arrows are extra suffering that is added to the first hurt. The implicit message is that all first arrows in life would be avoidable if we were just smarter if life were fairer. Using second arrows distracts us from simply being with the pain of having been shot in the first place. Ruminative shame can function similarly—the self or other criticism of shame can be seen as second arrow behavior and as such, protects us from direct experience of the "crack" when the shame hits and "desire implodes" (Jacobs, 2020).

To go back to the cab for a moment, only a few beats after I saw my "lizard face" in the mirror two familiar storylines began to run in my mind: my hideousness as a physical being, and what a joke it was to think that I could ever find and inspire love.

Given the assumptions regarding shame that I listed above, I have been in the practice for quite some time of seeing self-criticism and shame stories (all second arrow behaviors) as distractions perfected to dissuade me from following my desires into the world, and to keep from facing directly the fears that accompany desire. Knowing this, I actively practice listening for the wishes and fears that hide under critical thoughts, sometimes even saying to myself, "You get mean when you are scared. I've heard the mean stories before, but we never talk about your fear. What are you afraid of?" This line of inquiry often gets me to the question Robine suggests we ask when dealing with shame, "What were you wanting before the shame struck?" (2019).

Robine's question has been helpful here to reorient from the focus on self or other blame, and back to the fact that if there is shame, there is a conflict between what we were wanting and what happened. Robine emphasizes there is also someone we wanted it from—someone is implicated (2013, pp. 247, 250)! When we can name the thing we wanted from someone—that is, our desire—we touch the place where the shame contraction started. And, this line of inquiry leads again to Yontef's observation that for shame to develop there is a figure that gets interrupted—something in our experience does not find welcome. The interruption itself is the act of shoving the surprise and hurt aside; our attention becomes absorbed with the familiar (but always devastating) dreadful feeling of being unwelcome here. These interruptions leave us with a negative sense of self, or what can feel like inherent unworthiness.

The shame process takes over and keeps us from working directly with the "interrupted figure" Yontef mentions. In my case, the interrupted figure was a desire for love. Desiring at all clashed with my preference for self-reliance. I had taught myself early and well not to want what I couldn't be sure to get because to do so had been, and would ever be, humiliating. Hoping to find and inspire love in my fifties entailed exactly the sort of risk I *knew* to avoid. With the preening and the easy optimism I had enjoyed that night before I went out, I had pushed past the part of me that knew better, acting instead as if I were a person who could dance easily and casually with my desires right out into the world. The "crack" and resultant shame came to tell me of the "disharmony" between that easy approach and the terror that *wanting love* also holds for me.

## What a Panic Lens Revealed

In Francesetti's description of a panic attack—the "crack in the continuity of experience" marks a total break between a known world of one moment—and the world one lands in a moment later (2018). Even though when I heard his lecture I did not think I had ever had a panic attack, Francesetti's conceptualization of panic resonated deeply with me. The "crack," he explained, "reveals the need for the other." It reveals a cry that went unmet and was silenced, and then forgotten long ago. Panic *attacks* when the cry can no longer be ignored (or, perhaps more precisely, the "cry" attacks causing panic...).

A few more points Francesetti made about panic attacks:

1.  The reason developmental challenges or relational losses trigger panic attacks in some people and not in others has to do in part with the awareness a person has (or doesn't have) of their vulnerability—of their desire for and need for support. Knowing one needs support is preventive for panic attacks; the more the "need for support was delegitimated, the higher the risk for panic disorder" (2018).
2.  As Francesetti noted, "panic" is not a clinical word, instead it is derived from the god Pan. The long-ago forgotten needs, or "forgotten call,"

Francesetti explained, refers to the god Pan's birth experience. Pan's mother was so frightened by her baby's man-goat appearance that she fled leaving the newborn Pan all alone in the woods. Pan cried for her, but she never responded. When Pan's father, Hermes, finally retrieved him, he put Pan (in all his strangeness) on display for the merriment of the other Gods. Francesetti contends that "Pan's birth is the story of being born into a world of immediate, radical loneliness. He was overexposed and left without the protection and support needed for a comfortable transition from this moment into the next" (2018). Having a "silenced and then forgotten call" in one's history is a common factor in panic attacks (2018).

3.  Citing Panksepp's work, Francesetti points out that "instead of being a fear experience, panic is at its root an experience of profound solitude, it is an experience of acute loneliness" (2018). Panksepp refers to it as the Panic/Separation System,[2] and contrasts it to the Fear System (Francesetti et al., 2020).

4.  Francesetti stressed that with fear and anxiety there are increased levels of cortisol and adrenaline, but this is not the case with panic. Panic and anxiety respond to different drug therapies as well. And unlike anxiety, panic is initiated by an "attack of solitude," not fear (2018, 2020).

As I was listening to Francesetti's lecture, the story of the taxi came to mind and I realized that I had skipped right over the moment of the crack, that moment between *the familiar now* and *the surprising next*. I had named the desire that preceded it, and had worked with the shame part of the experience that followed it. But, I had ignored the actual "crack."

Until now, I had explained the lingering sense of unsettledness I experienced that night with the simple fact that the body can take a long while to calm down. I'd been blindsided and suffered a big shame hit, and it often takes hours or even days to settle and to trust it is safe again after we are shaken in this way. Understanding panic in the way Francesetti described it caused me to wonder if the reason my body wouldn't settle was that there was something hiding in the "crack" that had not yet been heard. I began to reconsider the taxi incident. Could it have been a panic attack?

I could see my experience as panic, but I could also see it as shame. It met the criteria for panic, but it was also certainly a shame response. So was it one? Or both? Or does it matter? Is there something that links shame and panic?

## What Is that "Crack"?

My curiosity goes to the moment of the shift—the "crack." Shame, when it comes in a flash, and panic are related in that they have the moment of the crack or shift in the continuity of experience in common. The *what-just-happened?* or the *oh-no-not-this-again* feeling rises after the "crack." The "crack" itself is often experienced as a flash of dissociation—a quick skipping over of that need we have not yet been able to know. The "crack" tells us of the interrupted figures, of the "silenced and forgotten calls," the existential angst. And it tells us that they are current, they are manifesting now. When the "crack" between worlds opens, and on the other side we find ourselves in panic or shame, we can surmise that there is something in that crack we learned to fear. The "crack" announces what has so far been interrupted and so, has not yet been adequately met, nor named, nor held.[3]

In the cab that night the world fell away—it was just me—suspended—nowhere to land. And later, even though I was with my friend, there was a way I couldn't touch her, a way that I was not reachable either. The experience was one of utter *aloneness* as distinct from loneliness. In loneliness I sense longing—I know what is missing (Jacobs, 2020). In profound aloneness, the world of people is already gone. I have no thought of reaching out—there is no point—there is no one there. The fear comes after the utter aloneness hits (Francesetti, 2018, 2020). Perhaps after that moment of shift, whether the dysregulation takes the shape of panic and fear of craziness or physical death, or it takes the shape of shame and one's own unworthiness, has to do with enduring relational themes (Jacobs, 2017b) and the habitual ways we make meaning. At root, both shame and panic and that moment of shift have to do with the lack of connection and support, the lack of welcome and fit between me and my world.

Certain lenses help me edge closer to understanding it: Lynne Jacobs talks about "a traumatized state of mind" (lecture, 2007) we can experience, and which aptly describes the agitation we find ourselves in as we navigate this after-the-"crack" world. In a "traumatized state of mind" (TSM) we are in a state that is distinct from our more typical competent way of functioning. And, when we are in a calm and more competent state we can recognize the TSM as a "trauma pocket," as distinct from who we are and how the world is. But, when inside of a TSM our competent self seems like a fraud, and the world is seen as inhospitable both now and forevermore. Some of the ways we can recognize we are in a TSM is by noting the changes in time, possibility, and complexity. In a TSM time is sped up and we feel our survival is at risk—things feel dire and like we had better act NOW to save ourselves; but time also feels paused and the current state is felt to be without movement, and it feels eternal. "Complexity collapses" such that nuance, gray areas, or degrees of good or bad cease to register with us (2007). We can very clearly see everything that is bad. And we can see that good, if it ever really existed, has evaporated. Thus, good outcomes are impossible to imagine. It is hopeless. Optimism seems naïve at best, and at worst it seems idiotic, irrational, or dangerous.

The body tightness we experience in the moment of the "crack" can be intense. When our needs are ignored or worse, rejected, we experience a "no" from our world. Most people sense their body tighten when they hear a "no."[4] Whether the "no" to our needs is said aloud, or with a look, or is just anticipated—our needs are "delegitimated" (Francesetti, 2018) and we tend to tighten muscularly to withstand the "disharmony" or shift in contact that accompanies this rejection. This type of "no" activates the threat defense system (aka fight, flight, freeze, faint) in the body (Siegel & Bryson, 2018, pp. 3–4).

Polyvagal theory provides a way to understand the suddenness and intensity of the physiological state change we experience in a "crack." With this lens, a sense of safety is the primary ingredient for a smooth "crack-free" flow from one moment to the next. As we sense danger, we move from a calm state to fight or flight and, if the danger persists to a "life-threat" level, we can move to freeze or faint. At any time when safety is perceived, our bodies will begin to down-regulate back into a calm and connected state. "Polyvagal Theory leads to an understanding that to connect and co-regulate with others is our biological imperative. We experience this imperative as an inherent quest for safety that can only be reached through successful social relationships in which we co-regulate our behavior and physiology" (Porges, 2017, p. 51). This system is not voluntary—it is ongoing and operates below our conscious awareness via neuroception:

> We need to distinguish 'neuroception' from 'perception.' Neuroception evaluates risk in the environment without awareness. Perception implies awareness and conscious detection. Neuroception is not a conscious process; it is a neural process without a dependency on awareness. Neuroception is dependent on a circuit that evaluates risk in the environment from a variety of cues and triggers and shifts in autonomic state to adaptively deal with the cues. Within Polyvagal Theory, neuroception was postulated as a mechanism to shift the autonomic nervous system into three broad states defined by the Polyvagal Theory (i.e., safety, danger, life threat) and to emphasize the potent role of the mammalian social engagement system, including the face, heart, and myelinated vagus, in down-regulating both fight/flight and shutdown defense systems.
>
> (Porges, 2017, p. 68)

Another crucial lens is that of implicit memory. Like neuroception, implicit memory operates outside of our awareness. "The kind of memory that enables us to ride [a] bike is called *implicit memory*; our ability to recall the day we learned to ride is *explicit memory*" (Siegel, 2010, p. 148). Explicit memory *feels* like a memory in that it comes with a time and a place (or at least hints of these.) In contrast, implicit memory *feels* like it is born of the current situation only—people often mistake implicit memory for intuition (Siegel, 2010, p. 151).

Examples can help us understand how implicit memory can inform our reactions. Sonia's older brother died in a bicycle accident when they were teens. Many years later, Sonia's toddler son was riding a tricycle (very safely) on their enclosed patio. Sonia felt terrified. She *felt sure* her son could be badly hurt if he wasn't very careful! Her husband was confused and annoyed by the intensity of her reaction. Sonia herself loved bike riding and was excited to teach her son to ride. But, seeing *a boy she loved on a bike* triggered her. Another example, I worked with a teen boy with severe Trypanophobia (e.g., fear of needles) who needed a medical intervention that required weekly blood tests. As we worked, it became clear that he was particularly terrified of the moment the needle would be withdrawn. During one session an old memory arose: he was six years old and had an enormous splinter in his toe. It was so big his parents took him to the doctor to have it removed. He shook as he spoke of the moment his pediatrician pulled it out. This "forgotten" splinter memory seemed to be implicitly informing his reaction to needles now. And, Siegel writes that the expectations created by implicit memory, "...when isolated and unintegrated might be the neural foundations for the mental suffering of PTSD" (Siegel, 2017, p. 173).

Implicit memories can be triggered when a current situation has thematic or situational similarities or resonances to a past experience that has not been fully integrated (Siegel & Hartzell, 2013, pp. 15–18). The intense reactions and dysregulation of "crack" experiences are often fueled by implicit memories.

There is a therapeutic reason we tend not to spend time dealing directly with the "crack" in worlds—at least at first. We need to help the patient (or ourselves) settle, to recover our sense of being safe—or at least safe-enough before we can go back and revisit that moment. The "crack" occurred that night in the taxi because I was "acting" braver than I was. There was a desire/danger bind[5] operating outside my awareness—my vulnerability and my need for support were secrets I was still keeping from myself. They burst forth as a "crack" and quickly took the shape of a shame attack. I am reminded of the way psychosomatic symptoms (such as migraine) can rush in to prevent us from facing a difficult emotion (such as anger with my scary father). Through bodily sensation, being jarred this way jerks us right past a need we learned to fear and not recognize as our own (Sarno, 1991, pp. 47–50, 144–145; Francesetti, 2020, p. 80). But, not dealing with the "crack" is a missed therapeutic opportunity, and it is necessary to go back to it if one is to learn to ride these "crack" experiences with greater resilience and less suffering.

I have known the term "existential angst" and I grasp its meaning and have a certain respect for it. But, fear of death and fear of utter and everlasting aloneness are much more terrifying when they are experienced in the body than the names and definitions we use for them can convey. In a "crack" experience, the terror of desire need bursts forth for such a brief moment, and then leaves so much for us to deal with in its wake, that it risks going unheard again. It wasn't until I had in hand the lenses I discussed above (i.e., of shame, panic, and the "crack") that I could then go back to that moment in the taxi when the world came apart and could really see and feel it. I needed to be bolstered before I could go further. I also needed my therapist. I needed her assurance that we could find our way back from the edge before I would get close to it.

## How Common Are the "Cracks"?

That taxi incident stands out as an extreme version of this sort of body hit when something shifts. But, but this "crack" between worlds is not uncommon, and it is not an experience that is linked only to shame and panic. I experienced the "crack" as an actual jolt in my torso—as if I had been shoved—but I think everyone has known the clunk in one's chest or stomach as some new fact lands and changes the world. A typical day may contain many small moments when our bodies register the degree to which our expectations are exceeded or dashed. I offer a few examples: years after graduating, Ben got an email from a college friend he'd secretly loved. As the content of her email *hit,* his heart swelled and he couldn't stop smiling; Daphne's long-time boyfriend told her he'd decided to move apartments without discussing it with her first. She had assumed she'd be consulted in a decision like that—she felt *dropped,* confused, and angry; Mary's routine medical procedure revealed an aggressive cancer that required immediate treatment. Her body *seized up* at the news and she floated through the rest of the appointment. We can also experience this in rarer circumstances and maybe more subtle knocks in the body. For example, this occurs when we slip in or out of an I-Thou experience[6]; and also when we slip into the easeful bliss of total belonging and interconnection that can happen during a good psychedelic trip or a satori experience.

What has been interesting to me most recently is the literalness with which the body registers these shifts in continuity. In the spring of 2020, as the pandemic was surging and George Floyd's murder was inspiring protests, several patients reported feeling discomfort in their bodies that they didn't recognize, or like. They described feeling unmoored and uneasy. With different people it had to do with a job loss and needing work, with how to be more politically active, with how to talk to relatives they didn't agree with, or with how to reconcile their own guilt about not having seen their part in racial and power dynamics sooner. It was very physical for them. To many, it felt like the old reality and the unknown new realities were jostling against each other and not finding an easy fit—the realities were un-align-able, and their unsettled bodies were telling the story of making the trip back and forth between different versions of the world and finding no place to rest. They were right. They were facing, many for the first time, the limits of their ability to make a plan and see it through, or to figure out a problem and take care of it. The world was fresh again, and they were not used to it, and were not yet finding their way in it.

I had a recent experience with a therapist friend that highlights how important it can be to stay with unsettledness. My friend, Lauren, was describing the impact a sudden shift in her mother's behavior had on her. In a moment, Lauren's mother moved from being able to see Lauren's side of a disagreement with her sister, to blaming Lauren for her sister's outrageous behavior. Lauren's mother had done this to her for all of Lauren's life. The mother was afraid to hold her other daughter responsible—so she always turned her anger on Lauren.

As familiar as it was for this to happen—it always landed with a jolt inside Lauren's body, and her habitual reaction was anger and intensely hurt feelings. Sometimes Lauren would protest, and other times she would burn with silent fury. This time though, as the shift in reality registered in Lauren's body, she paid close attention to its impact on her. She said the most striking aspect was that right after she lost her mother's understanding and trust "I felt so *unbalanced,* so *destabilized."* Lauren's equilibrium and poise evaporated, and her body wouldn't settle. Once Lauren was away from her mother she said it took her more than an hour to calm down and feel like herself again.

Lauren and I took a moment with this detail. I rocked as if jolted in my own body to feel into what she was saying. And as I did, it registered that this feeling of being destabilized was exactly right! It was accurate. Lauren's body was telling her, and me, about the impact it sustained when her mother changed the rules and the two realities were being straddled simultaneously and were at that moment, un-integrate-able. This was a life-long pattern between them, and our bodies responded to that sudden shift and the reverberations of it as Lauren told the story.

The being-unmoored motion Lauren and I shared told us of the experience of dissonance, which is the disharmony Robine (2013) mentions. The jolt and ongoing feeling of being destabilized was the truth about the experience of the impossibility of reconciling the understanding-mother of a moment ago with the blaming-mother now. Lauren's body was showing her what it was like to meet this sudden shift in her mother, and as we held it together she experienced a deep grief for this state of things and for how long it had been going on—and then a rush of gratitude for how strong she'd been all her life.

## Being with the "Crack" or "Hello, Crack"

After seeing it all this way, I have an easier time going back to the "crack." The image I have is of me and my therapist sitting on a bench together looking back toward that "crack" moment we have been discussing. I have recovered my calm. I am not afraid anymore of the shame and the panic I encountered. They are here as potentials, but they are not presently active or scary. I am, in this after-the-fact period, able to be interested in the "crack."

My therapist and I get up and walk back toward it. I can faintly hear the howl of terror that resides deep inside of it and gets louder as we approach. Fortified as I am by her presence and my growing understanding, I get on my knees as we move closer, and then down onto my belly as I inch up so my fingers can grasp the edge and my eyes can peer into the gaping darkness. The terror of utter and eternal isolation rushes up and engulfs me. Existential dread resides here, and so do the still howling cries that went unvoiced and unheld after the sudden death of my mother when I was a child. This terror is what grabs me in a "crack": the thing I fear most is that I am all alone and that no one will ever reach for me and pull me close. It was like that back then, but *this is not that*. *This* (i.e., longing for love at almost 60 years old) is not *that* (i.e., devastating loss in a family that eschewed grief). And, I am no longer nine years old. *This is not that.* The old and the current cries can be met and held and spoken of with my therapist at my side—we can be with them. When we are ready to leave, we scooch a few feet back before we stand up—the edge is still a scary place.

Understanding the "crack in the continuity of experience" is serving me well in this time of pandemic and so much unrelenting uncertainty. I have a reverence for the power and the terror in the crack between realities, and I recognize the terrain better than ever before. It starts with that jolt, that "crack" in the familiar world that throws us off balance and won't resolve easily. It is our body pointing us to the as-yet-unknown-ness of it all. The deepest desires—that it will be different this time—have gone out of our awareness and been forgotten. But they endure. If we can be interested in what we find here, we can tend to it and hold it. "It doesn't need to be healed, it needs to be held" (Foster, 2015) and named. And, when we can link it to our early wounds this can help us make sense of the enormity of our reaction. Usually, *this* is not *that*—it is scary but not dangerous. Usually, it is just what still needs to be recognized and welcomed "cracking" the world again. And the jolt in our chests is simply the feeling we get when it breaks through…

Hello, Crack.

## Notes

1 Francesetti, G. (2018). I have borrowed this evocative phrase from Dr. Gianni Francesetti, to whom I am indebted for having introduced me to a number of the ideas I explore in this essay.
2 Panksepp also refers to it as "PANIC (aka separation distress)" (2018, p. 7). I like this phrasing as well because it so strongly emphasizes the irreducibility of the relational nature of panic.
3 In a recent paper, Francesetti et al. write that Panic Disorder sufferers can "mentalize fear—to recognize and express it—but they are not able to mentalize the bodily signals indicating the lack of affective mediation in a situation of overexposure" (2020, p. 79). In other words, their relational needs do not register as such, and so are not discernable.

4 In a parenting workshop Dan Siegel asked participants to notice the impact of the word "no" as it was said 10 times or so. Most participants reported the "no" felt like a hit—they felt either reactive or shut-down by it. Then the word "yes" was repeated several times. "Yes" supported participants to feel more open and connected. Siegel and a co-author have since published a parenting book called *The Yes Brain* (Siegel & Bryson, 2019) that builds upon this idea.
5 A play on Yontef's "shame-guilt bind" (1993, pp. 498–499).
6 Martin Buber's term for a momentary encounter between people that is free of (I-It) objectification and constitutes a moment of unreserved engagement that touches "the essential being of both persons" (Hycner & Jacobs, 1995, p. 55).

## References

Brach, T. (2004). *Radical acceptance: Embracing your life with the heart of a Buddha*. Bantam.

Davis, K. L. & Panksepp, J. (2018). *The emotional foundations of personality: A neurobiological and evolutionary approach*. WW Norton & Company.

Foster, J. (2012). *From "De-pressed" to "Deep Rest": Depression as a Call to Spiritual Awakening?* https://www.youtube.com/watch?v=KPx0nN6aQj0

Foster, J. (2015). *Why haven't I healed or awakened yet?* https://www.youtube.com/channel/UC-kdgLYeqJyxR3eRHcKfK8A

Francesetti, G. (2018, Oct. 26–28). *Panic, Panic Disorder, and Anxiety* [Training Program 1, 2nd Seminar.] Gestalt Therapy and Phenomenological Approach to Psychopathology and Clinical Practice, Instituto Internazionale di Psicopatologia e Psicoterapia della Gestalt, Torino, Italy.

Francesetti, G., Alcaro, A. & Settanni, M. (2020). Panic disorder: attack of fear or acute attack of solitude? Convergences between affective neuroscience and phenomenological-Gestalt perspective. *Research in Psychotherapy: Psychopathology, Process, and Outcome, 23*(1), 87–101.

Germer, C. & Simon, T. (n.d.) *Chris Germer: The Power of Self-compassion*. Sounds True. https://www.resources.soundstrue.com/transcript/chris-germer-the-power-of-self-compassion/

Hycner, R. & Jacobs, L. (1995). *The healing relationship in Gestalt therapy: A dialogic/self psychology approach*. Gestalt Journal Press.

Jacobs, L. (2007, Jan. 13) *Traumatized States of Mind/Being* [Weekend Training.] Pacific Gestalt Institute, Los Angeles, California, USA.

Jacobs, L. (2017a). On dignity, a sense of dignity, and inspirational shame. *Psychoanalytic Inquiry, 37*(6), 380–394.

Jacobs, L. (2017b). Hopes, fears and enduring relational themes. *British Gestalt Journal, 26*(1), 7–16.

Jacobs, L. (2020, January 12). Personal communication.

LaPierre, A. (2018, January 12–14). NeuroAffective Touch Foundational Training [Training Program Module 1 of 5.] Los Angeles, California. https://neuroaffectivetouch.com/.

Lee, R. G. (2004). *The values of connection: A relational approach to ethics*. (pp. 163–171). GestaltPress.

Lee, R. G. & Wheeler, G. (Eds.). (2003). *The voice of shame: Silence and connection in psychotherapy*. GestaltPress.

Porges, S. W. (2017). *The pocket guide to the polyvagal theory: The transformative power of feeling safe.* WW Norton & Co.

Porges, S. W. (2018). Therapeutic Presence and Polyvagal Theory: Principles and Practices for cultivating Effective Therapeutic Relationships. In Porges, S. W. & Dana, D. A. (2018). *Clinical Applications of the Polyvagal Theory: The Emergence of Polyvagal-Informed Therapies (Norton Series on Interpersonal Neurobiology).* WW Norton & Company.

Robine, J. M. (2013). Shame. In Francesetti, G., Gecele, M., & Roubal, J. (Eds.), *Gestalt Therapy in Clinical Practice: From Psychopathology to the Aesthetics of Contact.* FrancoAngeli.

Robine, J. M. (2019, Oct. 16–18). *Narcissism and Shame* [Training Program 1, 4th Seminar.] Gestalt Therapy and Phenomenological Approach to Psychopathology and Clinical Practice, Instituto Internazionale di Psicopatologia e Psicoterapia della Gestalt, Torino, Italy.

Sarno, J. E. (1991). *Healing back pain: The mind-body connection.* Warner Books.

Siegel, D. J. (2010). *Mindsight: The new science of personal transformation.* Bantam.

Siegel, D. J. & Bryson, T. P. (2018). *The yes brain: How to cultivate courage, curiosity, and resilience in your child.* Bantam.

Siegel, D.J. (2017). *Mind: A journey to the heart of being human.* New York, NY: W. W. Norton & Company.

Siegel, D. J. & Hartzell, M. (2013). *Parenting from the inside out: How a deeper self-understanding can help you raise children who thrive.* Penguin.

Wheeler, G. (2000). *Beyond individualism: Toward a new understanding of self, relationship, and experience.* (pp. 5–11). GICPress.

Yontef, G. M. (1993). *Awareness, dialogue & process: Essays on Gestalt therapy.* The Gestalt Journal Press, Inc.

# Chapter 10

# What My Client Taught Me about Dialogic Presence: A Case Study of Client and Therapist in Relational Gestalt Therapy

*Armin Baier*

For a residential Gestalt therapy training program in the Spring of 2019,[1] the faculty theory presenters were asked to address the following topic: what has changed for you over the years since you've applied Gestalt therapy theory to your practice of psychotherapy and, especially, how do you apply the principles and developments of our theory, consistent with your style, in the clinical situation? I delivered a version of this piece then. As I write this down now, it will be over 40 years since I first encountered Gestalt therapy. I have to say I almost wouldn't recognize what I do now compared to what I thought I was doing back then.

But let me start by saying that I didn't begin by being a student of psychology or studying Gestalt therapy or Gestalt therapy theory at first. When I was in college I was deep into the process of coming out as a gay man, which probably sounds like I was out there experimenting sexually, when in fact what I was doing was withdrawing more and more from the world I knew with no expectation of how I was going to emerge from that. And in my junior year at school, I went to the counseling unit and tried to get some help. It wasn't until my senior year I was actually able to be assigned an individual therapist, a doctoral student/therapist. I have no idea what kind of therapy theory the therapist thought he was applying. I have to say in retrospect I think he knew nothing about being gay and nothing about the coming out process. To be fair, this was 1974 and it wasn't so much in the literature back then. But we struggled through the fall semester and at the end he said that he and his supervisor had decided I needed to have a family session. In good faith, I got my family to come with me during the Christmas break and we met with my therapist while his supervisor sat silently in the corner in the dark for the whole session. It was a bit traumatic for my family, with the therapist insisting that my father surely must have had an affair with someone in his office and the whole family forced to talk about this since that would not have been the kind of thing my family would ever talk about, even if it had been true. I think, when we left, we were all just relieved to have survived it; my family politely never mentioned it again. But when I returned to my next individual session with my therapist, he

DOI: 10.4324/9781003255772-13

announced to me that he had decided, with his supervisor, that he would not continue therapy with me. The reason he gave was my failure to come out to my family during that family session, which was something he and I had never even discussed before that moment. I was carrying so much shame at that point in my life and had so few supports that I didn't even know to object. I simply said goodbye, got up, and walked out the door. Although I considered suicide very seriously, I was able to back away from that and moved forward with my life, very slowly finding some supports and, after a time, some impulse to be open about my sexual orientation.

All this is really just to say that I had a great distrust of psychotherapists when I was referred to a Gestalt therapy intern five years later and suffering from depression and despair. I had attended law school in New York City and was starting to work as a lawyer and was very unhappy. I have only limited memory of what took place in that therapy, but I know that my very heterosexual therapist approached me with evident caring, acceptance, and an experimental attitude. (That therapist was actually very talented and has gone on to be an influential teacher in an institute.) After one year, my therapist checked in with me again and asked what I might actually like to do for a career. It suddenly occurred to me: I wanted to do what he was doing. I started to volunteer as a peer counselor at Identity House, a gay and lesbian crisis counseling center. The brilliant thing was that it was led almost entirely by Gestalt therapists from the New York Institute for Gestalt Therapy. Every volunteer had weekly group supervision with an emphasis on Gestalt therapy principles. I began to understand just how radical Gestalt therapy was, that it was founded on a concept that human beings, when not inhibited in their meeting with and interacting with the world, could grow and self-regulate without reference to "mature" or "healthy" development. In an existential world view, we could distrust the cultural imperatives, like heterosexuality, in order to creatively adjust as our individual needs required. Clearly, I thought this was my story, and Gestalt therapy was a revolutionary, creative means of releasing others from the pain of self- and societal-repression. I loved the peer counseling volunteer work I was doing, and I signed up to take a theory class at the NY Institute with Dan Bloom. Dan was a lawyer-turned-social worker and thus a role model for me. The seminar read Perls, Hefferline and Goodman, *Gestalt Therapy, Excitement and Growth in the Human Personality* (1994/1951), just that, and Dan had a way of making it as thrilling as I believed it would be. At that time in New York, you could practice therapy without a degree and so anyone could study at the Institute and start doing therapy in a private practice. I went a step further and followed Dan's route, taking part-time classes to complete a Masters in Social Work at New York University as well, graduating five years later. In addition to Dan's theory class, I also participated in Practicum at the Institute led by another instructor, which meant that I was doing and watching lots of supervised therapy demonstrations.

When it came to actual work in therapy, what I learned from practicum and from observing therapists strongly emphasized the experimental, direct and active/embodied therapy interaction. The text by Perls, Hefferline, and Goodman actually has very little to say about what the therapist is supposed to be doing. Much of what I learned to do came from the half of the book called Mobilizing the Self, essentially a series of self-explored experiments in contacting. At one point the text does say, "Our view of the therapist is that he is similar to what the chemist calls catalyst, an ingredient that precipitates a reaction that might not otherwise occur ... It does not prescribe the form of the reaction. What it does is to start a process, and there are some processes which, when once started, are self-maintaining or autocatalytic.... What the doctor sets in motion, the patient continues on his own." (Perls et al., 1994/1951, p. 262.)

From this, I came to believe that my job as therapist was to facilitate the clients getting in touch with their own feelings through direct experience, usually aroused by an experiment I was designing or proposing. I thought that my presence was about my ideas for the client's self-exploration, I was to be a kind of expert on experiencing, more than a co-creator of any relational reality in the moment. This could at times prove very supportive of the client's work, and often a client was able to express a new awareness of self that was facilitated by my interventions. Although the paradoxical theory of change had been proposed by Arnold Beisser at least 13 years before, I certainly never heard of it nor had I understood the idea that I was not to be a change agent. I also didn't really develop a truly phenomenological approach. I don't remember the word phenomenology ever being mentioned at that time. As a consequence, I never had any consciousness that I was discovering something, only that my client was. Nor did I imagine that I was changed in any way by the encounter, although I did believe that I was "improved" as a therapist by the growing skill of working experientially and experimentally. In fact, I never thought about my being in the room as a person in an encounter at all. What I think was true of my work was that I was accepting of my clients and their circumstances without judgment, and I believe this more than anything kept my clients returning to sessions with me.

But this could result in very awkward and perhaps even deleterious encounters. At one period during a social work internship in an outpatient psychiatric program, I was assigned to work with a 19-year-old woman who had been discharged from the hospital following her first psychotic break. She presented to me with a flight into health, mostly out of touch with the psychotic episode that had led to her being admitted to the hospital and believing that there was no longer any problem. My attempt in our first session at an empty-chair experiment resulted in an immediate return to the psychotic thought process. It was brief, but I sensed that I was out of my depth.

Around the time of my graduation from my master's program and as I undertook to start a small private practice, I left off contact with my Gestalt elders and peers in the NY community. I stopped my therapy, my dear Practicum instructor died of HIV, and my brief experience of the insistence on "aggressive expression and contention" at NY Institute gatherings and a conference, as rich as that may have been for those more experienced, triggered my as yet unprocessed shame, and I disappeared for a long while into my work at a substance abuse treatment agency and into my clinical work. It was quite a loss, as I left just as a major revolution was occurring in the Gestalt therapy world and, I'm told, at the New York Institute itself. So, without guidance from teachers like Dan Bloom, and in my avoidance of supervision, it was left to my clients to teach me some truths about the therapeutic relationship.

In the absence of good, orderly direction from my teachers and peers, my conception of therapy, and Gestalt therapy, in particular, began to change when I found myself way out of my experience as I encountered clients with life problems that seemed or were out of control, especially severe addiction and, of course, those dying of AIDS. I remember one closeted gay man, quite sick with AIDS, who worked in a city hospital supply room. At the point that he became more ill and dealing with his likely death, he wanted above all else in our therapy to convince me how important comic book literature was to his life and sense of self. I had to stop, listen and learn. And another gay man, son of farmers who worked as a maître d' and who was an amazing storyteller. He was terrified of dying as his AIDS symptoms increased, and despite my deep misgivings, he insisted that I learn a form of hypnotic regression so that he could explore past lives in our sessions. I finally gave in and let him lead me. He was sure that this would help him come to terms with his own dying, and in fact, it did. He died in apparent contentment.

But the story I really need to tell you is about what Betsy[2] taught me.

Betsy was first referred to me around 1993 by a coworker. She was a 31-year-old Caucasian woman, married, no children, living in the suburbs north of New York City. She was employed as a mid-level manager for an insurance company, handling purchasing contracts, and she was the only female manager. The presenting problem and the reason she was referred to me was that she had recently accumulated so much credit card debt that it seemed the only way forward was for her and her husband to file for bankruptcy. This was causing deep distress for her and she was feeling a lot of anxiety and shame.

Betsy and her husband had been married for about eight years, and they lived in the converted garage apartment of her mother's two-story suburban home. Any dreams they had of moving out to their own home seemed to be destroyed by the debts she created and the bad credit rating they would receive in bankruptcy.

From the moment I met her, Betsy's tone was sarcastic, caustic, critical, and ridiculing. Her obvious skill with language was usually put to use in finding new ways to make fun of other people, which seemed to give her much pleasure. She was generally friendly with me and seemed quite willing in the therapy, yet at the same time, she regularly made personal jokes about me and often had to have the last, sarcastic word. Periodically her anxiety would become very acute during our sessions, and then she would address me with an intense look I took as a kind of pleading with me to help her find any way out of her distress. I did my best to be the experimental Gestalt therapist, working in the moment with her experience, proposing experiments to investigate her anxiety and her anger. She tolerated this from me, but mostly I think I was the first person from whom she had received this much serious attention.

She couldn't tell me much about her credit card spending, describing it only generally, as if it had happened almost outside of her awareness. There was nothing else about her that seemed dissociated, but I did wonder about that. I imagined that it was just too shameful for her to discuss in detail. Most of our early work focused on coming to terms with her financial reality and taking the necessary steps to filing bankruptcy. This work would alternate with sessions in which she spoke sarcastically and bitterly about the demeaning way she was treated by her boss at work and the ways in which he seemed to take out his anger on her with the assignments he gave her.

By the end of the first year of our working together, she and her husband had their hearing at the Bankruptcy court. Betsy had come to trust me at that point and as we were leading up to the hearing she asked me in an almost infantile voice if I would please be there and sit next to her during the hearing. I'm not exactly sure why I agreed, but I actually went up by train and attended with her through the ordeal. Somehow, I naively thought this would be the end of the therapy: I had no idea what was about to happen.

As we still focused on her anger at work in her attempts to be treated with greater respect, Betsy also began and became willing, to open up to me about her life and some aspects of her childhood. She told me, for example, that as a child and an adolescent, she had been raised in a church-going family and throughout her childhood, her father was a volunteer youth pastor for her church community. Her father had died when she was about 20 years old. At the same time, it had also come out that she had an intense hatred for her mother. Although she and her husband lived on her mother's property, Betsy had not spoken to her mother for years, left the property every day through a separate entrance, and avoided any possible contact with her mother at all costs.

Very slowly and gradually, pieces of her story were revealed. Why did she hate her mother so much? Because, she said, as long as she could remember her mother hated her. Betsy said she was told throughout her childhood that she was evil, ungrateful, undeserving, uncooperative, not worthy of her family. She had one sibling, her brother who was a couple of years younger than her, who was constantly treated as the golden child and frequently showered with gifts. Betsy's experience was the opposite. When her brother got five gifts at Christmas, she was given one. She said that when she was six years old, in fact, her mother drove home the point by giving her nothing for Christmas except actual lumps of charcoal. Around that time, her mother also refused to celebrate her birthday.

I was using most of what I knew about an active experimental Gestalt therapy to explore her feelings about the past and the present with her at this time. She was willing, but also very stuck, becoming suddenly blank at times or simply dissolving into tears, insisting that there must have been something about her that was hateful, otherwise why would her mother have treated her this way. I honestly didn't know enough then to identify this as toxic shame, but I also thought it was my job to stay with her at the edge of this mystery and hoped we'd get closer and closer to her own underlying truths. I used empty chair exercises regularly to attend to, heighten and support her investigation of her emotional experience. It seemed helpful in some ways as she became more trusting in talking about some of what she experienced and in owning her own self-hatred around these experiences.

One day about 2½ years into our work together, she revealed to me that she had been having increased suicidal thoughts for about a month and that, as we sat in that session, she could not assure me that she wasn't going to go home and attempt to kill herself. Under the circumstances, I told her that I had no choice but to call for an ambulance to take her to the emergency room. She was tearful and did not want to do this, but she spoke as if from the voice of very young girl and clearly did not feel safe outside of my presence. In the end, she agreed to go, provided I would also be at the emergency room with her. I wasn't able to go with her in the ambulance, but I went to the emergency room and when I identified myself, the staff allowed me to join her in a locked holding pen that was a significant feature of the psychiatric emergency room. Betsy was finally admitted to the hospital and then released again after 48 hours to the continued treatment of her outpatient psychiatrist and me.

When Betsy started back in my office again, she seemed committed to looking at her childhood with new determination. It was clear there were things she was not telling me about yet, but it was also clear that there were gaps in our understanding that were filled in by mystification and self-blame. Not too long after the suicidal emergency, Betsy reported to me a dream she had had of being an infant in a crib and being strangled by hands around her throat. We explored this together for an entire session, but the work only left her frustrated. One day she had a new idea. She had recently run into a very old friend of her mother who was very close to the family, almost like a cousin to her mother. Betsy set up an appointment to have coffee with her, and during that event, she asked the woman what had happened that caused her mother to dislike her so much? In answer to that, the woman was embarrassed but truthful. She said that when Betsy was born, her mother was so upset that she'd given birth to a female that for at least a month after the birth she desperately tried to give Betsy away to any member of the family or friends who would take her. Betsy and I spent a lot of time staying with this new knowledge. Nonetheless, Betsy refused to offer herself any slack, insisting that in fact, she must have been an evil child.

And where was her father in all of this? It was only at this point, years into our work together, that Betsy began to disclose perhaps her deepest secrets, things she'd only discussed with her husband. What came out, in pieces of information, was that her father had sexually abused her beginning at the age of three. At least that was the first memory she had of that experience. These were not isolated molestation events, but rather relatively frequent assaults, often connected to her church events, and lasting until she was about 12 years old, when at her insistence she spent time only with a female youth counselor at the church. Betsy revealed that she had attempted suicide swallowing pills first at the age of eight and then again at the age of eleven. On both occasions her parents discovered her in a drugged state, but they kept her from going to the hospital and severely punished her for her behavior. At the age of eight, after the first suicide attempt, she tried to tell her mother about what was going on with her dad, but her mother of course would hear none of it, saying only that Betsy was lying as usual.

I can't say that I was terribly skillful in working with trauma at that time but I'm pretty sure, looking back, that even though I was very inept in my attempts to explore this with Betsy, I was sensitive to her moments of childish affect, confusion, despair, and anger. I didn't quite know where to go with that, but I believed that if we stayed with her ambivalence and the confusion aroused by her self-blame, she would get past this. She developed so much faith in me as a therapist at this point that she was willing even to suffer with my probably clumsy and excessive experiments in contacting and awareness.

At the same time, I must admit that my "revolutionary" ideas about the power of Gestalt therapy led me to assume that Betsy's insistence that I believe that she was fundamentally at fault and unworthy was wrong, and that with adequate work on her "awareness," she would come to see her worth and her value, just as I already did. I was unwilling to include the validity of Betsy's experience of herself; I would not permit it to be true. I believe I may have even argued with her about it. Lynne Jacobs has said, albeit in a somewhat different context, that "[a therapeutic] exploration [of a different experience of truth] may continue, but it cannot be a dialogue once one person's experience has been treated as having less truth-value than another's" (Jacobs, 2012, p. 65).

Betsy may have trusted me, but she was no longer willing to let me stay securely behind my wall of "superior knowledge," my belief that I was more equipped than she to direct her out of the inescapable box she was living in.

To whatever extent she trusted me, she finally got to the point of forcing me to drop my mask and just be with her in all of her anguish. I don't exactly remember how it started but I know that at one point we were in the session and she refused to speak to me. Instead, she looked at me enraged, then turned away and refused to respond to anything I said. It was clear she was very very angry, and she had every right to be. Every few minutes I tried to reflect what I was seeing in her and ask what was going on, but she just continued to stonewall me. This went on for the entire session until I told her our time was up. At that point, she turned to me with the affect and voice of a five-year-old girl and said tearfully and simply, "Could I have a hug?" She stepped toward me and put her arms around me with her head on my chest. My arms went around her shoulders for a moment, and then she stepped back and with a sad smile said goodbye. I was left feeling very vulnerable, sad, and full of self-doubt. But maybe, I thought, it was a breakthrough we had been aiming for.

The following week she came back and repeated the entire experience again. This continued session after session after session. I tell people that it lasted for a year, but in fact, I really don't know. I know that it lasted months and months. In the beginning, I worried about what to do. How should we start the session? Should I begin by asking about her rage? I tried numerous things but nothing seemed to make a difference because she refused to speak to me until she asked for a hug at the end. The more I tried to be the therapist, the more I failed. I felt responsible and helpless. At first, I felt completely incompetent, disempowered, and even accused ... but of what? I also felt alone. In fact, I had no therapist, supervisor, or mentor for years already, and I don't think I would have shared this even if I did have one. I had been physically present for Betsy at bankruptcy court and in the emergency room, but now she was demanding that I be personally, humanly present with her, to share with her wordless anguish and vulnerability, to know the visceral truth of her degradation.

I'm not too proud to say that it took me quite a while to catch on. There was nothing for me to do. Or rather, I was forced to account for the fact that I was also in the room, with all of my feelings, opinions, misunderstandings, needs. Over time I began (I was forced?) to drop my mask and open to my own sorrow, shame, and anger. I began to feel less like a therapist and more like a fellow mourner. I became very sensitive to the nuances of her non-verbal expressions of rage. I spoke less and less, and I felt less responsible for saying anything. But I never lost the sense that she was demanding that I stay attuned with her on this, second to second. As long as I was not authentically present to our therapeutic meeting, as long as I left myself out of the equation, she could not feel fully seen and received.

In his essay, Healing Through Meeting, Martin Buber wrote of what it means for a psychotherapist to be present in a dialogic meeting with a patient (Buber, 1957). He says that "...In certain cases, a therapist is terrified by what he is doing because he begins to suspect that, at least in such cases, but finally, perhaps, in all [cases,] something entirely other [than his science and theory, skill and experience] are demanded of him ... What is demanded of him is that he ... himself step forth out of the role of professional superiority ... into the elementary situation between one who calls and one who is called. The abyss does not call to his confidently functioning security of action, but to the abyss, that is, to the self of the doctor, that selfhood that is hidden under the structures erected through training and practice, that is itself encompassed by chaos, itself familiar with demons, but is graced with the humble power of wrestling and overcoming, and is thus ready to wrestle and overcome ever anew ... [In this process,] the necessity of genuine personal meetings in the abyss of human existence between the one in need of help and the helper has been revealed [to the psychotherapist.]" (p. 94).

At this point in my work with Betsy, Lynne Jacobs had already published on the subject of dialogue in Gestalt therapy, and Gary Yontef's discussion of dialogic inclusion and presence in his essential text Awareness Dialogue and Process (Yontef, 1993) had already been disseminated, but I knew nothing of them.

Lynne Jacobs has written a number of times about the dialogic presence of the therapist (Jacobs, 2009). In a more clinically nuanced account of what Buber requires, Jacob defines presence as a therapist's willingness to be open to a kind of engagement in which the patient can touch the therapist's subjective experience, both directly and indirectly. "There often comes a time when the empathic inquiry into the patient's experience leads to an apprehension that the patient seeks to meet the therapist's 'otherness.' If the therapist does not recognize that her 'otherness' is central to the therapeutic process (that is, a central factor in promoting the self-development of the patient,) then she may miss the signals of the patient's interest in her subjectivity. She may also underestimate the place of her subjectivity in the process of exploration, preferring to think of exploring *only* when she believes her subjectivity is a hindrance to the patient's progress" (p. 145).

Gianni Francesetti, writing of the "side-effects" of the therapist working with a client with melancholic depression, describes the therapist as "being in a depressive field, where time stops, space dilates and no co-created figure emerges; where the abyss makes the other unreachable and the body becomes heavy and barren. Being in a depressive field means feeling its weight, its nothingness, the lack of any direction whatsoever, loneliness, fear and extreme helplessness. The therapist's sense of helplessness can lead to feelings of anger. That anger may take the shape of self-deprecation ... or of a loss of faith in one's training and profession ... All this, of course, needs to be channeled back into the relational field and used for therapy, in the awareness that these feelings are a way of being-with the other, and so in such a situation it is already a therapeutic act .... it is this way of being present in the relationship that constitutes the therapeutic act in such situations, as by not giving up hope of reaching the patient, the therapist remains (frustrated and patient) in a position to be reached ... this kind of presence is the fundamental therapeutic act" (Francessetti, 2015, pp. 154–155).

Betsy seemed to emerge from the months of silent rage and agony as subtly and unexpectedly as she had started. She was never the type to have a lengthy discussion about what had happened between us or what she had gained from the therapeutic experience. Our work together then began to delve deeply into the sadness that had enveloped her whole life narrative. But even as I continued to explore her awareness of this with the experiential methods in which I had been trained, I believe I was present in that dialog in a new way. Buber was quite accurate in terms of my experience, when he writes, "The psychotherapist ... will return from the crisis to his habitual method, but as a changed person in a changed situation" (Buber, 1957, p. 95).

Ironically, this new encounter with I-Thou meeting in therapy caused me to doubt if I was, in fact, a real Gestalt therapist anymore. Since I was so erroneously out of touch with the Gestalt world and the current ideas of people like Gary Yontef, Lynne Jacob, Dan Bloom, and many others, I assumed that this was some other therapeutic method that I had learned in the trenches. Or it was just a recognition that I wasn't able to be the all-capable Gestalt therapist I thought I was supposed to be.

Not too long after this, Betsy began to make huge steps to change her life. Most importantly, she convinced her husband that it was time to leave her mother behind and move out of her mother's house. Despite the bankruptcy, they were able to finance a condominium unit. Shortly after that, she became pregnant for the first time. Betsy tried to rekindle a relationship with her brother and his family, but he was not welcoming once she moved away from their mother, and Betsy mourned the loss of family. On her job, she began to act as a mentor to younger women who were coming into the agency. She became involved with her church, heading a committee on distributing aid to families in need, and with her husband doing marriage preparation counseling with engaged couples. We continued our sessions for years, as she was diagnosed with breast cancer, had surgery, recovered. Finally, we agreed to stop, her life being quite full with meaningful relationships and activity.

Years later, again, my husband got a job in Los Angeles and I moved here in 2009. One of my goals in moving was to reconnect to the study of Gestalt therapy. By luck, I was directed to the Pacific Gestalt Institute. And in my first weekend of training, a fellow student mentioned Buber and "inclusion" and I asked, "What does inclusion mean." Suddenly, I began to understand that there was a whole body of theoretical work that gives form to the experiences of therapy that my clients had been pushing me toward. It felt like a great pillow that I'd landed on, and I've spent the many years since then trying to catch up on the deep reservoir of thought and writing that has created the relational Gestalt therapy world we live in today.

## Notes

1 Pacific Gestalt Institute, Winter Residential Training, March 2019.
2 Names, places, and other significant identifying information have been changed.

## References

Buber, M. (1957). Healing Through Meeting. In *Pointing The Way*. (pp. 94–95). New York, NY: Harper & Brothers.

Francessetti, G. (2015). Some Gestalten of Depressive Experiences. In Francessetti, G., ed., *Absence is the Bridge Between Us, Gestalt Therapy Perspective on Depressive Experiences* (pp. 137–204). Siracusa, Italy: Istituto di Gestalt HCC Italy.

Jacobs, L. (2012). Critiquing projection: supporting dialogue in a post-Cartesian world. In Bar-Yoseph Levine, T., ed., *Gestalt Therapy, Advances in Theory and Practice* (pp. 59–69). New York, NY: Routledge.

Jacobs, L. (2009). Attunement and Optimal Responsiveness. In Jacobs, L. & Hycner, R., eds., *Relational Approaches in Gestalt Therapy* (pp. 131–170). Santa Cruz, CA: Gestalt Press.

Perl, F., Hefferline, R. & Goodman, P. (1994/1951). *Gestalt Therapy: Excitement and Growth in the Human Personality*. Gouldsboro, ME: The Gestalt Journal Press.

# Chapter 11

# On Regret: A Relational Gestalt Therapy Perspective

*Peter Cole and Daisy Reese*

## Origins of this Chapter

This chapter had its origins in a dream. We were lying in bed, and Daisy woke up with a dream about Patrice, a surgeon and old college friend of Daisy's who had drifted out of her life following a painful rupture in their relationship. Daisy had referred a friend, Charles, to Patrice for consultation on a medical condition. The resulting surgery that Patrice performed on Charles did not have a good outcome, and Charles ended up suing Patrice. Patrice was deeply shamed by the whole incident, and although Daisy had reached out on numerous occasions to Patrice in order to begin a process of repairing the rupture that had occurred between them, a once very close, intimate relationship had now become cold and distantly cordial.

> *In the dream, Patrice was homeless. She came up to Daisy asking for a handout. When Patrice recognized Daisy, she flew into a rage, telling Daisy that because of her, the medical board had taken away her license and had thrown her out onto the street.*

As Daisy shared the dream, tears flowed. She felt terrible about the part she had played in these events. What could she do now? She felt helpless, wishing she could get in a time machine and take back the fateful referral she had made of Charles to Patrice. It was impossible to undo the damage that had been done. Patrice's apparent shame and her distancing from Daisy was now well beyond Daisy's control.

We sat with the feelings of deep *regret* evoked by Daisy's dream and we began to muse on the feeling of *regret* itself. As experienced psychotherapists, Daisy and I have ways of understanding, framing, and working with other commonly experienced feelings such as shame, envy, grief, or anger. We have ways of understanding these experiences both for ourselves and for our clients. We had no corresponding way of understanding how to work with *regret* that would be a support to Daisy in sitting with these weighty feelings. And so, we resolved that for our own sakes and potentially to add

DOI: 10.4324/9781003255772-14

some thinking around this to the Gestalt literature, we would embark on writing this chapter in the pursuit of a deeper conception of how to think about, feel, understand and hold feelings of *regret* in our own lives and in the lives of our clients.

## Introduction

In our work with clients, particularly those who are in later life, issues of regret are frequently weighty, painful, and difficult to integrate. Many of our clients struggle to cope with the reverberations of choices made or not made, with the impact over time of aware and unaware ways of relating, with the effect that their blind spots have had on them and those around them, or with a myriad of other ways in which regret may have formed in their lives. Regret is a phenomenon that typically develops gradually. It forms just outside the awareness of our consciously lived lives. It is the accumulation of that which has not come to fruition, that which has been frustrated, forgotten, or neglected. Regret can be a heavy burden for our later life clients and for ourselves as clinicians.

In this chapter, we will explore how the relational Gestalt perspective can help in our work with our clients who are experiencing regret. Conversely, we will explore how psychotherapeutic work around issues of regret can help illuminate many of Gestalt therapy's relational concepts.

We see varying levels of suffering among our clients who struggle with regret. For many, regret is a secret weight that they carry, invisible to the outside world. For others, regret shows up in depressed mood and increased anxiety. For some, regrets do not impair their functioning. For others, regret is part of a cluster of difficulties such as low self-esteem and avoidance that can impair the individual's capacity for coping and adapting to life's challenges. Regret and shame often reinforce one another – causing increased isolation and depression. When regret is complicated with shame, it is not uncommon to observe a pervasive sense of self that is colored by feeling unacceptable or less worthy than other people.

In the case example below, we discuss Janet, a woman for whom regret did not overtly impair her high functioning life. Her regret was held deeply inside, causing a pervasive sense of disappointment and failure in her life and causing her to feel "less than" others. In opening up to dialogue and connection around her regret in the therapy, she experienced a significant measure of healing in her sense of disappointment and failure.

> Janet is a very talented and brilliant 55 year old psychologist who has been married for 17 years. Janet spent her 20s and early 30s working short term jobs, attending college on and off, dipping into a variety of progressive spiritual and political communities and being involved in a number of short-term relationships. With many unresolved issues from

her family of origin – she did not feel ready for a committed relationship until she was in her late 30s. She met her future life-partner, David, when she was 38. Janet was now settling into her chosen profession of clinical psychology and had become much more clear about what she wanted in life. David was eight years older than she, had a young son, Mark, and had recently emerged from a bruising divorce, in which child custody was hotly contested. Janet became aware over time of a deep desire to have a child. David however was quite negative about having another child. He was already overwhelmed with his current parenting responsibilities which included helping his son Mark deal with the divorce and helping Mark deal with his unstable and angry mother.

Janet lacked the confidence to advocate for having a child with David. She got deeply involved in helping David support Mark in the emotional chaos following David's divorce, and let her support for David and Mark supersede her own needs. She later came to understand that her fear of abandonment by David had outweighed her capacity to stand up for herself. Janet gave in to David's reluctance to have another child without a vigorous and sustained dialogue with him about her desire for a biological child that she and David could potentially have together. Janet did not fully appreciate the magnitude of this life-choice at the time, but over the years, her sense of grief, regret, loss and anger grew until it became the impetus to begin therapy with me (Peter).

In the therapy it soon became clear that although Janet had achieved much professional success, she was anguished by regret around not having had a child. She felt ashamed that her friends had children and that she did not. She felt *less-than* others, and felt like a fraud when working as a psychologist with her clients' parenting issues. She felt that no-one would take her seriously because of her childless status. She secretly felt that her life was a failure, because to her, motherhood was the most important thing.

In the early stages of therapy, Janet vacillated between anger at David and feeling disappointment in herself around not having insisted that she and David have a child together. She described her lack of a child as a dark, empty place in her soul. Much of the therapy with Janet consisted of "holding a container" for her by engaging in dialogue around grief and regret. I made no attempt to reframe her experiences or try to make "lemonade out of lemons." We learned together to tolerate the emptiness and loss that she felt. I shared with her that I too have experienced deep regret and loss in my life – and while I did not share the specifics of those experiences, I communicated to her that I could resonate with the pain and depth of her regret.

Although the weight of her regret (and what it evoked in me) felt like more than we could bear at times, I tried to support Janet in bringing her regret into cognitive, emotional and somatic awareness. The purpose of this was not to wallow in her regret, but to *be* with these feelings in the context of our relationship, so that we could hold the painful feelings together and with relational support.

It is not the case that Janet thought consciously about her regret constantly. Her regret was working in the background of her experience: shaping it and influencing her conscious experiences in ways that were out of her awareness. A sense of emptiness, resentment and failure in the background of her experience had become part of the *structured ground* that shaped her foreground experiences. The filter of her structured ground shaped her experiences in ways both subtle and overt. In her relationships with women who were mothers, she would frequently distance herself because of painful feelings of envy. In her relationship with her siblings, she felt "less than" because they all had children. In her relationship to her elderly parents, Janet felt less important than her siblings because she had not continued the bloodline. In her clinical psychology career, Janet often struggled with countertransference feelings of inadequacy when dealing with her patient's parental concerns.

Over time, Janet came to accept her grief and regret as part of the texture of her life. She gradually developed the capacity to symbolize her regret, and began to view the desire for a child in the broader context of needing a greater sense of generativity in her life. She began to feel that she could manifest generativity in part by nurturing relationships that gave her a sense of continuity and meaning. When held relationally, (that is to say that when Janet and I held her feelings of loss, grief and regret between the two of us in the therapy), those feelings seemed to become more manageable and to take up less of a central position in her emotional life. Janet developed a more resilient sense of self-acceptance and balance that became the structured ground from which the foreground experience of regret came into relief, thus transforming the experience of regret from one of shame-based self-deprecation to one of experiencing her pain and disappointment as just one part of the fullness of her humanity.

## Regret as Part of the Structured Ground of Our Lives

For some of our older clients, the lived life is haunted by what might have been. The phenomenon of regret is inextricably linked with the human experience of our forward and one-way movement through time and the choices we have made as we have moved through our lives. Each choice we make along the way precludes all other choices we might have made. And so, especially for some of our older clients, the life lived is shadowed by the life that might have been had they chosen differently in areas such as career, education, love, or the ways they have treated others.

Frequently, in our middle-aged and older clients, regrets become part of the structured ground of experience. As Gordon Wheeler explains in Gestalt Reconsidered, "the personal subjective past is part of the structured ground, which conditions the dynamic creation of the present figure"(p.76) (Wheeler, 1991). Similarly, Jean Marie Robine states "it is not so much the figure itself that holds our attention as the relationship that the figure has with the ground that constitutes it and supports it" (location 999 Kindle edition) (Robine, 2015; Wheeler, 1991). In developing an awareness of the structured ground, subtle changes begin to occur in our clients' foreground experiences. When regret plays a large part in organizing the structured ground of our clients' experiences, it can be healing and transformative for our clients to experience their regrets as a shared experience, held together with the therapist in acceptance and compassion.

## Creative Adjustments, Structured Ground, and Unaware Enactments

As Perls Hefferline and Goodman state "psychology is the study of creative adjustments" (p. 230) (Perls et al., 1994). "Correspondingly" the authors continue "abnormal psychology is the interruption, inhibition, or other accidents in the course of creative adjustment" (p. 231) (Perls et al., 1994). The creative adjustments we make in childhood become part of our structured ground in adulthood and deeply influence our perceptions and behavior. In the case study below, we look at Steve, a man whose regret centered around sexual activity that up-ended his marriage.

Steve is a client who grew up in a rigidly religious Mormon home. His father was a high-profile college president and his mother was far more attuned to the social requirements of her husband's career than she was to parenting her five children. A live-in Nanny sexually abused Steve for many years. No-one in the family knew about, or attended to Steve's distress. Steve was under great pressure to be the ideal Mormon son – a role he outwardly performed to perfection in terms of his academics, athletics and religious obligations. His creative adjustment was to be a high performer on the outside, while secretly he was suffering the effects of long-term sexual abuse. In adulthood, these creative adjustments shaped Steve's structured ground – in which he experienced life as split between meeting the demands of a high achieving, successful, Mormon man, while splitting off his sexual life and needs.

It will perhaps come as little surprise that in adulthood Steve enacted the split between his achieving self and sexual self. He married a "nice

LDS girl" with whom he had four children and developed a high-powered sales career. Meanwhile he engaged in a wide range of clandestine sexual activity. When his wife found out about his secret sexual life, the walls came crashing down on him. After much struggle to save the marriage, they divorced. Steve's children, having been raised with the same morally rigid code of behavior as he was raised in, condemned Steve for his "betrayal of the family."

It was during this period that Steve came into therapy with me (Peter). He was racked with regret and remorse over his sexual behavior and the rupture in his relationship with his wife and children. Over time Steve learned to connect the splitting off of his *sexual self* from his *high performing self* with the creative adjustments he had made in childhood. In connecting the dots between his creative adjustments of childhood and his adult enactments, his self-condemnation began to soften. The regret that had evoked intense shame and self-loathing, gradually evolved into a symbol of the pain and trauma that had occurred in childhood due to his experience of neglect and long-term sexual abuse, coupled with his family's demands for high performance perfectionism. Both he and I were able to hold these feelings with compassion and understanding. In working his way through the shame and regret, Steve was able to begin to repair his relationship with his children. Over time, they too softened in their hurt, anger and condemnation of Steve. His relationships with all of his children were now on a much different, more human, more complex and more honest footing.

In working with regret, we clinicians often encounter enactments like Steve's. Some are less dramatic than his, while others are more extreme. The creative adjustments of childhood will almost inevitably shape in one way or another the choices we make in early adulthood. Sometimes those choices work for the long term. Sometimes they do not. When they do not, regrets may begin to form. Not uncommonly, the accumulation of regret over these life choices brings the client into therapy. The so-called mid-life crisis that many people experience is often connected with this form of regret. The young adult response to the original childhood situation may have appeared to have solved the original problems, but since the choices were often re-active to the childhood situation, and not part of working through or healing of the childhood issues, the choices made will sometimes boomerang and lock the client into a new set of problems (which in many cases end up repeating the underlying dynamics implicit in the original situation). In some cases, the client's regret will signal the need to make significant changes in their life circumstances. In other cases, the client's regret will symbolize a movement toward acceptance and compassion for all parties concerned and no overt changes in the client's circumstances will be called for.

## Regret as *Signal* – Regret as *Symbol*

In my (Peter's) 1998 article, Affective Process in Psychotherapy (Cole, 1998), I discussed two distinct ways we can process our emotional responses. The first is to process the emotional response as a *signal* that something needs to change in our world. The second is to process the emotional response as a *symbol* of broader issues in our lives that call to us for further integration. For example, if a person feels regret about how they have hurt another in the past, that can be understood as a *signal* that they need to change their behavior in the future, or that they need to make amends with the person they have hurt. Another example would be the regret a person might feel for not having attained advanced formal education. Integrating this regret may be taken as a signal that they need to go out and pursue a higher academic degree. Regret as *signal* is a call to *action* – remorse or sadness about past choices stimulates the individual to make more fulfilling choices going forward.

On the other hand, when working with regret as *symbol* we are not looking to improve the situation in any significantly actionable way. Instead, the movement is toward acceptance, self-compassion and a sense of universality in that many people have regrets that cannot be "fixed." For example, suppose a client feels regret for having been hurtful to another person who has subsequently died. In any practicable way, it would be impossible for that client to make amends to the injured other. When processing this as a *symbol,* the regret of having hurt another can be utilized as a doorway into growth and integration. It might be that the injury inflicted on the other was in part, an enactment of the pain the client had experienced in their own childhood. For the client, accepting that she has enacted her own pain by inflicting it on others may be an important step in the development of self-compassion and integration. There is wisdom in understanding that not everything can be fixed or repaired in this life. There is poignancy and wisdom in recognizing that to be human is to sometimes injure and sometimes be injured. This is a part of our human condition that we must learn to live with.

When processing as a *symbol,* the regret of not having attained advanced formal education, a person might work toward *acceptance* of this circumstance. Further, the person might recognize, with self-compassion, that in earlier phases of their life, they had not received the interpersonal support or coalesced the self-support necessary for the successful pursuit of advanced education. Further work may involve moving toward acceptance of the qualities of achievement and satisfaction they have attained in their life and a general coming to terms with both the limitations and opportunities they have been able to avail themselves of.

Below, we explore the feeling of regret in the context of Gestalt therapy's Cycle of Experience (Zinker, 1977, 1980). We present two abbreviated cases.

In the first instance, we will examine how regret can be understood within the Cycle of Experience as a *signal* that calls forth practical, concrete actions that the person can take to make changes in their life. In the second instance, we will explore how regret can be understood as a *symbol* leading to wisdom, acceptance, and a poignant sense of life's mixed bag of satisfactions and disappointments; successes and failures; connections and disconnections.

### Regret as *Signal* in the Cycle of Experience: Moving Toward Action and Change

Mary is 36 years old with a PhD in English Literature who is employed in a low-paid, high-stress Adjunct Professor role.

1   **Sensation** – Mary feels the weight of regret somatically – it is like a weight on her chest. She is aware of feeling a chronic sense of depression and heaviness in her body.

2   **Awareness** – When held in awareness, Mary finds that the somatic feeling of weight in her chest is connected with the feeling of regret. Mary regrets that she has spent too much of her life mirroring her father who has a very romanticized idea of an academic life for her. She is aware that she feels under-appreciated and underpaid in her academic career. As she stays with the flow of feelings, Mary becomes increasingly aware that she feels dissatisfied and unhappy with her academic career. She begins to be aware of a budding passion for psychology and psychotherapy, and starts to imagine what it might be like to become a psychotherapist.

3   **Mobilization of Energy** – Mary begins to awaken to aliveness around embarking on a new direction on her career path. After having successfully completed the arduous journey of earning her PhD in literature, Mary had never considered returning to school for another degree. Now however, she feels new energy in entertaining the thought of changing careers and pursuing a professional psychology degree. The thought of making such a big change had previously felt utterly overwhelming and impossible, but now she feels new energy for it. At the same time, on another level, she experiences exhilaration about emerging from her life-long confluence with her father's expectations, and finding her own, authentic direction in life.

4   **Action** – Mary pursues a Master's program in psychology, taking a courageous turn toward a new career path. She does the hard work of organizing her time, energy, and finances around this choice. Juggling her marriage, newborn child, work, internship, and school is intense, but she has the energy and determination to make it all work.

5   **Contact** – She makes exciting new connections with peers and mentors on her new career path. She makes better contact with her father, having

achieved a new separateness from him. She finds her internships and the work of psychotherapy to be a good fit.

6   **Satisfaction/New Equilibrium** – Having mobilized the energy to make a huge change in her life and having embarked on a new direction in her career, Mary feels a sense of satisfaction with her choices and finds a new balance in her life. She now has momentum in her new career and looks to her future with a rich, fulfilling sense of being on the right path in her life.

## Regret as *Symbol* in the Cycle of Experience – Moving Toward Acceptance

Aaron is a 70-year-old retired attorney

1   **Sensation** – Aaron has a mild, vague headache and a sense of wanting to tear up and cry. He is aware of occasional bouts of despair that can feel intense emotionally and somatically.

2   **Awareness** – As he stays with the somatic sensations, he connects them with a feeling of regret. The regret is in relation to his law career. He is aware that his first choice would not have been to become a lawyer. Aaron's father and grandfather were both attorneys, but his passion had always been for music. Aaron also got in touch with anger around the physical abuse he suffered at the hands of his father. Furthermore, Aaron is aware that he spent most of his adult life living as a straight married man, when in truth, he is and always was gay. It was not until his mid-fifties that Aaron came out. He feels great regret for lost time in his work and life.

3   **Mobilization of Energy** – As Aaron stays with the regret, he is aware of holding a mixed bag of feelings. His legal career has provided a comfortable retirement, and for that, he is pleased. He now can focus on his music – which is also pleasing. At the same time, he grieves the many years he spent in legal work that he found "soul-sucking" as well as the loss of the many years he might have spent developing himself as a musician. He also grieves the many years he spent living in the closet and the loss of authenticity and love that he might have experienced all those years.

4   **Action** – In the therapy, Aaron is able to actively grieve his many years of less than fully authentic living. He is now able to cry, express anger at his (deceased) parents in the empty chair, and mourn the fact that it has taken many years for him to separate out his needs, desires, and aspirations from those he had introjected from his parents.

5   **Contact** – Together in therapy, we hold Aaron's regrets. He is able to cry about the many years he spent "in the wilderness." We lament together that he will never develop the level of skill he might have on his cello had he devoted his life to music. We grieve together for his many years of

desperation, loneliness, and low-grade suicidality as a closeted gay man living in a straight marriage. Together, we hold his many regrets, not trying to minimize or fix them.

6   **Satisfaction/New Equilibrium** – Before doing the work of grieving for his lost time, Aaron had been living in despair. Now he moves toward a sense of poignancy and acceptance, which gradually takes root as a new baseline affective state. As he works through the forces that shaped him, he comes to see his father as both an angry man who physically abused Aaron, and also as a wounded man who was himself in a great deal of psychic pain. Aaron worked toward developing compassion for his own younger self. He came to forgive the young man who made the choices he made – considering with self-compassion that his younger self had many fewer resources, less support, and far less knowledge of himself and of life than he now possesses in his later years.

Of course, in real life and real psychotherapy, modes of processing the experience of *regret* do not fit so neatly into categories of *Signal* or *Symbol*. There is usually a mix of the two, but in our experience, the work typically leans in one direction or the other. In the above examples, Mary worked with her regret symbolically as well as working with it as a signal to change her life. Examples of symbolizing include her finding universality in the experience of needing to separate and individuate from her father's expectations. She also experienced the *archetypal* nature of change by relating her long and difficult journey away from the expectations of her family of origin to those of mythical heroes and heroines of old such as Odysseus who left home in order to embark on his life's journey. She developed self-compassion in her acceptance that the choices she had made were the best she could do at that time in her development. Finally, she allowed us to hold the regret together, in the contact and container of the therapy relationship, thereby moving the regret out of the solitude of shame and into the intersubjective and compassionate space of the therapy relationship. With all of that said, the work leaned into the realm of action, signaled by her regret, whereby she took definite steps to change her life and career.

In the case of Aaron, where the emphasis was on the *symbolic* nature of working with his regret, there was much in the way of action that he did implement in his life, signaled by his grief and regret about the past. Aaron retired from his work in corporate law and spent a great deal of time listening to and writing about music. Although he had developed mild arthritis and was not able to actively return to the cello, he placed his love of music at the center of his life and joined a community chorus which he greatly enjoys. He also found a loving male partner and takes great joy in living as an open and proud gay man. While all of these changes were highly significant, they did not erase the grief and deep regret Aaron felt for his many years of living out of alignment with his true self. So, while our therapeutic emphasis was on working with the regret as *symbol* and coming to terms with the many lost years, the work of change in the present, signaled by the regret, was woven into the work.

## From Barrenness to Enrichment in the Structured Ground

It is the movement from a structured ground marked by shame and isolation to the enriched ground of connection and dialogue that forms the relational essence of healing the experience of oppressive regret. The relational work between therapist and client enriches the ground from which the client's foreground experience of regret becomes figural. Thus, there is an opportunity for regret to be transformed. The regret is no longer experienced as an over-simplified representation of the client's badness or failure, but as an experi-ence far more complex: symbolizing many things such as the client's hu-manness, grief, disappointment, life's limitations and it's poignancy.

When working with regret as *symbol*, awareness of the regret does not lead so much to action as it does to acceptance and integration. As such, our symbolic work with regret places emphasis on the relational dimensions of Gestalt therapy. Here, therapist and client are involved in holding the pain of regret *together*, thereby opening the *regret* up to a felt sense of greater spaciousness, compassion, and shared experience. Working with an em-phasis on holding the regret relationally, between therapist and client, can be particularly helpful when the client has been carrying their regret in secrecy and shame. The depression or despair that frequently accompanies such regret can begin to soften and lighten when held in the shared humanity of the therapy relationship.

The relational emphasis is on *connection* as opposed to fixing. Where there was once a shame-based and underdeveloped structured ground in which the foreground experience of regret became figural: now, with the support of the therapist, and in relational connection to the therapist, the foreground ex-perience of regret begins to shift as the structured ground becomes supported and enriched. *Shame* told the client that they were alone in the experiences they so deeply regret. *Shame* told them that they were *bad* for having had such experiences. A relational connection to the therapist helps to change the isolation and self-deprecation that colors the background the regret is held in. Now there begins to be room for a sense of *connection* – that the client is accompanied by another – the therapist – in the experience of regret. Let us bear in mind here that the therapist's role is primarily to *resonate* with the client – not to interpret, reassure or minimize the pain of the regret. Instead, the therapist (who hopefully has engaged in personal psychological work on their own regrets), is able to connect with the client in a sense of shared humanity around the experience of regret and its inevitability in our lives.

Furthermore, a sense of the archetypal begins to emerge in the therapeutic joining around regret. Here, we borrow from the timeless work of Carl Jung (1980), whose understanding that the pathways of human experience have been charted in works of mythology and literature that have emerged from the human imagination since the dawning of human consciousness up to the present day.

> A client recounts a story, held in deep regret, about a terrible rupture that occurred within his family: a rupture that he played a significant role in and was partly responsible for. We talk about the rupture within his family and his terrible regret about it for much of the therapeutic hour. I share with him that I too have experienced ruptures in my family that I deeply regret. Additionally, I ask if I can tell him a story, which he agrees to hear. It is from The Baghavad Gita. There is a war between two factions of a great family. Arjuna is a warrior in a chariot and is a member of the family at war with itself. He does not want to participate in the battle. He has no desire to be part of this rupture between two factions of his family. His chariot driver, Krishna, who is an incarnation of the divine, understands Arjuna's repulsion for the battle, yet instructs Arjuna to be "in it, but not of it". By this, Krishna means that Arjuna must fulfill his karmic role in this battle between family factions, but he can approach the situation without attachment to hate, and with an understanding that compassion and forgiveness are qualities he can bring to the battlefield.

This begins to introduce the *Archetypal* to my client's experience of regret. It is not meant as a morality tale or as a spiritual lesson, but as an enrichment of the structured ground. Now – he has two facets of an enriched ground that support the foreground experience of his regret. First, there is my presence and connection with him. Secondly, there is a story from humanity's collective imagination that may help enrich his experience, and help him see his regret in the light of being a part of the human family.

A sense of self-compassion and self-acceptance are qualities that often flow naturally from the experience of relational connecting with the therapist around issues of regret. Having opened up to connection and broken down the walls of shame that held the regret locked inside, my client begins to feel that his experience, while painful, is part of the broader human experience and in some larger way may be part of what makes him human and subject to those experiences common to the human condition. Bringing in the *archetypal* piece adds an imaginal element to this sense of connectedness. Not only is my client connected with others in his experience of regret, but he is also connected to the stories of collective imagination that capture the shared experiences of our human condition.

Relational Gestalt therapy provides a strong theoretical foundation for psychotherapy with people who suffer from debilitating or oppressive feelings of regret in their lives. Its foundations in dialogue, intersubjectivity, contact, presence, and the paradoxical theory of change all support an approach that seeks connection and integration of these feelings rather than an approach that interprets them, minimizes them, or seeks to replace or extinguish such feelings.

## Countertransference Considerations

Regret takes a toll on the client. At the same time, it can be almost equally painful for the therapist as the therapist sits with the client grieving over regrets. It can be painful for the therapist to sit with the client's deeply held regrets, especially when the therapist's own regrets may be triggered. Regrets that act as *signal* can be enlivening and satisfying to work with for both client and therapist. There is still something that can be done. Action can be taken. Problems can be at least ameliorated if not resolved. When regret is seen as *symbol*, however, the path is much less clear and much more strewn about with thorns. At this point, regret comes too late: such as the man who didn't visit his mother as she lay on her death bed or the alcoholic, now sober, who grieves over lost family and much harm done.

In these situations, there is little in the way of practical help that the therapist can offer. Sometimes things really cannot be fixed or relationships repaired. As therapists, our work is to sit with the client, keeping an open heart, and being present to the client's intense feelings of grief and regret. It is vital that the therapist not distance themselves. It can be quite a temptation to "make things right" by trying to help the client look at the reasons that the events in question were not too disastrous or to highlight ways that the client did the best they could at the time.

An inevitable aspect of being human is the experience of failure. At various points in our lives, each of us has fallen short and caused harm to ourselves and others. In the face of the regret that the client holds in connection to their failures, the central task of the therapist is to resonate with the client's feelings. Often the therapeutic task is not to sympathize or fix, but to resonate – in the same way that a guitar resonates when a string is plucked. Ideally, the therapist can let the client's regret enter into the therapist's own being, which in turn may stimulate reverberations of the therapist's own regrets. It is therefore vital that we therapists continue to work on ourselves including our regrets. If we can tolerate, and even welcome such feelings in our own lives, then we are much better equipped to be relationally present and resonant with the client's regrets.

## Conclusion

Working with regret often stirs up complex and painful feelings for therapist and client alike. Helping our clients move through the experience of regret requires both therapist self-awareness and an openness to resonate with the client's pain. The difficult truth is that there is no shortcut. Regret that is explored and grieved in the shared space of the therapeutic relationship creates a strong and steady ground from which the client may move forward in their life. Working with regret may catalyze important change in the client's life or it might lead to greater self-acceptance and an appreciation of the poignancy of our human condition from which none of us emerge unscathed. It is by facing and embracing the pain of our regrets that we become better able to integrate them into a rich and contactful life.

## References

Cole, P. (1998). Affective process in psychotherapy: A Gestalt therapist's view. *Gestalt Journal, 21*(1), 49–72.

Jung, C. G. (1980). *The Archetypes and the Collective Unconscious*. Princeton, NJ: Princeton University Press.

Perls, F., Hefferline, R. & Goodman P. (1994). *Gestalt Therapy: Excitement and Growth in the Human Personality*. London: Souvenir Press.

Robine, J.-M. (2015). *Social Change Begins with Two*. Siracusa, Italy: Istituto di Gestalt HCC Italy. Kindle Edition.

Wheeler, G. (1991). *Gestalt Reconsidered: A New Approach to Contact and Resistance*. NY: Gardner Press

Zinker, J. (1977). *Creative Process in Gestalt Therapy*. New York: Brunner/Mazel Publishers.

Zinker, J. (1980). The developmental process of a Gestalt therapy group. In B. Feder & R. Ronall (Eds.), *Beyond the Hot Seat: Gestalt Approaches to Group* (pp. 55–77). New York: Brunner-Mazel.

# Chapter 12

# The Encounter Process

*Bruce Aaron*

The therapy groups I run tend to be highly relational; we focus on the current interaction between group members. These communications sometimes get "thick" or "sticky," which is to say the meaning of the intended message isn't always explicitly transmitted. This lack of clarity isn't just on the part of the receiver. When the listener doesn't quite get what is being said, the speaker is often lacking a well-defined sense of what they are needing to get across.

I want to emphasize that rather than being an exception to the rule, I find that when it comes to communicating messages that have some charge – which might as easily be the result of feelings of intimacy as they are of aggression – vague statements, which require interpretation in order to make meaning of them, are extremely common.

Encounter is a specific process I offer clients to facilitate interactions that are not leading toward any satisfactory conclusion (Yalom, 1995). For someone well acquainted with the Encounter process, the method can be used in a wide variety of challenging interpersonal situations. My close friend and colleague, Marilyn, regularly encounters me when she feels uncomfortable about some aspect of our relationship. An example: many years back, Marilyn informed me that she had called and left messages on my answering machine three times, yet I had failed to return any of them. My immediate reaction was to deny this. "I don't ignore my voice mails! Certainly not those of a friend!" But as she continued her Encounter, I began to think about how I get when life's responsibilities start to overwhelm me. When I start to fear I'm reaching a breaking point, it is specifically those I feel closest to, who I let fall through the cracks. As she spoke, my defensiveness softened as I started to recall her calls, my good intentions to respond, and the pressure I was feeling to attend to other matters. I hadn't recognized that she had phoned so many times without getting a response from me.

When I hear a certain tone in Marilyn's voice and I well imagine she is angry with me, I tend to feel tight in my chest, queasy in my belly, and an impulse to defend myself. But when I hear the meanings that she has made of my behavior – "Bruce, when I leave you three voice messages you don't respond, I imagine that you don't want to spend time with me any longer

DOI: 10.4324/9781003255772-15

and that makes me sad and angry!" – I immediately understand her feelings and easily empathize with her plight. I see how my actions could give the impression that I am not interested in spending time together.

By couching her present feelings in the context of the meaning she is making of the data, what otherwise might have been a confusing or hostile exchange, became an opportunity for mutual understanding and reconnection. This outcome would have been unimaginable in the absence of the Encounter process.

Although it takes courage to initiate the discussion, Encounter rarely fails to make clear what was previously opaque. And once worked through, the door to connection has been opened. Aside from coming in handy in moments of interpersonal challenge, the Encounter format also informs my clinical work. Many of the interventions I make in my therapy groups are portions of Encounter statements:

- "Margaret, what are you feeling as you say that?"
- "The story I'm making up about that Andy is that you don't consider having that beer the other night as 'drinking again.' Is that right?"
- "Glenn, what do you imagine is happening for Kathryn as she speaks in that tone of voice?"
- "I imagine you're feeling pretty angry at me right now, Michael."

*The Little Prince* stated that "words are the source of misunderstanding" (de Saint-Exupéry, 1943). I find that the fewer words used to explain oneself, the clearer the message rests in the mind of both the speaker and those listening. Making a statement brief is inherent to the process of structuring Encounter statements.

The Encounter process not only enhances communication by helping the *listener* understand what is being said. More fundamentally, the exercise supports the *speaker* in becoming clear about their own process. This most significant benefit occurs through the internal work required of the speaker to construct their Encounter statement, by means of which the essence of their situation becomes crystalized.

Encounter process is a means whereby a speaker shares their experience in such a way that the listener learns precisely how the speaker is feeling (about them), how the speaker came to their experience, the perceptions/beliefs that support those feelings, and what action the speaker wishes to take.

-----------------------------------------------------------------------------------

## The Four Components of Encounter Statements

The raw structure of the Encounter Process is simple:

"When you ..." "I imagine..." "I feel..." and "I want to...."

When encountering another, the first step is for the speaker to identify the sensory data they assembled in order to arrive at their current experience. This is the only part of the statement that refers to the receiver of the statement in any way. All of the other portions of the process solely apply to the speaker. Thus, when utilizing this technique correctly it is not possible to project. This first part of the statement is purely objective. It does not contain words that allow for any interpretation whatsoever. Thus, for example, "When you look sad" would not be an appropriate initial statement, as it is a conclusion drawn by the observer. But a purely objective observation such as: "When your eyes are aimed at the ground and your mouth is turned down..." makes a great opening report.

Many people are under the naïve impression that they simply take in objective information and are unaware that they actually organize the sensory data they receive. Clients regularly need help distinguishing the conclusions they come to (e.g., "you look sad") from the sensory data they have taken in (e.g., "your mouth is turned down"). Discovering this crucial distinction often depends on a therapist's repeated interventions which support client learning to discriminate between objective information and the meaning they are making out of that data.

Before continuing I want to mention that although I am labeling these as first, second, third, and fourth steps, that is only for the purpose of explicating the format. In actual experience, the steps may arise in different orders. Someone may become aware of their feeling or an impulse to take some action and only later come to recognize what is evoking that response. The order does not matter. What does matter is that all pieces of the process are acknowledged.

The second step in encountering another is for the speaker to articulate the meaning they are making of the sensory data they have taken in. It thus commonly begins with either "I imagine...," "the meaning I make of that is...," "and the story I tell myself about that is..." or "my fantasy is...." Thus in the above example, the statement might continue: "When your eyes are aimed at the ground and your mouth is turned down I imagine you're feeling sad."

This is the pivotal step in the statement, around which the process crystalizes. In our work as Gestalt therapists, part of the ground out of which we work is how we value supporting client awareness of self and their environment (Jacobs, 2006; Perls, 1992). How often do we hear statements such as "You made me angry!"? There is very little self-awareness evidenced in that statement. Truth is, there is nothing anyone actually does which makes others angry. What is reacted to is the meaning made of others' behavior. The reason people regularly respond differently to the very same situation is that each person organizes and thus perceives the situation differently. In other words, each person tells themselves a different story about the situation. How we respond emotionally to anything is based not on the occurrence itself, but on the meaning we make of that occurrence.

So, when a client says that a fellow group member is making them angry, I invite them to consider what they are imagining their colleague is intending. By posing: "What is your fantasy about this person's behavior?" the client is invited to bring their own meaning-making process into awareness. Once people begin to notice how their cognitive filter is organizing their current perception, they start to view themselves as active participants, thus taking responsibility for their experience.

Especially when difficult feelings are stimulated, by couching situations in terms of meaning that is being made, the feelings that get evoked can often more easily be understood. Thus, although I initially stiffened when I heard the angry tone in my friend Marilyn's voice, once I understood that she believed that I no longer wanted to be her friend, it was easy to understand how hurt and angry she'd felt. Stating the meaning being made in a situation is a necessary element in both understanding oneself as well as helping others to understand. It is also the perfect set-up for the next step in the process.

The third step in the Encounter process is acknowledging the feeling evoked. I am using the term *feeling* in a very precise way. "I feel you're not really understanding what I'm trying to say" is not a feeling. That is my perception of you. If I don't think you get what I'm saying, I might feel frustrated, or disappointed, or perhaps even helpless. Those are feelings. Even the statement "I feel tricked" isn't really a feeling. It is a statement about how I imagine a situation was set up to fool me.

I am a real stickler when it comes to identifying feelings and I want to be clear why I believe this is so important. One way to view the Encounter process is as a tool to clarify the contact boundary. People who are unclear about what is theirs and what belongs to the other, have little chance of authentically being known or of knowing anyone else (Polster & Polster, 1973).

When someone articulates a feeling, they are describing something that pertains solely to themselves. I sometimes say that a feeling fits inside of one's skin. In the statement, "I feel trapped," the information is actually about the situation the speaker is finding themselves in but does not convey what they are feeling about being in that situation. A feeling is an experience occurring inside of a person. Someone who reports that they are trapped will likely feel afraid or frustrated yet may need some help differentiating the way they view their situation from the sensations or emotions that are aroused.

Of course, feelings may be evoked as a result of a situation in which they are finding themselves; in fact, it almost always is. But that's not the feeling. The feeling is the energetic experience that is stimulated as the result of undergoing their circumstances. By teaching our clients about feelings and helping them notice and articulate the feelings in a responsible and clear manner, we are helping them become more aware and more whole, in the Gestalt sense of the word, inasmuch as they can then take ownership of their experience.

There is a major clue to ensure that a stated feeling is a genuine feeling. First, a feeling is always one word. As soon as a client uses a second word, I remind them to find the one word that best describes the feeling. This is especially easy to spot when the word "that" follows "I feel...." Whatever words follow "I feel that," is a thought and thus belongs in the previous step, "I imagine...."

Now we come to the fourth and final step: "I want to...." This is a statement of what behavior the speaker wants to take, not what they want someone else to do. If I am angry at you, I might say that I want to tell you to stop doing whatever it is you've been doing that's been hurtful to me. This step gives voice to the speaker's impulse or intent to take action.

This too can be an important element in helping clients identify aspects of themselves of which they were previously unaware. Spelling out the action the speaker wishes to take can be helpful in many ways. It might indicate a solution or at least a means of dealing with the challenging situation currently being confronted. It might also instill hope that something can be affected. But I think, most importantly, articulating the behavior they want to engage in helps instill a sense of responsibility.

When I invite a group member to make an Encounter statement, usually one of three situations is occurring. Either the person being spoken to doesn't seem to understand what the speaker is attempting to convey, the speaker is producing lots of words without any clear message crystalizing, or both people seem to keep missing each other in the course of their back and forth. When communication feels unsatisfying to the involved parties, or to the onlookers, typically the speaker's awareness is somehow lacking. One way to enhance their clarity is to utilize Encounter.

Frequently, the speaker will say they don't know how to begin. I explain that it doesn't matter which of the four segments they start with. I encourage them to begin with whichever piece they are most in contact with at that moment. So if all they know is that they want to run out of the room and hide, that's the perfect place to start the Encounter. Of course, that would be a direct lead-in to whatever feeling is evoking the desire to flee. Once one part of the statement is out on the table, the next segment typically follows organically. In this manner, while the Encounter flows, the speaker's self-awareness grows.

The Encounter process can be an exciting and energizing experience for the speaker, the listener, as well as any onlookers. Watching someone crystalize what they have been frustratingly attempting to communicate is a most satisfying phenomenon to observe. Even though it can seem intimidating at times, group members gain the courage and inspiration to start using clear and direct language.

Initially, the speaker might be aware only that there is something on the person's face that they are reacting to. In that case, I would invite the speaker to make an objective and specific description of what they're noticing. If the statement produced is, "When you make that mean look" I stop the process. There is no objective "mean" look, I explain. I assist the speaker to describe in detail what visual information they are actually observing that creates the impression that the person is mean. They might need support detecting the specific visual and other sensory cues which lead them to conclude that the person "looks mean," but that's the work of this model. Especially when the format is new, people will often need assistance formulating their Encounter statements.

Each segment that gets articulated offers the possibility of a budding new awareness. "Oh, yeah. When you squint your eyes and your mouth puckers out like that I imagine you're angry with me... (pause) and that makes me frightened."

Not only does awareness grow as a result of utilizing the Encounter process, but so does a sense of responsibility (see Latner, 1973). Let's return for a moment to the second step in this process, the portion that starts "I imagine...." I have referred to this segment of the process as pivotal, in that it is an act of creativity on the part of the speaker. Two people who witness the same event will often generate different emotional reactions, as each organizes the observed data in their own characteristic way, that is, they each make-up different stories about the event's meaning. In the above example, the speaker believes the person they are speaking to is angry. But another person seeing the same person squint their eyes and purses their lips might imagine that the person is concentrating very hard which might lead to feeling grateful – very different from "frightened." But each feeling flows directly from the story that the speaker is telling themself about the meaning of the event they are witnessing. This creates a situation in which the statement "You're making me mad" cannot occur. Once the speaker articulates their process of meaning-making, the feelings that get evoked as well as the action they want to take are now their own. There's no room for "You made me scared" in this process, only, "When I imagine you are angry, I feel scared and want to run away." That's taking responsibility.

Another word about the final segment of the Encounter statement. By identifying what action they want to take, the speaker's sense of personal response-ability (Perls, 1969) increases. The clearer they become about the response they wish to take, the more able they are to respond to the situation. Defining the desired action literally instills a sense of responsibility. Thus clients own more of themselves, becoming more whole, aware, and responsible.

## Encounter and the Three Zones of Awareness

The vastness of the concept of awareness, which I define as noticing one's experience in the present moment, can be an overwhelming notion for a Gestalt newcomer to practice in their everyday life. One way to make the awareness training a bit easier is to break the practice down into zones. The three zones of awareness have been articulated in Gestalt therapy theory (Perls, 1969). They consist of an outer zone, which comprises anything one might notice in their external environment utilizing their five senses, an inner zone of sensations and emotions, and a middle zone which includes one's thoughts, images, judgments, plans, memories, expectations, etc. After working with the Encounter process for many years it dawned on me that as the speaker identifies the four components of their Encounter statement they have, likely without realizing it, given voice to all three zones of their awareness.

To offer an Encounter statement as an example: "When you lean your head forward and stare at me holding your mouth wide open, I tell myself that you're amazed at what I admitted, and I feel proud and want to puff my chest out." The opening phrase: "When you lean your head forward and stare at me holding your mouth wide open" consists of data that has been taken in via the observer's sense of sight. As such it takes place within the outer zone of awareness. The second phrase, "I tell myself that you're amazed at what I admitted" encapsulates the way the speaker has organized their visual input and made meaning out of it, and is thus middle zone awareness. The pride expressed is, of course, an inner zone awareness, as is the expression of their impulse to puff out their chest. I think one of the elements that can make the work of identifying Encounter statements so fulfilling is that it rounds out the speaker's awareness in a way that most of us would not typically bother to complete.

## Factors to Consider When Inviting Use of Encounter Statements (ES)

1   One-to-one

Encounter statements are made from one individual to another. Group members often want to make the Encounter statement to the entire group. While it may be true that they have similar feelings toward many group members, this is usually a way to diminish the intensity of affect they are concerned about having or showing. In addition, it seems nearly impossible that someone feels precisely the same way toward each group member. I usually invite the person doing the encounter to make the statement to one person. Once that is complete they can decide if they would like to encounter someone else in the group.

2   Present tense

Encounter statements are made using present tense verbs. Even though the incident that evoked this moment may have occurred in the past, at the moment of the encounter we want to invite in as much contact as the participants can tolerate. Bringing situations linguistically into the here and now, which is a staple of Gestalt therapy, is one means of moving clients toward the goal of lively contact.

3    Start where they're at

When beginning the Encounter process the speaker may not yet have in mind all of the four steps. In fact, that's how it is supposed to be. If they already know what they are going to say, their awareness is already intact. The purpose of making the statement, aside from letting the other person know what is getting evoked, is raising self-awareness, which is the basic principle of Gestalt therapy. Encourage the speaker to start with whichever step they are most in touch. Be ready to assist them as they work to supply the missing elements of the Encounter statement.

4    Only objective data can be used

Recall that the first section of the statement that begins "When you..." needs to be completely objective. "When you look ecstatic like that" is an interpretation and won't work here. Some people need a lot of support around using their visual and auditory senses to identify what they are actually seeing and hearing that gives them the impression they end up with. "What are you actually seeing or hearing that gives you the impression that they are ecstatic?" might be a helpful prompt to offer. That might get the speaker to supply information like, "Well, when she smiles broadly and opens her eyes wide while tilting her head back, I get the distinct impression that she is thrilled with what she accomplished." This would now constitute not only a useful first part of the Encounter statement but the second segment as well.

5    Feelings are always one word

Remember that feelings are always one word. Don't get taken in when a client reports their feeling as: "I feel they tricked me." That is the story the speaker is generating. Encourage them to utilize that phrase in the "I imagine..." section of the statement and then noticing what one-word feeling gets evoked. Although an oversimplification, sometimes offering the menu options of: mad, glad, sad, scared, or ashamed helps.

6    What action do they want to take?

In the last section of the Encounter statement, which begins "...and I want to..." make sure the speaker identifies what they want to do, not what they want to have done. We don't want to encourage passivity or taking a victim stance. This part of the statement is about clarifying what action they can take in order to satisfy their current needs vis-à-vis the other person.

7    The listener does not respond

It is only natural for the listener to want to respond to what was said to them, about them. This response usually takes the form of explaining what they "really" intended to be conveyed by their behavior. What this amounts to is an attempt to deflect, negate, or at least minimize the speaker's experience. When it comes down to it, Encounter is never about the person being spoken to. It is about the speaker. It is the listener's job to hear what meaning the speaker has made and what feelings got evoked in them. If the person receiving the Encounter statement feels the need to respond, I suggest waiting a minimum of five minutes. Here's what this often difficult feat can accomplish: it becomes an opportunity to experience what it is like to be with someone who makes meaning of your actions that you did not intend. It also serves as a chance to experience boundaries and differences, and the realization that we don't all have to be the same in order to feel whole in ourselves.

## When Offering Encounter Might Be Useful

There are all sorts of situations in which making Encounter statements can be useful. As mentioned, I have friends with whom these sorts of exchanges have become regular aspects of our dynamic. I find Encounter to be a trusty guide especially when I am feeling uncomfortable or unsure of what to say, whether serving as a backbone for a complete four-step structure or as a more subtle influence in a communication informed by the process.

In Gestalt therapy, we are careful not to interpret clients' meaning or experience (Yontef, 1993). But when clients seem to need a bit of help making sense of their experience I often share the story I am making up about them based on the data I have gathered. I then invite them to let me know if I'm spot on or off the mark. And when I'm told that I'm off, it's the perfect lead-in for the client to let me know where I've gone astray, and what comes closer to their sense of the situation, which after all, is what the process is about in the first place.

Of course, a therapeutic situation such as group therapy is a perfect setting in which to encourage Encounter statements, as we have already seen. When clients bring up difficulties they are having with their partners, I may encourage the use of Encounter by offering a short instructional on the process and providing them with two copies of Encounter Guidelines (see the last section of this chapter) one for them and one for their partner.

## Considerations When Working with the Encounter Process

When anticipating whether to introduce the Encounter process, it is important to take into account some considerations. One important aspect to bear in mind is that it is a highly structured format that frequently demands intervention on the part of the therapist. Clients can get frustrated when told the way they are describing their feeling, for example, is actually not a feeling but a thought. If that challenge leads to a strong emotional reaction on their part, their relationship with the therapist may become figural in that moment, rather than with the person they were initially encountering. That is not a helpful situation. It is thus incumbent on the therapist to manage their interventions so that the initially intended communication remains the focus.

Parallel to that concern is the issue of spontaneity which can become compromised when the therapist has to intervene multiple times in order to support the client making the Encounter statement. The situation is somewhat like a toggle mechanism. On the one hand, the therapist's interruptions can detract from smooth and extemporaneous expression. On the other hand, once a truly clear statement is identified, the energy that gets generated may offset any temporary lag or awkwardness of communication.

The overarching goal of enhancing the speaker's contact with themselves as well as with the one they are encountering needs to be the therapist's guide in determining how much and what sorts of interventions are optimal so that the clarity and liveliness of contact are heightened.

## Open Encounter

Thus far Encounter has been described as a way of facilitating communication between two people. Over the years I have found that offering periods of "open Encounter" in my ongoing therapy groups can be valuable both in helping group members grasp the value of the process as well as experience a "bump-up" in their connectedness with each other. I may suggest at the start of the group that they may want to make time for "open Encounter" during the current session and ask when they would like to do that, and for how long. Typically 10–20 minutes seems optimal. Once it begins the agreement is that no one speaks unless they are ready to encounter a fellow member or myself. I remind them that one way they can identify that they have something or someone to encounter is by paying attention to their bodies: if their heart rate rises, their palms start to sweat, their breathing changes, or they notice anxiety rising, they may indeed have an encounter to make.

I reiterate that they can begin from whichever of the four steps of Encounter feels closest to them at the moment. They may be most aware of their quickly beating heart (feeling), their impulse to hide (the action they wish to take), the story they are telling themselves now about someone in the group, or what someone is doing that has sparked their reaction. Once the statement is completed the group returns to silence until someone else is ready to initiate an Encounter.

I also remind the members before beginning the process that when they receive an Encounter, they are not to respond. That is to allow the other's statement just to be, without challenging its veracity. After all, I explain, inasmuch as it is principally a statement about the speaker, not the one being spoken to, what a wonderful opportunity it can be to allow someone to have a view of ourselves that is not consistent with our own. This can of course be challenging, but the benefit of learning to experience boundaries and not needing to change someone else's experience in order to feel valid and whole are invaluable.

When a member wishes to make a statement to the whole group, even if it is applicable to all of the members, I request that they identify one member and make the statement to them. This one-to-one communication tends to heighten the liveliness of the contact and resultant sense of satisfaction.

Once the time for open Encounter is up, I ask the group about their experience and how it felt for them. This processing can also lead to some important learning for the group members and may help them in subsequent experiences with the process.

[The author would like to express his gratitude to Charlie Bowman who so generously assisted him with citations for this chapter.]

## Guidelines for Making Encounter Statements

*The Basic Structure:*
*When you ...*
*I imagine ...*
*and (so) I feel ...*
*and (then) I want to ...*

### "When you..."

Make sure you use truly objective data to describe what you are seeing, hearing, etc. For example: "You look angry" is not objective, but an interpretation. Identify actual sensory data you are receiving with your senses (hearing, seeing, etc.) which gives you the impression that the person is angry, e.g., *"When you purse your mouth and narrow your eyes..."*

### I imagine..."

Articulate the meaning you are making from the sensory data you have received. One helpful question might be "What story are you telling yourself [or] what is your fantasy about this person's behavior?" You might prefer to word this by saying: "The meaning I am making about that is," or "the story (or fantasy) I'm telling myself about that is..." e.g., *"I imagine you are angry at me."*

### "... and (so) I feel ..."

Feelings are always one word, Period! "I feel you're trying to scare me" is in fact, not a feeling, but a story you are telling yourself. It is the result of a cognitive process. If you need help identifying a one-word feeling, see if any of these basic feelings might work: Mad, Sad, Glad, Scared, Ashamed. e.g., *"and so, I feel scared."*

### " ... and (then) I want to ..."

This is where you identify an action you want to take given your current feeling state and/or the meaning that you are making of the situation. Be sure the action is not passive and being acted by someone else. This statement is a description of what action you feel motivated to take given the current conditions. e.g., *"and (then I want to run out of the room."*

### The Listener Does not Respond

When it comes down to it, an Encounter statement is never about the person being spoken to. It is about the speaker. (Boundaries.) Though it might not be easy, it is the listener's job to receive what the speaker is telling them. If the person receiving the Encounter statements feels a strong need to respond, I suggest waiting a minimum of five minutes.

### One-to-One

Encounter statements are made individual to individual rather than to a group of people.

### Present Tense

The Encounter statement is made using present tense verbs, even when the incident being referred to occurred in the past.

### Start Where You're At

There is no correct order in which the four components of the Encounter statement should be expressed. In fact, it is usually most helpful to start with the part you can most easily recognize. You can then use that one clear segment to identify the next, and thus piece together the Encounter statement as it evolves organically in your awareness.

------------

## References

de Saint-Exupéry, A. (1943) *The Little Prince.* Orlando, FL: Harcourt, Inc.

Jacobs, L. (2006). That which enables-support as complex and contextually emergent. *British Gestalt Journal, 15*(2), 10.

Latner, J. (1973). *The Gestalt Therapy Book: A Holistic Guide to the Theory, Principles, and Techniques of Gestalt Therapy Developed by Frederick S. Perls and Others.* New York: Julian Press.

Perls, F. (1969). *Gestalt Therapy Verbatim.* Moab, UT: Real People Press.

Perls, L. (1992). *Living at the Boundary: Collected Works of Laura Perls*. Highland, NY: Gestalt Journal Press.

Polster, E. & Polster, M. (1973). *Gestalt Therapy Integrated: Contours of Theory and Practice*. New York: Random House.

Yalom, I. D. (1995). *The Theory and Practice of Group Psychotherapy*. 4th edition. New York: Basic Books

Yontef, G. (1993). *Awareness, Dialogue and Process: Essays on Gestalt Therapy*. New York: The Gestalt Journal Press.

# Chapter 13

# Shame and Relational Gestalt Group Therapy: Restoring the Interpersonal Bridge

*Joan Gold*

Several months ago, I witnessed a client in one of my women's groups dare to tell her most shameful secret: Desperate to protect her children in ways she had never been protected, she told a lie about the death of their father that is still impacting their lives 30 years later.

Instead of being showered by judgment in her group, she found herself embraced. Several group members identified with her story, both as parents and as adult children looking back at their families of origin. "Wow," she kept repeating, shaking her head and looking stunned. "I didn't expect that."

When we returned to her experience the following week, she had this to say: "I'm not sure what happened to me but something's changed. I don't hate myself as much. Maybe my story actually makes sense."

As a Certified Healing Shame practitioner (*Lyon/Rubin Method*) and a relational Gestalt group therapist, this client's transformative moment is why I find the combination of shame work and group therapy so powerful.

Group therapy is a container for so many of the resources needed to heal shame. No intervention from a therapist could have come close to the impact of the group's compassionate response, a primary component of transforming toxic shame (*I'm a terrible person*) into healthy shame (*We are all flawed human beings. We have all been shaped by our childhoods, we all have regrets, and we are STILL worthy of being loved and accepted*) (Lyon, 2016).

In fact, group therapy shows us that our willingness to be vulnerable, to be seen in our imperfection – it makes us MORE lovable.

At its best, group therapy has the potential to provide a corrective emotional experience to those of us who carry shame at our core, allowing us to be seen accurately through kind eyes. From a relational Gestalt perspective, the focus is on "empathy, connection, dialogue and sensitivity to the vulnerability that accompany relationality" (Cole & Reese, 2018, p. 31).

For many of my shame-saturated clients, group is their first lived experience in discovering an alternative narrative to the one that says *I'm just not good enough/smart enough/fill-in-the-blank enough and that is why I am not loved*.

DOI: 10.4324/9781003255772-16

If shame is defined as the breaking of the interpersonal bridge – the connection between one loving human being and another that helps us grow up feeling seen and valued (Kaufman, 1974) – then relational Gestalt group therapy is the restoration of that bridge in action. "People need confirmation of their human existence and membership in the human race. This confirmation comes from interpersonal contact. Moreover, it takes new input to enable replacement of old introjected shame tapes" (Yontef, 2003, p. 370).

## A Therapist's Journey in Healing Shame

I decided to focus on Healing Shame (*Lyon/Rubin Method*) in my groups because of my own lifelong battle with shame. I grew up not knowing what was wrong, just that I was an eternal disappointment to everyone around me, and nothing I did to try to fix myself worked. None of my therapists identified the shame that lived at my center or, if they did, they didn't know how to work with it. I wound up in a locked mental facility at age 32; like many of my clients, I lived a very small life for far too many decades.

By creating a coherent narrative – a story one can live with and a way of making sense out of senseless reality – shame becomes a creative adaptation to certain kinds of childhood wounding. Unfortunately, it is the self that is sacrificed.

Utilizing the Healing Shame approach of identifying the four physiological reactions to shame (Attack Self, Attack Other, Deny, and Withdraw) as a centerpiece (Nathanson, 1994), I decided to put shame in the foreground of a small relational Gestalt women's group.

All groups have shame in the background, but because even the word "shame" is shame-full, it is easy for it to stay there. Every time I talk about shame, I feel my own lifelong burden lifting a bit more. One of the most important things to understand about shame is that it lives in the non-rational part of our brain. It does not respond to left-brain reminders like *I've done all these great things* or even *I'm a therapist now*.

Running a Healing Shame group (just like working individually with shame) demands we deal with our own shame, oftentimes in the middle of an actual group. I've learned over the years that making a mistake – a key shame trigger for many people including myself – is a huge opportunity for growth and a valuable learning opportunity for everyone. It is helpful for my own shame to be reminded that I am human and human beings make mistakes. And it is helpful for the group to watch me be open and take responsibility for what I did/didn't do. *If even therapists make mistakes, then it must be okay for me.*

It is both humbling and healing as a group leader to have to start a group with a confession: "I made a mistake. I am so sorry. Please tell me about your experience and what I can do to make it right." Often this is enough. Often group members will tell me this is the first time they have actually experienced a perceived authority figure taking responsibility for a mistake and being open to hearing about impact.

Just as lack of repair creates shame, repair diminishes it. In working with my own feelings of inadequacy as a therapist and human being, it is helpful to me as a group leader to remember no matter what I do in group, right or wrong, it will be useful for the group. This frees up my somewhat anxious energy to be a braver, more in-the-moment leader who takes risks that don't always land.

## Orienting the Group to Working with Shame

Because shame feeds on isolation, and most of us lack understanding about where it comes from and how it works, I begin with psychoeducation during the intake process to familiarize group members with talking about shame.

I usually start with the good news/bad news about shame, something I find myself repeating periodically to the group as a whole. Shame is a normal human emotion (good news). Because it is a normal human emotion, we can never get rid of it (bad news). What we can do is transform it from toxic – the shame that festers deep within and keeps us feeling small, stupid, and unworthy – to healthy.

Like healthy anger or healthy grief, healthy shame is necessary for our full functioning as human beings. We wouldn't want to live without healthy shame – what many people call guilt – because without it, we wouldn't know when we hurt someone's feelings, have been unkind or otherwise missed the mark. Healthy shame is about taking responsibility for what we are actually responsible for.

Toxic shame is a whole difference beast.

Andrea called the day after the group to let me know she was going to give her notice. "I'm just not feeling connected. I don't think it's the right group for me." A 45-year-old, single, web designer, Andrea came to the group to work on her lack of relationships. She had few friends and no significant long-term partner. She came from an alcoholic family and I knew from our intake sessions that her creative adaptation to avoid becoming a target was to always keep a smile on her face, her thoughts to herself, and to function flawlessly.

I commiserated with her frustration, noting how painful it must be to come to a group to work on relationships and discover a group of people that you couldn't relate to. I asked Andrea a question I've learned to ask many of my clients: "Is it possible there is a secret are you keeping from the group? Something you've wanted to say, but not been able to?" She was quiet for a moment, then I could hear her start crying. Andrea did indeed have a secret – hearing about other group members' relationships triggered her own lack and she was too ashamed to talk about it. With my support, she brought her secret back to the group and found herself met by acceptance. She has been an extremely active and connected group member ever since.

Andrea's impulse to leave/hide is one of the more prominent actions of toxic shame which often acts to shut us down and cut us off from all human contact (which is where it appears the shame is coming from). It is my personal belief that shame is responsible in many cases for what is often diagnosed as depression.

"Shame affect operates to reduce interest – excitement and enjoyment-joy, the affects that make us vital, lively, charming, fun, interesting, enjoyable, exciting, charismatic, thrilling, inspiring and appealing. If you wonder why someone lacks vitality, look first for the nearness of shame" (Nathanson, 1994, p. 155).

Any kind of difference has the potential to cause shame. There are the obvious differences such as age, race, weight, disabilities, and then there are the less obvious differences that can't always be observed, such as Andrea's difference – being single in a world that seems to exist in pairs – or another client's early experience of being told she just wasn't as quick as other children.

The **Attack Self** reaction to shame is the one we are all most familiar with, but shame also shows up disguised as **Denial** (dissociation, addiction, and the fawn/cling response), **Attack Other** (blame, contempt, criticism, and violence), and **Withdrawal** (isolation, depression, and mistrust).

Resources the group brings to each individual member's transformation from toxic to healthy shame include Humility (*It's okay to not know everything there is to know*), Responsibility (*We are not responsible for other people's actions, we are only responsible for own*), Big Picture (*Given the circumstances, you actually did the best you could*), Humor (*We can try our best to keep those ducks in a row but sometimes they just won't stop squawking!*), and Self-Compassion (*You tried your best and that's all anyone can ask*).

## How Making Shame the Focus of Group Work both Supports and Impedes Group Progress

When I first began to conceptualize my Healing Shame group, I was advised by a number of colleagues that I should think twice about including the word shame in the title. "It's hard enough getting a new group up and running," they told me. "The word shame will scare potential group members away."

But my instincts told me that putting shame up front was an integral part of the healing – you can't heal what you can't name. *I want the women to know what they're signing up for. I want them to know this thing that has ruled their life – this thing that hides behind words like lazy, stupid, silly, depressed, confused – is shame. And that shame has a narrative. We can name it, learn to understand it, reality-check it, develop compassion for it and give it back where it belongs.*

Roz, an early group member, kept showing up for the group on a wrong day. She always apologized and she always said the same thing: "I don't know what's wrong with me. I know this group meets on Tuesdays, there's no excuse." It turns out there was.

Each week Roz would get confused about the day and time the group started, would either get lost on the freeway or find herself uncertain which building in the complex we were in. Once she named her struggle and the group commiserated with how shame shuts down our thinking brain and puts us all in a freeze state, her struggle ended. She had never connected the fact that she had shame about coming to a shame group to her inability to get to group. Once we were able to process this experience, amazingly, she never showed up in my waiting room on the wrong day or time again.

After several years of running my Healing Shame for Women group, I started a second group specifically for women therapists in response to so many of them coming up to me after workshops saying: "I wish I could be a part of a group like that." It turns out therapists are not exempt from feelings of shame, inferiority, and "not-enoughness."

Shame is an extremely opportunistic emotion. For those of us carrying shame at our core, anything can offer an excuse for shame to take over. Sometimes it shuts the group down entirely. Sometimes it acts to create misunderstandings between group members that require careful navigation. For every shame identified in group, there seems to be a paired opposite. Some of the paradoxes we have dealt with in group include:

- Shame about not being enough and shame about being too much
- Shame about having unmet needs and shame about trying to get them met
- Shame about speaking up and shame about staying quiet
- Shame about having too many feelings and shame about not having enough feelings or the right ones
- Shame about holding secrets and shame about telling them
- Shame about being different and shame about not being different/unique enough

Part of the healing in Healing Shame is the women acknowledging and even laughing at these ridiculous double-binds ("No wonder we always feel so stupid!"). There is no way to win at the shamegame.

## Necessary Strategies for Holding Space and Surviving in a Shame-filled Environment

I learned quickly that I had to be a more transparent group leader in order to survive a Healing Shame group. The first night of my first group I was so overwhelmed by the shame in the room – mine, all six group members, no doubt the shame that lingered in the room from previous clients – that

I froze up and couldn't operate the credit card machine that I'd used every day for at least the previous five years.

I played it off in the moment (this was, after all, my first Healing Shame group) but eventually used this incident as an example of how shame can operate to shut down our bodies and our thinking brain.

Over the years I have learned and developed several strategies for keeping my head, and the heads of group members, above the shame-filled waters.

**Name it:** We call it by many names: *shame attack, shame vortex, the spiral, the pit*. Whatever it is called, naming shame is a powerful antidote to living it. Group members learn to call out their own mind-reads (*I'm thinking you guys are all laughing at me for being such an idiot*) to give themselves the opportunity to find out what is really going on. Often shame sits on top of other feeling states – grief, loss, fear – that block them from being processed. I remind the group that naming shame is the first step in supporting a change process that is organically waiting to happen.

**Experiments:** Experiments as utilized in Gestalt therapy help challenge group members' creative adjustments in the here and now and allow them to make contact with parts of themselves that have been minimized, denied, or forgotten. Deliberate, prolonged eye contact with other members, enactments, and two-chair work have been particularly helpful ways to deepen our work, helping clients to make more functional choices and gain new experiences through group interaction.

**Touch:** Touch has become an unexpected resource in both my healing shame groups. Not every group member is open to it, but for those who are, touch has been a way of gently challenging the isolation/counter-dependence that binds shame firmly in place. Several times group members who shy away from touch have become so moved by watching other group members sitting closely beside each other, shoulders touching or even holding hands, that their own hunger has awoken and they have asked to be included too.

**Note:** Human touch is one of our biggest losses due to the coronavirus. Now that we are all working online, I will ask group members to put their own hands over their bellies or hearts, or rub their palms together and hold them over their cheeks in order to create that soothing contact, skin to skin, that can bring us back into connection with each other and ourselves.

**Breathing/Movement:** At times, the shame has gotten so heavy in our small group room that I can feel the weight of it in my own body. That's when I know it is time for a breather: I will lead the group in taking slow deep breaths, stomping our feet, using sound healing/vibrational "medicine," playing catch-the-couch-pillow, or on one memorable occasion "toss the tissue box." Group members who are used to just gritting their teeth and surviving shame report being surprised we can pause such an intense experience to call in more resources, a real victory for healing shame.

**Therapist transparency:** Misery may love company, but shame avoids it. Talking about my own shameful experiences, in small doses, sometimes with humor but often without, has been a great equalizer for clients who have managed their shame through isolation. Knowing you are not the only one with shameful secrets is one of the most potent counter-shaming resources available (and having your therapist join you, even more so).

******

That client who told us about her lies at the beginning of this chapter has been in the group for close to two years now. She still struggles with shame and frequently needs the group to remind her that her story makes perfect sense given her childhood. That she has always done the best she could with the few resources provided. And that she is learning and growing from her experience, and enlarging her resources, which is all any of us can do.

Healing Shame groups are much more than support groups but the support offered to this client and all group members is a foundational element of their healing process (Lee's (2003) shame-support polarity) as well as facilitating the increased vulnerability and connection necessary for real change. Toxic shame – the shame that lives at our core – often travels side by side with complex trauma. Healing is not a quick process, but the healing is held steady in the container of love, laughter, authenticity, and connection that is relational Gestalt group therapy.

## References

Cole, P. & Reese, D. (2018). *New Directions in Gestalt Group Therapy*. New York: Routledge.

Kaufman, G. (1974). The meaning of shame: Toward a self-affirming identity. *Journal of Counseling Psychology*, 6, 568–574.

Lee, R. (2003) Shame and the Gestalt model. In R. Lee & G. Wheeler (Eds.) *The voice of shame: Silence and connection in psychotherapy*. Cambridge, MA: Gestalt Press. (Original work published 1996).

Lyon, B. (2016, November 12). *Transforming toxic shame into healthy shame*. Center for Healing Shame. https://healingshame.com/articles/transforming-toxic-shame-into-healthy-shame-bret-lyon-phd

Nathanson, D. L. (1994). *Shame and Pride: Affect, Sex, and the Birth of the Self*. New York: W. W. Norton & Company.

Yontef, G. (2003) Shame and guilt in Gestalt therapy. In R. Lee & G. Wheeler (Eds.) *The voice of shame: Silence and connection in psychotherapy*. Cambridge, MA: Gestalt Press. (Original work published 1996).

# Integrative Relational Approaches

# Integrative Research Approaches

# Chapter 14

# Embodied Relational Presence in Buddhist Psychology Informed Gestalt Therapy

*Eva Gold and Stephen Zahm*

Buddhist psychology and its practices invite us to meet ourselves, others, and all of life with mindful presence, compassion, wisdom, and love. This is foundational to the therapeutic relationship in Buddhist Psychology informed Gestalt Therapy (BPGT; Gold & Zahm, 2018). In this chapter, we look at how BPGT supports and enhances therapist embodied relational presence. A brief overview of BPGT provides context. Then we look at aspects of the resonance between Buddhist psychology and its practices and the field phenomenological and dialogical foundations that ground Gestalt therapy in the relational. We also point to potential new theoretical territory and consider how a BPGT perspective may expand what is possible in the therapeutic engagement.

## What Is Buddhist Psychology Informed Gestalt Therapy?

BPGT is based on Gestalt therapy theory and method, and informed by Buddhist psychology views and meditative practices, broadening Gestalt therapy's focus and extending its reach. The Buddhist psychology informed Gestalt therapist can bring both knowledge of Buddhist psychology views, and the experiential understanding that comes through following the path and its meditative practices, to the therapeutic engagement. In BPGT, Gestalt therapy's dialogical relatedness, field phenomenological method, experiential and experimental focus, attention to natural regulation, and goal of increased awareness remain central (Gold & Zahm, 2018). However, additional processes can also be attended to, including Buddhist psychology's understanding of the cause of suffering, and path to liberation from it. Meditative and path practices can be integrated within Gestalt therapy's experimental framework, both in and outside of the session. This can help focus attention on present moment experience, support increased awareness, or explore the cultivation of beneficial qualities such as loving, kindness, and compassion.

BPGT emerges from the organic synthesis of essential convergences in Gestalt therapy theory and Buddhist psychology views, as well as convergences

DOI: 10.4324/9781003255772-18

of Gestalt therapy method and the methods of mindfulness meditation—a foundational practice of Buddhist psychology (Gold & Zahm, 2018). Convergences of views include the view of human nature, the recognition of interconnectedness, understanding self as a process, how suffering is created, and what is curative. The convergences of the method include a field phenomenological focus, attention to present experience, and the importance of being with "what is" for increasing awareness and creating the conditions for organic change. These convergences allow for seamless integration while maintaining the holistic integrity of each system (Gold & Zahm, 2018).

Buddhism offers what is, for many, a spiritual or religious practice. However, our view—supported by many Buddhist practitioners, writers, and teachers—is that what Buddhism provides is a *psychological* understanding of ourselves. It includes practices and a path of inquiry to increase awareness. And, although it suggests ways of understanding the world and our experience, this is not an imposed belief system. Rather, it is pragmatic applied psychology that, like Gestalt therapy, privileges what we can know and apprehend directly through our own experience. Throughout our writing, we refer to Buddhist psychology rather than Buddhism to clarify this. And although what is considered "spiritual" is often seen as separate from the "psychological," we see these as interwoven, each fundamental in actualizing our human potential.

The Buddhist psychology informed Gestalt therapist's degree of integrating Buddhist psychology depends on both the therapist's and the patient's experience, orientation, preferences, and direct relevance to the work. The therapist's own study and meditation practice inevitably shift his/her/their worldview and way of being and experiencing self and other, and this will of course influence what the therapist brings to the therapeutic relationship. Also, some patients now come to therapy as meditation practitioners, familiar with Buddhist psychology, or with aspirations to pursue these practices. This may influence what is the foreground for patient and therapist, as well as therapist choices. The therapist may also opt to explicitly bring a particular perspective, to suggest experiments integrating meditative practices in and out of session, or to work directly with processes Buddhist psychology identifies (Gold & Zahm, 2018).

### Benefit of this Integration

Gestalt therapy, like other Western therapies, addresses our individual/relational psychological issues and patterns. This work can clarify and resolve internal conflict, expand self-experience, and support authentic contact, alleviating distress and symptoms, and contributing to personal growth. However, as essential as this work is, from a Buddhist psychology viewpoint this is still a limited outcome. Buddhist psychology recognizes that we will continue to suffer no matter how much personal psychological work we do because human suffering goes beyond our own psychological issues (Yeshe, 1998). Freedom from this suffering requires understanding the causes and conditions that contribute to the creation of it, and this is Buddhist psychology's central concern. The universal challenges that all humans face must be recognized and addressed to reach our potential for what Buddhist psychology sees as our capacity for true mental health and well-being. This essential difference offers an added perspective for Gestalt therapy and for what can be addressed in the therapy process.

Freud once described the result of psychotherapeutic treatment as transforming neurotic misery into normal unhappiness. Existential humanistic approaches, including Gestalt therapy, aimed higher, recognizing that increased self-awareness and a healing therapeutic relationship could lead to a more authentically lived and richly satisfying life. Buddhist psychology reaches further still. With its broad views and experiential prescriptive path, it addresses humanity's universal challenges, pointing us toward an expanded understanding of our human potential. Since it does not include the personal/relational psychotherapeutic work that is also essential, BPGT bridges the two, enriching both, and creating a unified therapy approach with new possibilities for application and inquiry.

## Support for Embodied Relational Presence in BPGT

Of course, the study of Buddhist psychology teachings, and the expanded awareness developed in the meditative practices offer benefits quite apart from the practice of psychotherapy. However, we have also both found this path and its practices influencing and supporting embodied presence and relational connection in the psychotherapeutic encounter, as they deepen the capacity for qualities such as wisdom, compassion, equanimity, and love. Relational Gestalt therapy underscores the importance of these very qualities in the therapist that have not generally been given the emphasis in Gestalt therapy that is warranted by their impact (Yontef, 2002). In this section, we consider aspects of how BPGT can support Gestalt therapist's field phenomenological and dialogical practice in ways that contribute to and enhance embodied relational presence.

### Mindfulness Meditation

In mindfulness meditation we pay attention to our immediate experience, to "what is" as it is arising in the moment. The meditator is not seeking a particular state like calm or relaxation, and we are not practicing for a particular goal, nor do we try to make something happen. Instead, we recognize and allow what is happening as it is happening. The invitation is to bring an open curiosity, to just be with experience, and also to recognize when we want to resist it, judge, fix, or change it. We notice the difference between being with actual present embodied experience, and when we are off in memory, fantasy, and other thoughts. This increases awareness and offers insight into aspects of ourselves, our habitual and reflexive patterns, and the nature of our experience that would normally remain out of awareness.

One of the four foundations of mindfulness, mindfulness of the body, guides the meditator to connect with the felt sense of embodied experience, bringing us right into the present moment. Turning bare attention to bodily sensation and perception allows experience to clarify and reveal itself more fully, as we attend to the detail and nuance of actual experience, not our thoughts about it. This also reveals the embodied nature of emotion and the inseparability of body/mind. We get better at attending to subtleties, like the way the in-breath feels different from the out-breath, or how the space between the end of the exhalation and the beginning of the next inhalation is an opportunity for more complete release of one breath and more fully receiving the next. At times we can sense the body as the field of movement and energy that it is, freed from an idea or image of the body as solid or static. Slowing down, stillness, and silence support the unified attention needed for this increased awareness. Concentration meditation, a partner practice to mindfulness in which we consistently bring attention back to the object of concentration, also strengthens the ability for sustained focus.

These practices are training in connecting to and staying with experience moment to moment. As we are more attuned to ourselves, we also become more resonant with others and the world around us, so the therapist engaged in these practices becomes a more sensitive instrument. This kind of mindful embodied presence is ineffable, not easily quantified or defined, but we recognize it when we sense it in ourselves or experience it in another. It involves being fully "there" in our own body, open-hearted and emotionally available. It can include more exquisite attention to nuances of not only the patient's emotional experience, but of their physicality—what is expressed in posture or a gesture, or the slowing or quickening of the breath. The therapist may more naturally support the patient slowing down and mindfully tuning into and staying with bodily experience as well (Siegel, 2007). Organic interventions that are experienced by the patient through a "felt sense" of being joined by the therapist can make all the difference in how an intervention lands, and the resulting contact, the essence of "healing through meeting."

## Compassion

Self-compassion and compassion for others arise naturally in mindfulness practice. Compassion is the result of directly meeting our own or another's pain or suffering, without resistance. As we sit with ourselves without our usual distractions, emotional or physical pain can become foreground. Whether physical or emotional, we work with allowing and meeting the raw experience of pain as it is. This can include things like locating the feeling in the body, breathing with it, opening to it, softening around it, or creating more space for it. With physical pain, this might be deconstructing the generality and noticing throbbing, sharpness or dullness, constancy, or intermittency. Abiding with grief, loss, sadness, hurt, fear, loneliness or despair, and developing more self-compassion, tenderizes us, opening our hearts more fully to the pain of others. Compassion emerges naturally as we grasp the universality of the pain of the human condition.

The simplicity of meeting our own pain and suffering directly without needing to do anything about it is also a reminder of the healing power in this process. As waves of sadness or grief wash over us and we stay with ourselves, we may experience the sense of wholeness and embodied connection that comes with allowing what is. And often the waves can leave a sense of relief or even gratitude in their wake. These experiences deepen faith in staying with what is painful as healing and transformative, also strengthening the capacity for embodied presence in the face of another's pain. This increased confidence and trust in this process helps us to be fully present with and to support our patients in doing this as well, as we find our way to a deeper more present-centered and embodied connection to ourselves and the other, moment-by-moment and breath-by-breath.

*Phenomenology and Equanimity*

Like Gestalt therapy's phenomenological method, mindfulness meditation prescribes attending to experience as it unfolds, bringing open non-evaluative attention to whatever arises. The practice involves "noting" or describing what is observable rather than explaining, interpreting, or making assumptions. This increases awareness of our moment-to-moment creation of subjective experience within the context of field influence. Noticing when we *are* caught in explaining or interpreting, we can become aware of and note or bracket preconceived ideas, evaluation, and biases. This also allows us to see if we are with our experience or our ideas about it. In meditation, we can directly recognize the transient and shifting nature of experience, as well as seeing where we are objecting to or trying to fix or change ourselves, or our experience. Becoming more familiar with this process, we are more likely to recognize it in our interactions with patients, and to see when our patients are doing this themselves.

This practice naturally develops equanimity. When equanimous, we maintain an embodied sense of stability whatever comes. Desires and preferences are clearly seen as such, and we are not caught up in attachment to being "for" one experience or "against" another. To the extent that we can embody equanimity, it offers spaciousness and capacity for a truly open and non-discriminatory receptivity, a grounded center from which we can be present with all arising conditions. Equanimity takes acceptance to another level, as we not only accept but embrace all experience. Equanimity frees us from the need to control for a particular outcome, helps us see that we do not know what the next moment will bring, and allows more ease with the not knowing.

As Gestalt therapists, the phenomenological method is foundational to what we do. We value and aim for this stance even as we notice and attend to the obstacles in holding to it. Developing equanimity in meditation supports us in this, making it more embodied—more a part of who we are. Equanimity increases therapists' capacity to meet and be present with all of what both they and the patient are experiencing, including whatever relational challenges emerge. This can create new relational ground and deepen awareness as patients sense an acceptance that allows them to open more fully to the therapist and to themselves. Equanimity allows us to step into an even more radically descriptive, non-interpretive, and non-evaluative therapeutic stance where biases about and evaluation of experience are diminished—the embodied essence of Gestalt therapy's phenomenological practice.

## Field Perspective and Interconnectedness

Gestalt therapy's field perspective reminds us that any component of the field affects all others in a complex interactive relationship and that the field is never static. The patient-therapist relationship is understood as a co-created field of mutual and reciprocal influence. One of Buddhist psychology's three "givens" of material existence is the truth of impermanence, which includes recognizing interconnectedness. This is the understanding that everything arises as a result of causes and conditions that are interconnected, interdependent, and always in flux. We grasp this experientially in mindfulness meditation practice, as we connect with the ongoing flow of sensation and perception, seeing that movement and change are constant and that no experience lasts. We also develop more of the felt sense of interconnectedness, recognizing that we are deeply interdependent with all of life, other beings, the air we breathe, and the planet that sustains us.

Bringing this awareness into the therapy relationship helps us stay connected with this sense of our interdependence, and co-regulation. It also reminds us that we do not have to make change happen, but that it is always happening, and we are more primed to notice even small or subtle shifts in ourselves and in our patients. We can be more attentive to how these are experienced in the relational field in the moment, and how no two moments of contact are exactly the same. We keep in mind that any relational experience or new awareness in therapy may have a profound and far-reaching impact. In this co-created relationship, we also see that the therapist's understanding and capacities contribute to field conditions that can allow for a new depth of relational connection including shared moments of awakening, as we describe in the following section on the expanded BPGT perspective.

## Dialogue, Buddha Nature, and Cultivation of Heart Qualities

Gestalt therapy's model for the patient-therapist relationship is based on Martin Buber's philosophy of dialogue (Buber, 1958). The dialogical attitude (Hycner, 1985) informs the Gestalt therapist's understanding of what is healing in the therapy relationship. This involves the aspiration to hold the other as a "thou," to feel the patient's experience as if from the inside, and an apprehending of the patient's whole being. It also includes therapist presence—the openness to being authentic, vulnerable, and to being seen as we are. Rather than trying to change the patient, or being attached to a role or self-image, the therapist is willing to be moved and touched by a real encounter.

Buddhist psychology recognizes the buddha nature in all human beings. This reflects each person's potential for compassion and wisdom and includes our innate capacity for transformation and awakening. So, any engagement between two people can be seen as two buddhas meeting. There is a resonance between this view and Gestalt therapy's dialogical attitude. "There is a sacredness in the I-Thou relationship that goes beyond the very important goals being sought in therapy, and beyond the content and process explored during therapy sessions" (Edelstein, 2015, p. 441). Recognizing the universality of buddha nature supports the Buddhist psychology informed Gestalt therapist's aspiration toward non-hierarchy, recognizing interconnectedness, and a complete turning toward the other, allowing us to more easily let go of aims and to be present with the sacredness of whatever emerges in each unique moment of contact.

Buddhist psychology also includes practices for cultivating qualities such as loving-kindness and compassion that are inherent in us but can be further developed. As we described earlier, compassion is naturally enhanced in mindfulness practice, but it can also be more directly nurtured. Loving-kindness meditation increases the capacity to open our hearts, to wish ourselves and others well, or to help us to connect with this intention. The BPGT therapist can practice this with a patient in mind, and it can be integrated in the therapy work (Gold & Zahm, 2018). Compassion practice directly attends to helping us see that others' pain is not separate from our own. "Compassion is not a relationship between the healer and the wounded. It's a relationship between equals. Only when we know our own darkness well can we be present with the darkness of others. Compassion becomes real when we recognize our shared humanity"(Chodron, 2010, p. 50). The practices also help us keep in mind that these qualities are innate in our patients as well, and we can be alert to opportunities when experimenting with exploring them may be useful in the work. This perspective and these practices support a full turning toward and embracing all of our own and our patient's humanity with an embodied dialogic attitude that comes from the heart.

## BPGT—An Expanded Perspective

So far the ideas we have talked about support and enhance what Gestalt therapists already do, and can help us embody our field phenomenological and dialogical practice. Now, we venture further from the beaten path, as we look at an expanded theoretical perspective, and point to new directions for what can be addressed and explored in therapy, further deepening the therapist's capacity for embodied relational presence, and expanding contact possibilities.

### Pain and Suffering

Buddhist psychology points to the difference between our actual immediate experience and our relationship to it (Fronsdal, 2011). Immediate present experience is sensory and perceptual, in the moment, embodied (Stevens, 1971). Our relationship to experience is in our thoughts about and reactions to it, opinions, evaluation, and judgment. This might be liking and wanting to hold on to a pleasant experience. Or, it might be not liking and rejecting an unpleasant experience or rejecting an aspect of ourselves. For example, the immediate experience of sadness can include sensation such as welling in the chest, pain around the heart, or tears. The relationship to the experienced sadness might be in thoughts or reactions like "I don't want to feel this" or "Crying means I'm weak." This relationship can include self-blame "It's my fault I'm sad, I screw up relationships" or future predictions like "I'll always be alone."

Within this distinction, we find Buddhist psychology's understanding of the difference between *pain* and *suffering*, and the insight that *suffering is in our relationship to any experience, not in an experience or event itself.* Life's unavoidable pain emerges in what is present, embodied. The added suffering is in our beliefs, ideas, resistance to, or the stories we tell ourselves about an event or experience. When we are in opposition to "what is," we suffer. In the example above, the pain is in the embodied sadness, and the suffering is in the added ideas and thoughts about it. So while pain in life is inevitable, suffering is optional. *However, only by becoming aware of this process and recognizing our in-the-moment creation of suffering can we have more choice in it.* This does not mean suppressing or trying to get rid of these responses. It does mean increasing awareness of how we are relating to ourselves and to our experience, and recognizing that this "relationship to" is not the same as the experience itself.

For the Gestalt therapist, there is nothing new in attending to present embodied experience. From the beginning, F. Perls exhorted us to "lose our minds and come to our senses." We know that it is in restoring connection with embodied emotional experience and present contacting that increased awareness, healing, closure, and transformation happen (Perls et al., 1951). And, like Buddhist psychology, Gestalt therapy is based on the understanding that if there is a chance of healing what is painful, we must first experience it fully (Beisser, 1970). The Buddhist psychology perspective and Gestalt therapy's understanding of creative adjustments and resulting boundary processes are also parallel. The "relationship to experience" would often be where we see these boundary processes manifesting—reluctance to be with what is, the avoidance, denial, and disowning of aspects of authentic experience. So, of course, the context of patient's lives, meaning-making, and working with boundary processes continue to be an essential therapeutic focus. However, what *is* new in BPGT is the added perspective of recognizing this distinction between pain and suffering. It can influence the therapist to pay attention to how and where this process is seen in therapy, as we become more discerning about noticing the difference between actual experience and concepts--a difference that can be subtle at times. And we can then see more clearly where content, context, and story are elemental, humanizing, and enriching to the unfolding therapeutic contact, and conversely where these may interrupt staying with present embodied feelings, and the potential for a deeper relational connection.

After decades of practicing Gestalt therapy, one of the ways we have both found ourselves influenced by Buddhist psychology is in this understanding of pain and suffering. We are more attuned to observing this process in therapy, and have seen the benefit of bringing patients' attention to it. So, as we address therapeutic themes and relational processes, we also at times observe and point out the process of in-the-moment creation of suffering. Often, the patient becomes aware of the "optional" nature of it—what is being added. This opens up a new opportunity for experimental phenomenological exploration in a relational collaborative process, for example facilitating the patient moving between elemental pain and added constructs, to highlight the difference. This recognition may be even more easily accessed in BPGT work than in meditation, since the Gestalt therapist is leveraged to work with process, experiment, and awareness in this way, harnessing the power of this integrative perspective. This understanding also underlines the value of supporting the patient to stay with pain at times when this can allow deepening of a present embodied focus, opening up to transformative experience and healing contact. The case example later in the chapter illustrates aspects of this.

### "Selfing" and Identification

In Buddhist psychology, inherent in the suffering found in the relationship to experience is a reified sense of self. Buddhist psychology's understanding of "not-self" refers to the absence of an essential, enduring self-entity. The belief in a solid separate "self" is seen as a misunderstanding. This in no way denies our sense of personal continuity of self-experience over a lifetime. However, Buddhist psychology points us toward recognizing the process of "selfing" in which a dynamic experience of constantly changing process is erroneously sensed as an entity that contains the ongoing experience.

Buddhist psychology and Gestalt therapy converge in understanding self-experience as an ever-changing, experiential, field-dependent phenomenon. They both recognize self-as-process, the "how" rather than the "what," and both use process language to describe this, while also acknowledging the human reflex toward self-reification (Gold & Zahm, 2018). They also both recognize that as we reflexively learn to identify with narrowed ideas of who we are, that this influences our sense of who others are, and our ongoing experience of what the world is. Both systems see that as this process itself remains out of awareness, this is limiting.

Although converging in this understanding, the two systems emphasize different aspects of it. Gestalt therapy sees identifying with authentic self-experience as essential to healthy ego functioning. At the same time, it is understood that a fixed and rigid self-sense limits awareness, responsiveness, and the capacity for interpersonal contact. In contrast, Buddhist psychology points to seeing through identity construction and holding experience as less personal. "The sense of identity ... is regarded by the Buddhist tradition as an elaborate construction project ... in which the continually arising data of the senses ... are channeled into structures and organized into schemas that support an entirely synthetic sphere of meaning—a virtual reality" (Olendzki, 2005, p. 244). BPGT reconciles this apparent contradiction by looking at these perspectives not as mutually exclusive, but as synergistic. We propose that the patient's capacity to connect to authentic self-experience establishes the foundation that can clear the way for looking more deeply into the nature of self-experience, the essential insubstantiality of it, and the potential freedom in this (Gold & Zahm, 2018).

### Looking for the "I"

In mindfulness meditation, we discover just how we take the arising and passing away of thoughts, feelings, sensation, and perception to be a coherent, continuous, and solid entity or self. But when we look directly for the "I" within actual present experience, it is nowhere to be found. Although we are a physical body with consciousness, this sense of a solid "self" is created. And when we ask the question "what is actually here in awareness right now?" we discover no solidity, but a movement and flow of sensory experience and thoughts. Our roles and identifications—who we think we are—are not to be found either, since these are also created constructs. Instead, what we find in actual experience, what we can be directly aware of, is bodily sensation and perception—the touch of a breeze on the face, or of clothing on skin, the feeling of pressure where the body meets the cushion we sit on. We feel the movement of breath, the heartbeat, hear the sound of the meditation bell. Then there are thoughts that come and go—memories, ideas, concerns, fantasies, no more substantial than a wisp of smoke—and a consciousness that abides with it all.

Seeing this selfing process in action, we can hold these created identifications more lightly, less confined by set ideas about our own self-experience, others, and the world as we perceive it. Although roles and labels are absolutely necessary for pragmatic living, we can start to see them within the context of an actuality that is beyond these. Generally we remain unaware that our created identity, shaped and confined by the context of our lives and experience, exists within this boundlessness (Rinpoche, 2019). Our habitual patterns of thought obscure this awareness, but it can be revealed as we connect with actual present moment experience, beyond thought and concepts. Although Gestalt therapy understands self-experience as fluid and field-dependent, Buddhist psychology offers a more radically field phenomenological perspective allowing destructuring of all concepts and identifications. By more clearly recognizing the field-dependent nature of all experience as Buddhist psychology does, Gestalt therapy may more fully live up to the potential of its field theory (Wolfert, 2000).

### Clinical Application

For the BPGT therapist, access to this wider lens can offer an essential perspective and more freedom to explore and question when we find ourselves caught in a fixed view of ourselves, our patient, or the relationship. We can also hold this clarity for patients when their experience is of being "stuck" or seeing themselves in a narrowed way. This understanding also supports equanimity, helping us to explore how the patient experiences us, with less attachment to any viewpoint or outcome. We can more easily remain open to and curious about ourselves, our patients' responses to us and ours to them, and the relationship as it unfolds in the moment.

There are also times the therapist can facilitate patient and therapist dropping into a more pure experiential moment together, freer of beliefs, identifications, and filters. Buddhist psychology directs our attention to the "unaware grounds" that we take as given, but that are themselves creations (Wolfert, 2000). A BPGT exploration may allow early creative adjustments to be seen through this lens as well. Although originally essential for psychological survival, the contemporary iterations of these in restrictive boundary processes can be seen not only as limiting *but as actually insubstantial* (Gold & Zahm, 2018). As the patient and therapist deconstruct the conceptual scaffolding these were built on, they may be recognized for what they are, at times allowing the patient to see through the whole "construction project" itself. To paraphrase Einstein, in order to solve a problem we need a different mindset than the one that created it, and this access to an expanded level of awareness and freedom can open up these new vistas.

*Jonah entered therapy in his early forties. He had been a meditation practitioner on and off for a number of years. He had a history of early abandonment and loss, and believed he was inherently unlovable, alien, and different from others who had been loved and cared for. This sense of self-informed what he thought relationships required of him, and what he could expect from others. Over the course of more than a year, he explored these enduring themes, and the related introjective and retroflective processes in a traditional relational Gestalt therapy. Jonah became more aware of the function the belief about himself as unlovable had served, and how it continued to color how he was with others. He gained some clarity about how this emerged in current relationships including with the therapist, and over time this had less of a hold.*

*During a session in which Jonah was exploring this theme, he moved more deeply into the pain and grief of his early losses than he had previously. The therapist supported Jonah staying with this, suggesting just opening to and making more space for it. Noticing when he started to move away from his present experience and into thoughts about it, the therapist suggested that he experiment with bracketing these, and coming back to his in the moment embodied experience. As he was able to do this and stay with it longer, he had a sense of "something letting go," and the sense of self that had been his foundational scaffolding dissolving, leaving just pain, tears, and a sense of "groundlessness." After a time, Jonah's tears subsided and his breathing steadied. Patient and therapist continued in a space of silence and sustained eye contact infused with a deeply felt sense of presence and connection for both. Later in the session, Jonah described the feeling of "wholeness" and flood of self-compassion that had come up as he connected with the depth and intensity of his lifelong pain. He also reported a new experience of lightness in just "being with" the therapist with "nothing required."*

In this example, we see Jonah's suffering in the "relationship to" the pain of his early losses. The relational connection with the therapist supported Jonah in feeling the depth of his pain in a way he had previously avoided. In intentionally bracketing off thoughts and staying with the present embodied pain, he could clearly experience the difference between these. This was key to seeing that the belief about unlovability was a construct and without substance. When Jonah was embedded in this self-view, it seemed solid and real, limiting awareness and interrupting the contact that was ultimately transformational. This work opened the door to an expanded experience with the therapist in which self-evaluation (lovable or unlovable) became irrelevant, supplanted by the power of being fully with himself and the therapist as the therapist was also fully with him both free of limiting ideas. Of course, the earlier work done in therapy was the foundation for this further exploration.

Gestalt therapist Ruth Wolfert has also pointed to how Gestalt therapy can encompass this kind of expanded experience. She proposed *being* as the "… (F)inal, fully lived stage of contact. *Being* signifies dwelling in moments of unity, where the splits of mind, body, and external world are healed …" (Wolfert, p. 82). She goes on to challenge Paul Goodman (Perls, et al., 1951) who wrote that this final stage of full contact lies beyond therapy, and is only to be experienced, not examined, or otherwise explored. She saw this as limiting Gestalt therapy unnecessarily, and proposed that, with the integration of a Buddhist perspective, we can extend the experience of *being* and the opening of deeper grounds "… allowing moments of full contact to flower into fuller awakenings" (Wolfert, 2000, p. 82).

One opportunity for this may be in extending the time between final contact and the emergence of the next figure. Here, there is a void, pregnant with all possibilities, and the potential for firmly held constructs to loosen and lose their valence and for something novel to arise (Wolfert, 2000). This consciousness shift encompasses the expansiveness of pure awareness beyond content. "This is a time when the past is gone and the future is not yet; a time of profound newness when all things are possible" (Wolfert, 2000, p. 83).

Buber's I-Thou moment also encompasses this quality of *being*, involving sustained presence and immediacy. More freedom from the usual constraints and limits of thinking and concepts, and a relaxation of deliberateness allows access to the full emptiness of surrender to the between, to what is emergent in the contact moment. "The dialogue that Buber describes is also a transcendental process … For Buber this development toward the higher reaches of existence was a product of his basic trust of the sphere of the 'between' … a surrender to the forming moment rather than an attempt to control what will happen next" (Jacobs, 1989, p. 35). Although Buber described these moments as occurring through grace, not something that could be aimed for or intentionally created, our perspective provides another take on this. That is, by attending to the particular elements of the relational field that we have described, can we create the conditions for these shared moments of awakening that are always potentialities, and that can be accessed at times through an intentional figure-ground shift to a more content free presence?

### Expanded View of Natural Regulation

Through a BPGT lens, we can consider this as *another aspect of natural regulation*. Here, we recognize that any mind-created construct or identification may interrupt our potential for wholeness and fuller connection with our self-experience, others, and the world. We can consider all identifications as fixed *gestalten* limiting fluidity, perceptivity, and responsiveness (Gold & Zahm, 2018). This does not diminish the importance of context, story, history, and conceptual understanding or the many ways of contacting that are part of the therapeutic process. However, as we open more deeply to simple presence this can create added freedom in the relational field, expanding possibilities for connection and transformation.

## Conclusion

In bringing Gestalt therapy and Buddhist psychology together, BPGT potentiates the depth and power of each, creating a whole that is more than the sum of its parts. Buddhist psychology views and meditative practices can help us develop more of an embodied experiential connection with Gestalt therapy's foundational ground of field phenomenological and dialogical practice. An expanded view of natural regulation can support patient and therapist accessing and abiding in present moment non-conceptual transformative experience. The therapist's access to this perspective, and capacity to embody this expansive experience, supports entering into the therapeutic engagement freer of limitations, creating new possibilities for embodied relational connection. To touch this experience with our patients we must first discover it in ourselves.

## References

Beisser, A. (1970). The paradoxical theory of change. In J. Fagan & I. L. Shepherd (Eds.), *Gestalt therapy now* (pp. 77–80). New York: Harper Colophon.

Buber, M. (1958). *I and thou* (R. G. Smith, Trans.). New York: Scribner.

Chodron, P. (2010). *The places that scare you: A guide to fearlessness in difficult times.* Boston, MA: Shambhala.

Edelstein, B. (2015). Frames, attitudes, and skills of an existential-humanistic psychotherapist. In K. K. Schneider, J. F. Pierson & J. F. T. Bugental (Eds.), *The handbook of humanistic psychology: Theory, research, and practice* (pp. 435–450). Thousand Oaks, CA: Sage.

Fronsdal, G. (2011). *Dharma talk.* Woodacre, CA: Spirit Rock Meditation Center.

Gold, E. & Zahm, S. (2018). *Buddhist psychology & Gestalt therapy integrated: Psychotherapy for the 21st century.* Portland, OR: Metta Press.

Hycner, R. (1985). Dialogical Gestalt therapy: An initial proposal. *Gestalt Journal, 8*(1), 23–49.

Jacobs, L. (1989). Dialogue in Gestalt theory and therapy. *Gestalt Journal, 12*(1), 25–67.

Olendzki, A. (2005). The roots of mindfulness. In C. K. Germer, R. D. Siegel & P. R. Fulton (Eds.), *Mindfulness and psychotherapy* (pp. 241–261). New York: The Guilford Press.

Perls, F., Hefferline, R. & Goodman, P. (1951). *Gestalt therapy: Excitement and growth in the human personality.* New York: Dell Publishing Co., Inc.

Rinpoche, Y. M. (2019). *In love with the world: A monk's journey through the bardos of living and dying.* New York: Penguin Random House LLC.

Siegel, D. J. (2007). *The mindful brain: Reflections and attunement in the cultivation of well-being.* New York: WW Norton & Company.

Stevens, J. (1971). *Awareness: Exploring, experimenting, experiencing.* Moab, UT: Real People Press.

Wolfert, R. (2000). Self in experience, Gestalt therapy, science and Buddhism. *British Gestalt Journal, 9*(2), 77–86.

Yeshe, T. (1998). *Becoming your own therapist: An introduction to the Buddhist way of thought.* Boston, MA: Lama Yeshe Archive.

Yontef, G. (2002). The relational attitude in Gestalt therapy theory and practice. *International Gestalt Journal, 25*(1), 15–35.

# Chapter 15

# The Here and Now of Sandtray Therapy: Sandtray Therapy Meets Gestalt Therapy

*Karen Pernet and Wendy Caplin*

## Introduction

This chapter will introduce sandtray therapy and will discuss the intersection of Gestalt and sandtray therapies in working with adults. Included are sections on the Gestalt Cycle of Experience and Gestalt concepts that we have found most relevant to sandtray therapy. We have included two case studies illuminating how the contact cycle and concepts come to life in sandtray therapy and speak to the relationship of therapist and client. Additionally, we will describe the use of sandtray for therapists to explore their own culture in a way that avoids defensiveness and creates an interesting and exciting journey into self-understanding.

## Sandtray Therapy

In sandtray, you stand before a tray filled with sand. Your hands connect. You choose from a large collection of miniatures representing everything needed to build a world and place them in the tray. In the sand (ground) you create a scene (figure). From abstract to concrete, powerful metaphors emerge; the most therapeutically powerful are those that are self-generated.

Sandtray therapy is a process-oriented experience, which activates the senses, emotions, creativity, and intellect. The sandtray therapy process creates a place where the expression of needs and wants are not dependent upon words. Using a container of sand and a world composed of miniatures, the creator builds a three-dimensional picture, which comes from different levels of consciousness. The therapist and the builder of the world are co-explorers. Sandtray is for people of all ages, from pre-schoolers to seniors (Boik and Goodwin, 2000).

During a sandtray session, the therapist is both witness and guide, creating space for the builder to bring to awareness what they have created. The therapist creates safety through the presence and empathic curiosity. Margaret Lowenfeld, developer of Sandtray therapy said "Sandtray's power lies in the gradual revelation to the patient through his own work,

DOI: 10.4324/9781003255772-19

accompanied by the understanding of it, which is meditated to him (her) through the therapist, of his (her) inner experience"(Lowenfeld, 1979).

In our current understanding of the brain and of interpersonal neuro-biology, the witness is the safe presence allowing the builder to create with their right hemisphere and to verbalize the experience with their left hemisphere, integrating these two ways of being. The right hemisphere is the land of implicit memory, emotional experience, sensation and body awareness, intuition, metaphor, felt sense, autobiographical narrative, and play. The right hemisphere only knows the present moment – a melody and a rhythm without words. The left is the land of language, logic, making meaning, spoken narrative, a calendar containing past, present, and future-the words of the song, but without melody or rhythm. Together the song has melody, rhythm, and words. The right and left hemispheres working together create a holistic experience; body and mind, working together to bringing deeper meaning to the surface (Badenoch, 2008).

## Gestalt Therapy

Fritz Perls, Laura Perls, and Paul Goodman developed Gestalt therapy in the 1940s. At its core it is a phenomenological method of awareness in which the therapist and client perceive, feel, and act in the present moment, rather than through interpreting the past. It is not that the past doesn't affect the present, but rather how it is affecting the present. Therapists and clients engage in dialogue (dialogic relationship) with each other, communicating their perspectives-verbally and non-verbally. The differences in these perspectives are discussed and are the material of experiments that the therapist offers during the session. The goal of therapy is for the client to become aware of self as being presented in the present time and place. The client learns how they can make changes through deeper acceptance of self. This process is known as the Paradoxical Theory of Change (Cole and Reese, 2018).

The focus of Gestalt therapy is primarily on the process rather than on the content, thus on what is happening (being done, thought, and felt) rather than on telling the story; it focuses on the whole embodiment of the client's experiences in the moment as well as those of the therapist, and on the connection between therapist and client (Cole and Reese, 2018).

## Gestalt Cycle of Experience and the Process of Sandtray Worlds

An interesting approach to the intersection of sandtray therapy and Gestalt therapy is to look at the interplay of The Gestalt Cycle of Experience (Zinker, 1977) with the unfolding process of the cycle of a sandtray session. "...the Cycle gives us a schematic of the life history of an impulse in iso-lation" (Wheeler, 2003). In sandtray therapy, we see the cycle evolving in a relationship (therapist and client) rather than in insolation. A trusting relationship between therapist and client is critical. The therapist acts as a guide (not a director)and co-creator by providing both direction (versus directing) and support. In essence, the therapist acts as a shepherd through the Gestalt Cycle – supporting, guiding, standing next to the client, and creating a safe place where both awareness and change can occur.

The cycle of contact/experience was formulated as a way to explain the experience of contact – a figure emerges from *the* ground until it is satisfied and then returns back to the ground. In Gestalt theory, figure is what surfaces for you at any given moment *out of* that which becomes the focus of interest. Ground is the entire experience of your world from birth to the present moment. An emerging figure could be a word, a memory, a smell, an awareness of something in your body, or something from the environment. It is your ground/background that shapes an emerging figure.

Sandtray therapy is a modality that creates a three-dimensional experience of figure/ground formation. As the figures (miniatures) emerge from the ground (sand) the opportunity arises to help the client develop good contact by working through fixed gestalts, unfinished business, and disturbances of contact which interfere with healthy functioning.

The Gestalt Cycle of Experience demonstrates how figure/ground dynamics shift during the experience of contact. Zinker (1977) describes the experience in the following sequence: sensation, awareness, mobilization of energy, action, contact, and withdrawal/satisfaction.

Below is a description of a sandtray session divided into seven stages. The progression of each stage is paired with each phase of the Gestalt Cycle of Experience.

The unfolding of a cycle can occur over the arc of the session (macro) as shown below but also as smaller cycles (micro) within a session.

### Introduction

When a client walks into my office, they are greeted by a wall of shelves filled with miniatures. I introduce sandtray as a therapeutic modality – their reactions may vary (excitement, intrigue, fear, interest, disinterest). I invite them to look at the miniatures and explore the sandtrays. I encourage them to run their hands through each tray to experience their visual and tactile differences (fine white, beach grainy, paprika color, wet).

### Exploration (Sensation)

During a session, something (hazy) begins to surface – a sensation (restless fingers), feeling (anxiety) or no feeling (numb), somatization (head/neck ache), image (baby/candle), or a thought/memory (not crying at the funeral of a parent).

*For example, Sally, a 30-year-old white woman, has a significant history of severe depression, suicidal thinking, and cutting. In session, she talks about struggling all week not to cut and her desire to do so in the moment*

### Invitation (Awareness)

As a developing figure holds sufficient attention, a need emerges. A figure begins to develop and from that a need arises. It becomes lively and of interest to the client or therapist. The therapist helps to bring it into sharper focus and awareness. A clear figure emerges. The therapist invites the client to create a sandtray to further explore what has emerged.

*I (Wendy) prompt Sally to identify where the desire to cut might be in her body. Sally reports that it is in her chest. To deepen this and make a clearer figure, I ask her to put her hand on her chest and describe her experience. Sally says it is a large heavy weight pressing down on her chest. I decide to explore this further using a sandtray session as an experiment.*

### Setup (Mobilization)

During this phase, the therapist facilitates mobilization to heighten the dynamic of figure/ground formation in movement toward contact and learning along the way where disturbances in contact may occur. There are two parts to this phase – the suggestion by the therapist and the creation of a world by the client. Suggestions are either non-directive or directive.

*I gave Sally a directive suggestion; I have also included an example of a non-directive suggestion to illustrate the difference.*

A nondirective or spontaneous suggestion could be an invitation to look at the miniatures and "select those that speak to you, allow your hand to direct you to an image, pick as many as you like and create a world in the sand." This allows figures/projections to spontaneously emerge.

*I invited an adult male client to create a sandtray. He thought the whole idea preposterous. He randomly picked 7 miniatures and haphazardly placed them in the sand. He leaned back, crossed his arms and looked at me as if to say "there!." As I guided him through an exploration s world, he was completely amazed at the "figures" that emerged and the meaning he came to make of it. We continued to work on this one sandtray for three more sessions.*

A directed suggestion may focus on something that emerges during the exploration or invitation phases. The therapist proposes holding on to a certain thought, feeling, situation, sensation, or memory as the client picks images.

*I invited Sally to hold the feeling of weight on her chest as she picked miniatures.*

## Creation (Action)

The client is invited to choose a sandtray, to sit and place the miniatures in the sand to create a world. The therapist sits quietly as this process unfolds. When the creation seems complete, the therapist gently suggests the client sit quietly and take in their world. They may choose to rearrange, remove, add figures or leave it unchanged.

During the creation, both the therapist's presence and the boundaries of the sandtray create a safe holding environment. The therapist observes the process as it unfolds. For example, the therapist notices the emotional responses of the client or the therapist, the organization of the world, how the sand is arranged, images hidden or enclosed, a safe or unsafe environment. Although the therapist forms impressions that may later be expressed as observations, they are careful not to interpret based on their own projections of the world.

*Sally picked 5 images. Four were placed at each corner of the tray - an alien, a fetus, Elmo in a boat, and a large polar bear with Inuit children on its back. However, it was the image in the center that immediately captured my attention: a cartoonish boy with an oversized mouth, jaw wide open in a scream, small arms held out to the side. When I asked Sally where the energy was, she pointed to the screaming boy*

## Processing (Action and Contact)

During this phase, the client is invited to share their world with the therapist. The client may spontaneously tell a story or comment on each figure or sit quietly. The therapist may encourage the client to reflect on the world by inviting them to tell a story or contemplate the images. At all times the therapist stays aware of the client's body language and emotion. They may encourage a client to slow down, to pay attention to their body or how they are feeling. If the therapist notices disturbances of contact or creative adjustments that interfere with contact, they may create experiments within the sandtray, as illustrated in the example below.

*When Sally indicated the energy was with the screaming boy in the middle, I encouraged her to tell me about the figure. When she said that it represented the weight sitting on her chest, I invited her to have a dialogue and learn more about this part of her. Sally picked up the image and with my support a dialogue ensued with Sally taking both parts-herself and the figure. I sensed from Sally's history and the dialogue that "retroflection" and "introjection" were at play. Sally became more aware of the meaning of the weight. This was the beginning of a long process of undoing retroflection and rejecting the introjects.*

With the client's agreement, the session comes to an end. The therapist and client leave the sandtray and move back to their seats.

*Post-creation (Satisfaction)*

The therapist and client are no longer in the sandtray experiment. During this time both reflect on the experience. The client may spontaneously talk about the experience or the therapist may encourage reflection. It may be that no discussion occurs and the two sit quietly. This figure or the issues involved will reemerge in future sessions until there is resolution.

*Take Picture (Withdrawal)*

The therapist will take a photo of the sandtray; the client may request it or may take their own picture. After the client leaves, the therapist carefully returns the images to the shelf.

## Gestalt Concepts and a Sandtray Narrative

To illustrate the connection between Gestalt therapy concepts and sandtray therapy.

I (Karen) am highlighting two sandtrays and then reviewing the concepts prominent in the trays.

### Narrative

Sarah, a 65-year-old white woman, came to therapy because she was experiencing trauma symptoms from a near-fatal accident during a vacation in China several months before. Sarah was frustrated that Gene, her husband, seemed weary hearing about the accident although she was still recovering physically and emotionally. In general, she struggled to express her emotions, often retroflecting anger. During our first session Sarah, speaking rapidly and urgently, told me the story of the accident. Although I knew that the verbal account wasn't healing in itself, I felt her need to tell the story and did not slow her down.

As therapy proceeded, Sarah was increasingly aware that the trauma from the accident continued to affect her. Following the accident, she felt a dissonance between her likable social self and her private sad and aggrieved self. In addition to physical and psychological pain, she found herself growing distant from Gene.

She requested using sandtray to work through the trauma. As the trays evolved over time, her aloneness, fear, anger, and pain became figural. This was Sarah's story. She led and I followed, as what I call a curious witness. My comments and questions arose from her creations, her words, and how she embodied her work.

Sarah suffered internal injuries which were challenging to diagnose and treat. In-tray after tray, she showed various ways that she was isolated and her basic needs were not met. Communication was an ongoing problem because of the dependence on their Chinese travel agent whom they did not trust. Most painfully of all Sarah did not feel supported by Gene.

The sandtray series of 20 trays began with the accident and ended with the return home. Midway through, Sarah became clear of the intensity of her disconnection from Gene. She believed that he did not comfort her when she was in pain, did not understand how terrifying the medical treatment was, and did not insist the insurance pay for the special equipment she would need to return home. She feared she would die if she followed the medical plan in what she saw as an inadequate hospital with a headstrong, inept young doctor who was insisting on surgery. Sarah's perception was that Gene did not fathom the gravity of the situation and was unwilling to speak up to protect her because his lack of assertiveness and fear of conflict overrode her needs.

Two sandtrays she created in the middle of the series demonstrated the power of the modality in bringing the issue into the forefront, as figural. I was becoming frustrated because unless Gene was involved in therapy, I did not see how this problem could be resolved. I doubted that he understood Sarah's issue with him.

In the first tray, Sarah initially placed miniatures representing herself and Gene in separate beds, looking away from each other. She placed miniatures of fire (pain) next to her. Medical figures were at the edge of the tray. She placed a figure of a woman in agony, behind her bed. The overwhelming sense of the tray was Sarah's isolation.

As Sarah described her tray and how alone she felt, both of us were increasingly aware of her anger. As she was talking, she picked up the figures of her husband and her doctor and forcefully placed them with their heads in the sand. In the final scene, Sarah lay in the bed in pain, and her husband and the doctor, feet in the air, heads in the sand. She titled the tray "I'm in Pain and My Husband Doesn't Get It." She enjoyed doing this. Outward expression of anger does not come easily to a retroflector. I accepted her intense emotions. Although I wished I could help, I knew Sarah's own experience of her feelings was an essential part of healing.

The following week, Sarah created another sandtray-a scene in which she was even more estranged from her husband than in the previous tray. Again, there were two beds. She placed herself in one bed, in pain, symbolized by the fire covering her eyes and her body. Again, the figure representing agony was behind her. She put Gene in the bed adjoining hers. She placed a screen between the beds so they could not see each other. She then put a box on top of him to further their disconnection. As I witnessed her creating the tray, I could sense her rage, pain, and fear. She placed the doctors at a distance so that she was isolated in a sand world full of people.

Sarah stopped at this point and began to talk about the tray. She expressed her anger, her loneliness, and angst. I stayed present and connected.

At one point, she hesitated, took a breath. I wondered what was coming next. She put her hand on the box covering her husband and then froze for a moment. She said she couldn't move his figure or change the scene. I was surprised. We explored her response. As she regained movement, she realized that in addition to re-experiencing her own pain, she was also experiencing her husband's emotions. Underlying his crippled response to her illness was his inability to make things better. She became aware that he was as trapped as she was. Both of them were terrified that they were unable to get the medical help she needed and she might die. Her fixed gestalt, her belief that he was not protecting her, shifted and there was literally movement. She moved the screen separating them, lifted the box off of him, and brought him closer to her. She rearranged the medical figures so that helpers were more available. Lastly, she removed the fire over her eyes, which had been blinding her. She could now see the world around her. She created a new scene, with connection, healing, and hope. An amazing shift in awareness, making the unseen, seen. She titled the tray "I'm in Pain and My Husband Gets It."

Both in her life and in her sandtrays, her relationship with her husband shifted, as she continued to choose figures representing their connection.

### Gestalt Concepts Illustrated in the Narrative

1   Gestalt concept: Phenomenology. A perspective focusing on the person's experiences of themselves and of their world. Thus it is the person's awareness, based on their perceptions, feelings, experiences, contact functions, and relationships that are important (Cole and Reese 2018).

Sandtray: The sandtray is a creation of the builder's inner self, often including the effects as currently perceived of past experiences. The therapist's exploration focuses on deepening the understanding of the tray with the full participation of the client. Together, they look at the relationship of the tray and current life. There is no interpretation by the therapist (DeDomenica, 1988).

*In the above narrative, Sarah's sandtrays brought an unresolved trauma into the present. She decided how much of the story to tell at any given session. In the two trays described, she recreated an unresolved situation from her perspective. Change was up to Sarah, if and when she was ready. My role was to witness, to be curious.*

2   Gestalt Concept: Here and Now. "Now" starts with the client's current understanding of the situation, which is alive in the present whenever it occurred. "Here" is the space where the person is in the moment (Cole and Reese, 2018).

Sandtray: The sandtray is created in the moment, bringing focus on the presenting issue. In the processing with the therapist, the relevance and meaning of the tray is deepened (Boik and Goodwin, 2000).

*In Sarah's sandtrays, her story was alive in the "Now" of the session. She re-experienced intense emotions in the present. The "Here" is the creation of the story in the sandtray and in the context our relationship. The work brought resolution to an ongoing issue in which her pain and isolation blinded her to her husband's suffering. At the end of the second tray, when she had an embodied response to his fear as well as to her own, her resentment melted, replaced by compassion.*

3   Gestalt Concept: Figure/Ground. That on which the person focuses is the figure – it stands out. The rest is the ground. If one changes perspective and focuses on something else, that part will be the figure and the rest, the ground. It is also important to note here that the figure never stands in isolation from the ground. Perspectives change and therefore the succession of figure and ground is continuously changing. Ground is also the sum of the person's experiences in life (Cole and Reese, 2018).

Sandtray: Literally the ground is the sand and the figures and their placement become figural. The exploration of the tray reveals that what is figural for the person- what is present in the tray. The process is assisting the client to deepen in her understanding of her creation.

*As Sarah chose the pieces, they became the figure. As she arranged and rearranged them in the tray the figure/ground changed. Sandtray allows for many ways to create and recreate what is figural, but the ground is always there, literally.*

4   Gestalt Concept: Awareness, Fixed Gestalts, Paradoxical Theory of Change. Gestalt therapy focuses on the present, in bringing forward what is in the room with the client. Past experiences, often in childhood, lead to creative adjustments. When they continue as part of our being, we react to the present as if it were the past. This becomes a fixed gestalt. The combination of a safe therapeutic relationship and growing awareness of one's fixed gestalts is the key to change. Awareness plus connection leads to growth.

Sandtray: Issues surface through externalization, metaphor, and a safe relationship with the therapist. The story unfolds in the contained world of the box of sand, in the creation of scenes, through the choices of figures, and the dialoguing between therapist and client (Homeyer and Sweeny, 2016).

*Sarah was aware of simmering resentment toward Gene and saw it as justified and unfixable. In childhood she learned that anger was not safe. She was a retroflector, turning anger inward. As she experienced her emotions, her heightened awareness led to a sudden shift from resentment to compassion. This is an example of the paradoxical theory of healing: in order to change, a person must first fully experience their stuckness.*

Gestalt Concept: I-Thou relationship: From Martin Buber- The relationship in Gestalt therapy is one of the essential healing factors and grows out of authentic contact between the therapist and client. Relationship is an end in itself, not a means to an end (Cole and Reese, 2018).

Sandtray: The therapist is witness and guide, fully present, aware of their own somatic responses, distinguishing between resonance with the client and their own reactions (Timm and Garza, 2017).

Timm and Garza (2017) "likens it (sandtray) to an umbrella built for two. Within this protected space, emotionally meaningful contact takes place and nourishment and intimacy can exist."

*As Sarah created her trays and told her story, I was present, and at the same time, aware of my own thoughts and sensations that might interfere. For instance, at the end of the first tray, when there was no resolution to her anger, I witnessed it and silenced my desire to help her find a solution. Finding a solution would have met my need, not hers.*

5   Gestalt Concept: Experiments are a key element of Gestalt Therapy. What can be brought into the room, into the relationship between client and therapist is key. There is never a right or wrong way, only tension between safety and stretching. The therapist creates the experiment in the moment.

Sandtray: Experiments are part of the process. The tray is an experiment - creating what is happening with the builder in the moment. After the tray is created, the dialogue and the changes in the tray are a continuation of the experiment.

*In this example Sarah's need was to safely re-experience the trauma, with me as witness. I thought of the whole process as an experiment in bringing the part of her past that was impinging on her current functioning to life. If I had felt that she were stuck, I might have suggested a specific experiment, such as having her voice her husband's thoughts to heighten awareness of the fixed gestalt.*

## Cultural Sandtrays

As therapists, we are often encouraged to pay attention to the culture of our clients – especially when their culture is different from our own. Defined as a broad multidimensional concept that includes ethnicity, race, gender, religion, language, social class, sexual orientation, and so on, culture has a major influence on our own lives. This is often ignored or minimized in our training and practice (Hardy and McGoldrick, 2008). I (Karen) developed the Cultural Sandtray as a means for therapists to take an inward cultural journey by using figures in the sand for non-verbal exploration, examination, and discussion. Questions of implicit and explicit influences on our work can be openly discussed. The following examples offer a glimpse into the power of these trays: a gay Asian therapist used a family of pandas leaving a Chinese temple and journeying to the Golden Gate Bridge in San Francisco as a profound statement of his story as an immigrant and of the divergent treatment of his sexual orientation; an African-American therapist divided her tray in half, with a river of blood (red ribbon) separating the sides... one side representing life in Nigeria – full of joy and connection and the other side life in the US – drugs, child abuse, death, and alienation; a white therapist practicing in an upper-middle-class area used her tray to explore a childhood marked by poverty. Each of them had the opportunity to share the ways that their ethnicity, class, sexual orientation, etc. affected their relationships with their clients.

One can imagine many productive discussions that could ensue with the use of Cultural Sandtrays.

Sandtray can potentially provide a safe arena to discuss what is often felt as unsafe and to sidestep defensiveness when issues such as privilege, prejudice, and structural racism arise. Social justice is an important component of Gestalt therapy and the use of Cultural Sandtrays can bring those issues safely into the here and now. While the Cultural Sandtray can be used with individuals, using it in a group provides a rich setting for listening, dialoguing, and growth.

## Conclusion

Our goal in writing this chapter has been to build a bridge between sandtray therapy and Gestalt therapy. There has been very little written on this subject and we are glad to have had the opportunity to make this contribution to the literature (Armstrong, 2008; Oaklander, 1988; Stevens, 2004). Our intention has been to describe sandtray sessions in a way that brings them to life and that connects our method of working with sandtray with Gestalt therapy. Additionally, we have introduced the concept and methodology of creating Cultural Sandtrays. We hope we have whetted your appetite and that you will continue to explore sandtray therapy.

## References

Armstrong, S. (2008). *Sandtray Therapy: A Humanistic Approach*. Dallas, TX: Ludic Press

Badenoch, B. (2008). The Integrating Power of Sandtray. In *Being a Brainwise Therapist* (pp. 220–243). NY: W.W. Norton & Co.

Boik, B. & Goodwin, E. A. (2000). *Sandplay Therapy: A Step-By-Step Manual For Psychotherapists of Diverse Orientations*. NY: W.W. Norton & Co.

Cole, P. & Reese, D. (2018). *New Directions in Gestalt Group Therapy: Relational Ground, Authentic Self*. NYC, NY: Routledge: Taylor and Francis Group

DeDomenica, G. (1988). *Sand tray world play: A comprehend (Intensive guide to the use of sand tray play in therapeutic transformational settings)*. Vision quest Into Reality, Oakland, CA 94602.

Hardy, K & McGoldrick, M. (2008). "Re-Visioning Training in *Re-Visioning Family Therapy: Race Culture, and Gender in Clinical Practice* (pp. 442–460). NY: Guilford Press.

Homeyer, L. E. & Sweene, D. S. (2016). *Sandtray Therapy 3rd Edition*. NYC, NY: Routledge: Taylor and Francis Group.

Lowenfeld, M. (1979). *The World Techniques*. London: George Allen& Unwin.

Oaklander, V. (1988). *Windows to Our Children*. New York: Gestalt Journal Press.

Rae, R. (2013). *Sandtray: Playing to Heal, Recover, and Grow*. NY: Jason Aronson.

Stevens, C. (2004). Playing in the Sand. *The British Gestalt Journal, 13*(1), 18–23.

Timm, N. & Garza, Y. (2017). Beyond the Miniatures: Using Gestalt Theory in Sandtray Processing. *Gestalt Review, 21*(1), 44–55.

Wheeler, G. (2003). Contact and Creativity: The Gestalt Cycle in Context. In Amendt-Lyon, N., & Spagnuolo Lobb, M., *Creative License: The Art of Gestalt Therapy 163-180*. NY: Springer.

Zinker, J. (1977). *Creative Process in Gestalt Therapy*. NY: Vintage Books.

# Chapter 16

# The Mountain and the River: Stillness and Flow and the Art of Therapy

*Christine Campbell and Jack Fris*

## Introduction

In December 2016, Jack had a double lung transplant. There was a nine-month period when we were awaiting a transplant, awaiting lungs from a donor, when Jack was very sick. We both worked hard every day to keep him alive. We were frightened and exhausted most of the time. Art was one of only a few things that really supported us, and in response to which we felt that we were living and not dying. That experience has stayed with us and we have often wondered about what was happening then.

So many of the usual supports had changed for each of us – our sense of effectiveness day to day, feeling good in our bodies, the capacity to look ahead and to plan, our sense of connection to the mostly healthy and relatively happy people around us. Music, poetry, and literature sustained us when other, more typically sustaining things fell away. Artistic experiences seemed to have the power to make a profound meaning of our suffering and to support connection.

We formed a book group that met every Tuesday night at our house. There were eight of us. We did not read a book on our own and then get together to discuss it. We only read when we were together, aloud, taking turns. The book was Finnegan's Wake by James Joyce. This took many months – several months leading up to the transplant, and more during Jack's recovery. Certainly, what makes this so moving to us is the commitment of these friends, who came every week at the end of their workdays. They helped carry us through that time. The book carried all of us.

If you are familiar with Finnegan's Wake you will know that much of it is all but incomprehensible. The very first page makes no sense at all. There are 60 to 70 world languages used, but not 1 at a time. They are all mixed in like a chopped salad, along with invented words, and portmanteau words in almost every sentence. There are countless arcane references to literature, myth, religion, etc., woven throughout. It's like reading aloud a book in a language that you neither understand nor speak. It is content without content. One can study a page for hours, arrive at a theme, and yet end up

DOI: 10.4324/9781003255772-20

further away from understanding the book. Several scholars have settled on the idea that Finnegan's Wake is about a mountain in love with a river. It was not an easy book to read aloud; each of us struggled to imbue meaning to the words we spoke to each other. But there is a vitality that emerges when you read this book – the cadence, the emotional tone, the sounds, are sensual, humorous, always vibrant.

Surprise! The always shifting ground of the book seemed to be holding us. Its spaciousness created room for each of us, giving us a way to be with each other that for two hours a week transcended our fears, and our desperate sense of everyday having and losing.

We were still all afraid, and we were willingly, purposefully stepping into mystery. There was a communal acceptance of our limited ability to know. Once we let go of knowing, we could play. All responsibility for having a penetrating insight – gone. Like a Gestalt experiment – because we did not read ahead of time – we were in the moment. Some of us played with accents. When there was a song one of us spontaneously began to sing, and others joined in. There was a short play within the book. We quickly assumed parts and made adjustments as we went along; the women landed on the sofa and together made a chorus.

Interacting with the book's gibberish felt the same as interacting with God's gibberish, or the inarticulate universe, that was taking Jack's life. The book is art, and by reading it aloud we created more art from it. The group assumed a position of active passivity, a *middle mode*, that was a lot like what we do as therapists with our clients. We did not pathologize the book – turning it into a problem to be solved. The book provided a structure within which we could experiment. We let go of any sense of authority, of any particular outcome, and were able to be with what was happening. Jack was dying, Christine was carrying him, and everyone assembled was terrified. The unspoken question was, "Are we going to run from this or try something we never tried before?"

## The Creative Process

There is a similar creative process at work in making art, in encountering art, in working with clients, and in living every day. How these processes are similar is relevant and supportive to our work. Here are some qualities of an artistic process:

A willingness to stay in the process, i.e., to not abandon a figure of interest, even when that figure is difficult to clarify, and its direction is unknown

> A reliance on one's own experience as the path of clarity
> A willingness to tolerate uncertainty while at the same time owning what one knows

An ability to follow one's interests, inclinations, and intuitions
A sensitivity to and an ability to flexibly respond to the limitations of a situation
A resistance to the imposition of influences from the dominant culture
The self-discipline to hone skills, to stay focused, as well as an ability to let go of an agenda, and to relax in the work
Openness to a flow rather than or in spite of self-doubt and self-criticism
A willingness to experience vulnerability, and to trust in the process of life

When we review our list, we see that each item on it is also indispensable to our therapeutic work. The qualities that are essential to an artistic endeavor are equally essential to the Gestalt therapy process (Zinker, 1977).

Consider this quote from the playwright, Samuel Beckett, "To be an artist is to fail...." (1983, p. 126) Note the absence of a "sometimes." Beckett embraces our perennial task of doing something that never triumphs, that can be only partially understood, as we endeavor to articulate that which eludes words.

Beckett's thoughts on failure are particularly useful to us as therapists, "Ever tried. Ever failed. No matter. Try again. Fail again. Fail better." (Beckett, 1986, p. 78) This statement is not ironic; it is to be grappled with as written. Failure is not a motivational or instructive experience on the way to success. It is in the topography of our very humanity, not a place we come to and go from. We never transcend our humanness, and certainly do not ask the client to do so. When we engage with our clients with our full presence, practicing inclusion to the extent the moment can bear, our failure, our humanity, resembles its closest relative love. This is the same love we are in the thrall of as artist and audience.

A sense of failure in therapy is inevitable since we can never say with certainty what has been the healing factor for our patients. The paradoxical theory of change instructs us to avoid aiming toward a particular outcome. The more we try to change, to be something we're not, the more stuck we become, and that change happens when we accept and fully embody our present experience (Beisser, 1970). When we try to change we are often self-rejecting, interrupting our own process, and creating conflict within ourselves. When we can accept our own experience in any given moment, we allow for a flow, a spaciousness that creates optimal conditions for change. This is a grounded place to be, a supported place that gives us traction for our next step.

When we stay with what is happening, tolerating uncertainty, and allowing our own vulnerability to failure, we become both humble and bold! Our better failures become generative for our patients.

So the artistic qualities we have identified remain relevant even when a therapeutic process flounders. Artists are committed to their work. They keep going. As therapists, we can see that we are helping. Our clients change, become more at ease with themselves and their world. Yet, on a daily basis, we do not often feel so successful. There are positive moments, but also much doubt. Like the artist, we keep going. We have a sense that what we are doing is worthwhile, that next time we will get it just right, and perhaps more importantly, we have faith that there is a process of healing at work. Our engagement in the process and our commitment to the relationship is perhaps our greatest service.

When in our work we have a sense that something is building, that we are ready with the key next questions, we can feel crestfallen by the client uttering "no." We may imagine our house of cards has fallen and all is lost. It is then that, like artists, we improvise with the pile of cards before us. When we set our imagination free while attending faithfully to each card, a previously unseeable move becomes apparent. Likely in some way, we will fail again. Hopefully, we will fail better.

*CHRISTINE:*   I work with Paul, a young man who has longed for, and felt entitled to exquisite attunement, both from me and from his friendships; to be understood without needing to explain; to finally get what he never received from his narcissistic mother. In one session he was disappointed in my response to him, pointing out that I seemed to have left the immediacy of the moment between us to describe my conceptualization of his predicament. My excitement in the telling felt threatening to him, "When you're energized like that, actually when you string together more than two or three sentences, I feel that you leave me. I become invisible. *Momentum is my enemy.* Whenever it happens I withdraw." Although I believed that Paul's wish for perfect and effortless attunement could never be fulfilled, that it was a source of ongoing disappointment, in fact, a loss to be grieved, I also recognized that his complaint was legitimate. Imagining that I was offering clarity and hope, I had avoided the pain of a moment, stepping out of it by conceptualizing his dilemma – where it came from, how it might play out outside the room, and how it might be healed. I felt shame and regret. I had let him down again! At the same time, I felt defensive; his criticism hurt. I acknowledged how I had let him down, remained genuinely curious about my impact on him, and shared some of his impact on me. Holding the complexity of the experience between us created an energetic intensity that we each felt poignantly. Sharing my experience, and being willing to set it down to meet his, without making either of us wrong, supported a moment of intimate connection. No longer invisible, Paul felt this as an affirmation of his experience, and as a moment of satisfying contact. Similar instances emerged as therapy progressed, so that he began to trust that the two of us would continue wanting to meet each other in this intimate and more satisfying way. He very quickly began to negotiate "good enough" connections with others as well.

> "It could be argued that every time we begin a conversation, there is an implicit critique of what both parties have previously taken for granted. Nothing – whether ideology or emotional conviction – survives interpretive dialogue intact. This is especially evident in clinical work, where an ongoing inquiry into previously held "facts" or "emotional truths" creates disruption. Modest and patient work in a hermeneutic spirit can, I believe, transform devastated life worlds into possibilities for shared understanding" (Orange, p. 107).

The art of therapy, then, is not so much in the graceful delivery of a well-timed and articulated interpretation, but rather in a commitment to the work even when it is clumsy, awkward, messy, and discouraging.

## The Middle Mode – Dialogue and Experiment

In Gestalt therapy's seminal text, Perls, Hefferline, and Goodman address a balance inherent in the creative process, that between creativity and structure:

> "With bright sensation and play in the medium as his central acts, the artist then accepts his vision and uses his critical deliberateness.... The artist is quite aware of what he is doing - after it is done, he can show you the steps in detail; he is not unconscious in his working, but neither is he mainly deliberately calculating. His awareness is in a kind of middle mode, neither active nor passive, but accepting the conditions, attending to the job, and growing toward the solution" (PHG, 1994, p. 22).

We do not have to forget everything we know in order to be creative, to meet our patients and the moment fresh. Actors memorize their lines so that they become automatic, they think carefully about their character's history and motivations, they try on different emotional tones for their lines, they block out their movements on the stage. Once the performance begins, they are not thinking about any of this, so that they can interact spontaneously and authentically with the playwright's words and with the other actors in the scene. Likewise, a painter studies perspective, color theory, stretches canvas, and mixes paint, before the first encounter with the empty canvas. In our work we have clear guidelines for our practice. We educate ourselves, immerse ourselves in theory, train and rehearse, but when we sit with a patient, these become background to our presence (Zinker, 1987). We can usually – not always, but usually tell you later why we made the choices we made.

*JACK:*   I had a retirement age client who was dealing with grief, regret and fear. She was self-employed and her work was drying up. Many of her old customers were dying. Mary was talking about the dear friends she had lost, and how empty her world was. She then remembered fondly a therapist she once had.

> "He was the only one who believed that I could breathe underwater!"
> Taken aback and confused, I sought clarification."What?"
> "Yeah. I can breathe underwater. I always could."
> I was stunned. As the moment expanded, her eyes were simultaneously imploring and rebuking me, each in an infinite intensity.
> "Oh no," I thought. "I can't believe this. I don't want to hurt her, but I have to, and it isn't fair." I couldn't collude with her in a fantasy.
> It was then that I asked myself, what if...? In the space of the now open moment I rushed through my mind and stumbled upon fantastic things that I had experienced. I was six years old, running in the grass on the side of my home. I remembered realizing that if I lifted my legs just so, I could fly! Or was that a dream I always had?
> Mary can breathe underwater, I said voicelessly. Her voice came in.
> "What, you don't believe me?
> I heard myself say, "I do."
> Now she was curious, "You do?"
> In a strange place, simultaneously embracing fantasy and still holding onto my truth, I said, "You're doing it now. In all the dread and desolation surrounding you, you're doing the impossible, you're alive. You're doing it."
> "I love that," she said.

My strong belief is that this worked because creativity is a byproduct of presence and inclusion. My "yes" was not aiming to fully join her in a denial of death, any more than it was to distract her and sneak in a cheap substitute. I'd said it out of respect, to include her experience. It was art because it took in the world and asked, "What happens if...?" Yontef and Schulz (2016) underscore this idea in their discussion of dialogue and experiments, where they assert that everything we do is an experiment.

It is in these fraught moments that the therapist must hold his or her own sense of vulnerability, and take a leap into the unknown. Met with an obstacle, Jack's own incredulous response, he jumped in. He surrendered to not knowing, open to experiment with what the client was bringing, and offering in return his own way of making sense, one that affirmed her wholeness and deepened their contact.

When we trust in our own experiencing, as we have said that we think good artists must, and when we stay with it a little longer, it tends to complexify. Lynne Jacobs writes,

> *"Complex experience changes focal attention from discerning differences and clarifying boundaries, instead to an appreciation of the infinite richness of each moment that moves through time, with no clear demarcation of past into future, of inter affective influence that can never be fully assessed, and of the flow of complex figures, one into another"*(Jacobs, 2011, p. 95)

What constitutes our experience is co-created, infinitely complex so that our understanding of it is always provisional. The world keeps turning, there is always a new horizon, and so our understanding must continue to evolve. When art puts us in a relationship with the ineffable, it provides a support for us to tolerate uncertainty and complexity, and to even celebrate it.

Consider this poem:

The Red Wheelbarrow, by William Carlos Williams (1923, p. 74)

so much depends
upon

a red wheel
barrow

glazed with rain
water

beside the white
chickens

Here William Carlos Williams is unapologetically moving toward relationship with his audience. He does not provide us with an abstraction. He offers his direct experience. He does not articulate, does not even hint at its meaning. Every reader must bring his or her subjective experience to it. He seems to have intuited this, but did not aim for it when he wrote "so much depends upon...."

What depends on the red wheel barrow?

The poem has the feeling of a here and now engagement with life. The red wheel barrow, the white chickens are the poet's figural experience. What depends on it, is Williams' ground, how he makes meaning, and he doesn't tell us that. But he wrote it for us. Each of us makes meaning with our own ground. Perhaps the direct experiencing is his reason to live, and the poem is a wide-open invitation for us to engage also, to enter into a relationship with his words, to take the time to allow our own experience to complexify, to perhaps contemplate what it is we live for.

## Presence as Generative

Much art gives us a strong personal sense of the artist. We stand in front of a painting and there is a sense of transparency, immediacy, and connection as if the artist were standing close by. We are in contact; we are in a relationship. This largely comes down to presence for the artist, in the same way, that it does for the therapist with a client.

Martin Buber's concept of Dialogic Presence entreats us as therapists to show up as ourselves, one flawed human encountering another – *to be* rather than *to seem* (Hycner & Jacobs, 1995). We give up our attempts to manage our patient's impression of us, instead of staying open to the possibility of a kind of contact that allows the patient to encounter our subjective experience. As the process of contact moves forward, there is a surrender to the moment, rather than an attempt to control, for either party, what will transpire – there emerges a trust in "the between." How we hold our own vulnerability in the face of the other is central to the presence and to creativity. A dialogic encounter supports integration and affirms the person's wholeness.

A similar, counterintuitive methodology is suggested by Feldenkreis,

> *"Most people spend their whole lives using their strengths to cover up and hide their weaknesses. They expend tremendous energy in keeping themselves a house divided. But if you surrender to your weakness, therein lies your pathway to genius. A person who knows and utilizes his true weakness, and uses his strength to include it, is a whole person" (as cited in* Leri, 1993, *p. 51)*

When we think about great artists we see that this is true. Bob Dylan does not have a conventionally pleasing voice, and he is not a virtuoso guitar player or harmonica player. These supposed deficiencies actually come together and create the esthetic that we call Bob Dylan and become what we love about him. With acceptance of his own artistic experience, he stayed true to his vision, and allowed his unique contribution to be fully realized. Think of the very talented therapists you have known. They are certainly not talented in *every* aspect of the work. It is their imperfections that make them unique, and their fallibility offers a point of connection.

Our authentic presence provides an opportunity for a more complex experiencing, and relationship to emerge. You will remember the song All

Along the Watchtower that was a hit for Jimi Hendrix in 1968, and you may or may not know that it was written by Bob Dylan (1967). When Jimi Hendrix did a cover of the song (Jimmy Hendrix Experience, 1968), he transformed it. Touch the link or point your phone camera at the QR code below to listen now to the first few lines, about 30 seconds worth, from each version (Figure 16.1 and Figure 16.2):

Hendrix's version is not a reverential cover. He was not behaving like a Bob Dylan acolyte. He was fully present in the song and made it his own – this unique thing that most people do not even recognize as a Dylan song. Of course, he could not have done this without Bob Dylan's lyrics. Hendrix likely could not have written those words, yet being moved deeply by them, he conjured something primal and transcendent. Legend has it that in an interview years later Dylan reported having written the song during a lightning storm, and he remarked that it was uncanny how Hendrix had unknowingly brought the storm to life. Hendrix manifested something that

*Figure 16.1* First Dylan: https://song.link/xpqrm0nvdqfjp

*Figure 16.2* And now Hendrix: https://song.link/2h0f5h52fnfqv

was latent in Dylan's version. This aspect of Dylan's ground became figural for Hendrix.

Dylan loved Hendrix' version, and is frequently quoted as saying, "It's Jimi's song now." When Dylan said this, he was not talking about theft. Hendrix had listened carefully to what Dylan created, and his version created something more than the sum of its parts. When Dylan wrote this, he had the poetry certainly – larger than life archetypal figures, the joker and the thief – with which he created a drama, replete with biblical references, but he did not compose the kind of grand musical architecture that would sound as aspiring as his lyrical ideas. Instead, he strummed an acoustic guitar and brought in his harmonica of uncertain pitch. Hendrix too brought in his limitations. Despite his prowess as a guitar player, he is doing someone else's song. Contemporaries in the pop genre rarely cover each other's work. There is an implicit humility in this act. Whatever hubris there may be in this, there is also creative play.

Here we see how presence generates the next thing. Each artist brought his subjective experience, as it shows up in the song. Because each is fully present, there is reciprocity. Our presence is generative. Our engagement as whole humans brings out the wholeness of the other. A new thing emerges that is greater than the sum of its parts.

*CHRISTINE:*   When Paul and I approach something very painful, he can still get scared and mistrustful. He becomes watchful, scrutinizing my responses, essentially asking, "Is this safe for me?" In this mood, he continues to point out ways that I disappoint him. I get excited, or I intellectualize, steering us toward an abstraction, or I don't get what he is saying the first time and he has to elaborate. It could be any of these things, and he is usually right about what has happened. I have become increasingly open to hearing from him because experience has shown me that exploring these perceived therapeutic missteps is often ripe territory for us. Sometimes I am the one to point one out. I will notice he has subtly withdrawn, and ask about it, e.g., "I wonder what was the impact on you when I said......." These moments, initially threatening, with my openness to explore, now create a kind of safety Paul never knew in his family of origin. No one was interested in his experience, in fact the feedback he got from his mother obfuscated his experience and left him bewildered and ashamed. He is building tolerance for these moments of understanding that are very intimate experiences for both of us. More recently he wondered whether I was being completely forthright by being so agreeable when he questioned me. He was very worried that he might be alienating me. At first, I reassured him that this was not the case, but he persisted. I paused, took a breath, and noticed my body. I sensed fatigue, and let myself settle into it. There was an ache in my chest. I decided to give voice to the sensation, not knowing for sure what I would say, "There's a feeling in my chest...that wants to say 'Why are you doing this to me? I'm tired, and this is hard. Can't you just be nice to me?'" I was sincere and he could hear the emotion in my voice. I said, "I want to talk about what happens between us. I'm very open to whatever you want to tell me. And if you want to know whether or not you can hurt me, the answer is yes, you can." This delighted him! He said he felt much safer with me knowing that I was human, that he had an impact on me, that he mattered this much to me, and especially that I would tell him so. "I like your honesty," he said. "I feel calm." With Paul, I had to let go of being the therapist I wanted to be, and become a fellow, flawed human in the room. This was risky for both of us (and certainly in many therapeutic situations these kinds of personal disclosures are not what is called for). In this case it gave him something to push up against. The situation went from "I am helping you," to "We, together, are doing this," further building his trust in the possibility of being met in the world as a whole, unique person, relied upon and worthy of trust.

## I and Thou

It seems like the most cringe-worthy hyperbole when an athlete gets called an artist, but Michael Jordan, with his boldness, his revolutionary above-the-rim style, and his improvisational skills, is arguably best understood with that word, and his transformation from mere MVP to NBA champion, adds a unique perspective to our inquiry.

Michael came into the league a young superstar and immediately began hauling the Chicago Bulls into the playoffs each year. Watching him levitate the sport off of the hardwood was like listening to Coltrane summon a world out of the pop confection of *My Favorite Things.* Yet despite his ferocious drive, his unparalleled talent, the da Vinci like flying machine he imagined and manifested, the Bulls fell short of the championship every year. It became clear that Michael's unguardable game was in one small but critical way guardable, because it had a predictable feature – in the final quarter, Jordan was never going to pass. His coach, Phil Jackson, saw the flaw and compelled Michael to accept a most illogical strategy – in the clutch, the best player on the floor must surrender the ball. He pointed out repeatedly that

John Paxson, a moderate NBA commodity, was always open during the times when three or more defenders collapsed on Mike. In game five of the '91 championship with the Lakers, Jordan made this most improbable improvisation. He surrendered. He still used all his artistry. He was fully present in his aerial ballet with its trickster choreography, asking entirely authentic questions of the Laker defense, but he added a great new trick. He made the ball disappear. He let go of being MICHAEL JORDAN, and in doing so found something even better – dialogue, play, a team. Jordan asked Paxson a genuine question, and Paxson began making 3's. This new creative play bewildered the Lakers. Paxson went 8 for 8 in the fourth quarter and the Bulls won their first championship. To make his first masterpiece, Michael had to use what was in front of him, rather than forcing an agenda. He never stopped being Jordan, but with Jackson's help he found Paxson and spoke to him in I – Thou mode.

## Conclusion

When we trust that we are artists we place our faith in the service of creativity and connection. We learn again and again that our need to be correct leads to errors and our errors can lead to corrections. We have a new chance every hour, every moment. In our simple embrace of paradox, in our counterintuitive hunches, like a river in love with a mountain, we bring forth what already is, by being near, by regarding, and being regarded, by flowing with the terrain and sitting in silence.

*Christine Campbell and Jack Fris are married and live in Los Angeles.*

## References

Beckett, S. (1983). *Proust and three dialogues*. Grove Press.

Beckett, S. (1986). *Nohow on*. Grove Press.

Beisser, A. (1970). The paradoxical theory of change. In J. Fagan & I. L. Shepherd (Eds.), *Gestalt therapy now: Theory, techniques, applications* (pp. 77–80). Science and Behavior Books.

Dylan, B. (1967). All along the watchtower [Song]. On *John Wesley Harding* [Album]. Columbia Records.

Hycner, R. & Jacobs, L. (1995). *The healing relationship in Gestalt therapy*. Gestalt Journal Press.

Jacobs, L. (2011). Ethical inspiration and complex experiencing. In Bloom, D. & Brownell, P. (Eds.), *Continuity and Change: Gestalt Therapy Now* (pp. 93–99). Cambridge Scholars.

Jimmy Hendrix Experience. (1968). All along the watchtower [Song]. On *Electric ladyland* [Album]. Reprise Records.

Leri, D. (1993). Learning how to learn. *Gnosis Magazine, Fall, 1993*, 49–53.

Perls, F., Hefferline, R., & Goodman, P. (1994). *Gestalt therapy: Excitement and growth in the human personality*. Gestalt Journal Press.

Williams, W. C. (1923). *Spring and all*. Contact Press. p. 74.

Yontef, G. & Schulz, F. (2016). Dialogue and experiment. *British Gestalt Journal*, *25*(1), 9–21.

Zinker, J. (1977). *Creative process in Gestalt therapy*. Bruner/Mazel.

Zinker, J. (1987). Presence as evocative power in Gestalt therapy. *Gestalt Review*, *1*(2), 3–8.

# Index

Note: Page numbers followed by 'n' denote endnotes